SOLSTICE SHIFT

"I have seen the sun during total eclipse, when the outline of the moon before its fiery face was of exactly the right size to precisely cover its diameter—no more, no less. . . .

"The placement of earth, sun, and moon in orbits just the right distances from one another to give creatures on the earth's surface the illusion that all three are the same size is a stretch of coincidence so enormous I cannot help but read it as a signature."

— Ken Carey
from *"Where Do We Draw the Line?"*

WERNHER KRUTEIN/PHOTOVAULT

SOLSTICE

SHIFT

Magical Blend's Synergistic Guide to the Coming Age

with Commentaries by
Ken Carey, Jean Houston, David Spangler, Shakti Gawain
Barbara Hand Clow, Michael Grosso, Lynn Andrews, Neale Donald Walsch
Sirona Knight, Douglas Rushkoff, P.M.H. Atwater, Robert Anton Wilson
and Eleven Others

Edited by John Nelson

Photo Illustration by Wernher Krutein

Edited by John Nelson
Photo Illustration by Wernher Krutein
Graphic Design by Rosie Smith/Bartered Graphics
Cover Design by Jonah Tobias
Cover art: photo selection by John Nelson
photo compositing by Wernher Krutein
Interior photos provided by Photovault

For information write:

Hampton Roads Publishing Company, Inc.
134 Burgess Lane
Charlottesville, VA 22902

Or call: (804)296-2772
FAX: (804)296-5096
e-mail: hrpc@hrpub.com
Website: http://www.hrpub.com

If you are unable to order this book from your local bookseller, you may order directly from the publisher.
Quantity discounts for organizations are available.
Call 1-800-766-8009, toll-free.

ISBN 1-57174-063-5

10 9 8 7 6 5 4 3 2 1

Printed on acid-free paper in the United States of America

Credits for Author Portraits: *Jean Houston by Martha Swope; Marsha Sinetar ©David Torres; Ken Carey by Terry Stout; PMH Atwater by Barney Barnett; John Nelson by Linda Berardi; Neale Walsch by Roger Holden; Shakti Gawain by Max O'Neil of Mill Valley, CA; Jean Houston by Martha Swope; Michael Langevin by Deborah Genito.*

Contents

Foreword

by Michael Peter Langevin

It is with great pride and enthusiasm that I invite you on *Solstice Shift's* most amazing journey, a guide into the unknowable future. For seventeen years, *Magical Blend* magazine has been dedicated to the premise that in today's kinetic world our lives fall between our highest hopes and our deepest fears. *Magical Blend* has been dedicated to instilling hope in and transforming our fears about how the future will unfold. In many ways, *Solstice Shift* is an amazing monument to that effort. Here we have brought together twenty-three of our most tuned-in writers and asked them to tap into each other's spiritual and creative energies and write a synergistic book about our transition into global or planetary consciousness.

I am extremely pleased with the results of our effort: a guidebook that not only charts the coming tumultuous changes in our personal and collective lives but also gives practical instruction on how to flow with them. I can only hope that it reaches those open to its message and able to apply its lessons.

There are several themes that recur, each time from a different perspective, and warrant particular notice in this brief foreword. Although none of the writers claim to know exactly in what form the future will unfold, all, in their own ways, optimistically feel that the challenges can be met with a global response, and that the new communication technologies will unite us in our effort to solve planetary problems as diverse as environmental abuse and resource shortages. Others, such as Jean Houston, point to the new "mythic" reality, that "it is our privilege and our particular challenge to witness and assist a new story coming into being." But, as David Spangler reminds us, "If humanity is entering a new world and a new consciousness, if a transformative shift is truly going on, then...we must be awake to it and be part of it." We must become active participants; we must co-create the future, and not expect to be miraculously transported from here to there.

Another major theme is the blending of male and female energies. And it is only fitting that the book should open with Ken Carey staring into a starlit night and questioning the limitations of our male-dominated technological world: "How technologically dependent can a species become without destroying its environment? ...How complex can the organization of our lives become before we lose the joy that makes living worthwhile?" And should end with Peg Jordan stating, "As a future resident of the next millennium, I seek to harmonize these two worlds. The masculine world I've learned to live outwardly, the feminine world of my retreat. And, in this time of tremendously accelerated change—social, political, economic, and spiritual reinvention—there is a desire to bring both worlds, both selves, into harmony and wholeness."

In its essence, this book is a prayer. It is a group prayer, an unselfish gifting of its authors' talents, their prophetic and visionary capacities, and the wisdom and insight that flow from them. But, as a prayer, it is also a communication with the creative forces of the universe, beseeching them for their help, guidance, and realignment. I believe it is in putting aside their own opinions, prejudices, politics and opening themselves to inspiration, that our authors, whom I'm proud to be among, have demonstrated the special capacity that we will all need to flow with the changes ahead: the ability to recognize our limitations and the humility to open ourselves to guidance and inspiration.

Introduction

by John Nelson

The idea for *Solstice Shift* is that if the assembled writers—all humanity—are connected at a higher level, and if they choose to focus on the same topic—the same endeavor—at the same time, allowing themselves to be *inspired,* then the result would be essays—works—that reflect each writer's—person's—point of view but also blend together to form a cohesive whole. The implication of this concept is that we are both individual and collective beings, that within each of us is a soul-self or essence-self that expresses both our individuality and our higher connection to all life. Interestingly, actually almost predictably, this implication was recognized by many of the writers who, when faced with the chaos of this time of great crisis and transition, urged us, or even shamanically summoned us, to connect with our souls as the guiding principle of our lives.

So, from this book's inception, when Michael Langevin came to me with the idea for an anthology of original articles by *Magical Blend* contributors and I came back with the idea to have the writers sit down on Solstice Day '96 and write a book together, the book's synergetic concept and how that was actualized became its own message. To borrow a phrase from the '60s, the media was in fact the message, or least a contributing factor. To understand what the process of writing this book and the form it took actually tells us about humanity's collective fate as we move into the next millennium, allow me to first outline the steps that were taken to bring it to fruition.

Since we were asking our writers to tap into that collective or higher group self, to allow themselves to be inspired and to implement the ideas that came to them, even if doing so meant working outside their normal parameters, it required an extraordinary group of writers. Michael Langevin chose, from hundreds of contributing writers to his magazine, those he felt most capable and willing to share our vision and work with us to realize it. Many responded immediately to the idea and signed on; others found it too precious or New Age-y and declined. A little less than a month before Solstice Day, Michael had gathered together twenty of the thirty projected writers; at that point, *Magical Blend* put the names of all the authors into a hat and drew chapter assignments. Again, the idea was that each writer would pen an article synchronous with their position in the book. They were given only their chapter numbers and a general theme: the coming shift to global or planetary consciousness and its consequences for humankind. None of the writers knew each others' chapter positions or the nature of their contributions.

By June 20, Solstice Day 1996, we had gathered more than thirty writers to participate in our "experiment in consciousness," as we were to refer to the book project in the months to come. On that day the writers sat down like Jerry Snider, legal pad in hand, to write their articles; or sat under a starlit sky like Ken Carey to gather their inspiration, or were inspired by a walk on the beach like Neale Donald Walsch, or a series of prophetic dreams like Michael Langevin. Others attended Solstice celebrations: Joan Wilcox at Devil's Tower, Wyoming, and Barbara Hand Clow at Findhorn, Scotland.

And then, as many of the writers, having gotten their ideas, or had their visions on Solstice Day, began to write their articles, something interesting happened. My experience was probably the most extreme; I had driven up and down the Blue Ridge Parkway on Solstice Day, had meditated on my power spot—a rock outcropping over a 3,000-foot drop—and had gotten a handle on what I wanted to write. But, when I sat down to write my article, I found myself channeling a message—one that covers familiar themes but with a different voice. This was an unique experience for me; I write from a deep place, usually in an altered state, but I had never consciously channeled in this manner. Other writers reported starting with a general topic in mind and writing something entirely different, or having their articles take unforeseen twists and turns. Michael and I were excited; it sounded as though our "experiment in consciousness" had succeeded.

And then the articles arrived; most of them were brilliant but twice the requested length. However, some of the writers did not complete their assignments, while a few sent in canned material on their special topics, and one or two wrote cutesy send-ups of the book's idea. Welcome to the New Age. As the book's editor, I was sufficiently daunted by the task ahead of me to file the articles away for three months until I could clear the space to tackle the job. I started editing a few days after the Winter Solstice. Immersing myself in the material over the Christmas holiday, I discovered in the first few articles a voice, a tone, or a like-frequency, despite their differences of style and content, that became easy to identify—when I went deep enough. By tuning into this frequency, I began to prune the overly long articles, and it became obvious to Michael and me which articles were not in tune with the overall flow and needed to be excised. We finished with twenty-three articles; any doubts about violating the intent of our project by not including all the "serious" articles—we excluded three of them—was answered by the cohesion of what remained, as well as the synchronistic sequence of the chapters as they were originally assigned—we just moved articles up to fill in the missing spots.

The result is a series of articles whose organization is mythological—as opposed to the linear amplification of a theme—following, as Jean Houston defines that structure in her chapter, "the more mythic and organic principles of discontinuity, simultaneity, and multiple associations." As with other myths, Houston would advise us to "look for flow patterns rather than for linear cause/effect explanations." Again, the book's structure reflects the seemingly chaotic conditions of modern life, or its emerging mythic reality, but also reveals that beneath the surface turbulence is an associative form of organization or meaning. Our challenge in reading this work, as it is in dealing with our increasingly chaotic lives, is to find the centers, the "strange attractors" of modern chaos theory, around which everything flows.

As with the authors of this work, who reached beyond themselves and incorporated a perspective broader than their own individual points of view, we have all acquired, whether we use it or not, a new capacity of the human psyche. It comes, Jean Houston claims, with our transition from the Promethean myth to the myth of Proteus, the shape shifter. "The sea god Proteus was capable of taking on all manner of shapes, forms, and purposes at will. This is us today, suddenly like Proteus, having to take on other cultures, other ways of being, ways of knowing. We have to become Protean, highly resilient and creative. . . ."

The new technologies require and develop this Protean quality of the human psyche. They also reflect our transition from top-down authoritative social structures to more egalitarian societies, demonstrated, for example, in the realities of the internet. As Douglas Rushkoff tells us, "Although technology may have been put in place to contain nature, and the media may have been put in place to contain populations, they became too developed in their own rights to be contained themselves. Our techno-mediated infra-structure became too complex for anyone—William Randolph Hearst, Rupert Murdoch, or Bill Gates—to control." We are no longer getting our messages from the social-political-religious programmers, but are creating our own meaning. The "institution" of television is a perfect example. "In the old days," Rushkoff tells us, "the TV image was unchangeable. Gospel truth piped into the home from the top of some glass building. Today, kids have the experience of manipulating the image on the screen. This has fundamentally altered their perception of and reverence for the television image [or the 'Gospel According to']. . . . Kids with camcorders don't even bother to watch prepackaged programs. They just make their own." And, as with any "synergetic" experience, from scanning the internet to reading this work, we don't look for meaning, we create it.

This brings me to the final quality engendered by the mythic "chaotic" structure of this work and its comment on our times. The enormous complexity of contemporary experience, or the viewing of complex synergetic works of art, creates fractures in the human psyche. No single ego structure is flexible enough to contain it all. Again, Houston tells us that "to prepare for these world changes, the human psyche, I believe, is manifesting many different singularities of itself. . . . I think if schizophrenia is the disease of the human condition, then polyphrenia, the orchestration of our many selves, may be our expanded health." Michael Grosso refers to it as "creative dissociation." He would ask us to "assume for a moment that the evidence shows that our everyday persona is a mask for many hidden layers of human potential. This raises a fascinating question. Maybe we can learn to consciously dissociate from our normal, less-developed selves. It may be possible to reconnoiter the hidden regions of our other, more comprehensive minds. The power of dissociation may be the psychological equivalent of Einstein's equation $E=mc^2$."

Are we moving toward, as the book and its structure suggests (one can hear in all the articles the faint echo of single voice) a more comprehensive organization of the human psyche at the collective level? Is our transition into the next global or planetary level, as we address in this book, the movement toward collective organization? Douglas Rushkoff tells us, "It's no secret to anyone who has gone online, on a vision quest, into psychedelic space, a meditative journey (or even onto the pages of *Magical Blend* [or *Solstice Shift*]) that the next obvious evolutionary step is for human beings to coordinate, somehow, into a single 'meta'–being. That's the whole human struggle: to find group awareness, but without losing what we cherish as 'individual' awareness." That is the great challenge facing us, and we will make that transition only by connecting with our soul-selves, where, as I say in my chapter, "[when] you release yourself to spirit, you will find that, instead of losing your sense of individuality, your uniqueness, you will begin to realize, in ways you cannot even imagine, a sense of identity that, as your body now includes myriads of organic cells, encompasses galaxies."

WERNHER KRUTEIN/PHOTOVAULT

Chapter One

Where Do We Draw the Line?

By Ken Carey

"Why does the earth's axis point to one of the most conspicuous stars [Polaris] in the sky? . . .

"This convenient alignment, so useful to navigation, might be dismissed as a random anomaly if it stood alone, if it were the only such improbable coincidence involving the positioning of the earth and her nearest celestial neighbors. But there is another. Sun, moon—and the shadow of the earth when it falls upon the moon—all appear to be the same size. . . .

"Who left the moon for a sign? Who pointed earth's axis at so bright a star?"

This hemisphere's revolution toward the warmth of tomorrow's sun has left today's sun far below the western hills. Seeking shelter beneath the same ridge of oaks and hickories, a nearly invisible, sliver-thin moon trails in its wake. The year's longest day has passed; its shortest night has begun.

"Once in a blue moon," they say. So it happens again this June: one month, two full moons. Thirteen lunar months might better suit the rhythms of ocean, blood, and bones—with an annual solar holiday to celebrate the random, the unpredictable, the seeming coincidental, and of course, the cyclical rounds of seasons. Tonight, the summer solstice coincides with the waxing of the month's second full moon.

Perhaps at this very moment, our planet's northern axis is reaching its most sunward point. The heavy breathing of damp Ozark air seems to slow until I can almost feel the interval of pause, the microsecond of absolute rest, the utter stillness before directions change to shorten the days; and these mountains, in the heart of our northern continent, lean back toward the crisp and cool renewal of an inevitable winter's sway—still (in our annual circuit round the sun) millions of miles away.

Arriving at my destination, I make myself comfortable in the center of a hilltop clearing surrounded by forest stretching farther than the eye can see. To the south, just beyond the tree line, the wooded land drops off sharply into Flat Rock Hollow, a seasonal creek bed of pools and springs that transforms to raging whitewater during heavy rains.

Stretching out on my back, head propped against a contour of stone, I look upward into a sky of brilliant stars. What tremendous energy they represent—these flaming points of light that arch across the night! Each is a sun, the center of an energy system as unique and mysterious as our own.

Enjoying an exceptional view of the Milky Way, my thoughts drift with the drift of my gaze until I realize that I've been staring at the North Star and recalling those nights, when, lying awake in my sleeping bag, I have watched the sky spin slowly around this ancient travelers' guide—this fixed point of reference, seemingly stationary among the revolving dance of constellations.

On those nights, I would observe Polaris motionless, while every star in the sky swung around it in a slow and lazy arc, as if our North Star were the center of their universe, the hub of their wheel, or the illumined hand of some skillful star child swinging them 'round and 'round on a woven string of gravity and light years. Of course, the earth's rotation on its axis creates this effect—or so they say—overeager, it seems, to consider the matter closed. Yet this standard explanation begs the question: why does the earth's axis point to one of the most conspicuous stars in the sky?

Polaris is extraordinary. Few stars of such brilliance exist in a night sky as random and varied as ours. The laws of probability suggest that the earth's axis had a far greater chance of pointing to some faint or nearly invisible star, or to a portion of the sky void of visible stars. But our planet's northern axis is zeroed in like a tracking beam on a highly visible supergiant, 6,000 times brighter than the sun. Chance?

This convenient alignment, so useful to navigation, might be dismissed as a random anomaly if it stood alone, if it were the only such improbable coincidence involving the positioning of the earth and her nearest celestial neighbors. But there is another. Sun, moon—and the shadow of the earth when it falls upon the moon—all appear the same size.

I have seen the sun during total eclipse, when the outline of the moon before its fiery face was of exactly the right size to precisely cover its diameter—no more, no less.

The sun's diameter is 400 times greater than the diameter of the moon; its mass, 1,998,000 times greater.

The placement of earth, sun, and moon in orbits just the right distances from one another to give creatures on the earth's surface the illusion that all three are the same size is a stretch of coincidence so enormous I cannot help but read it as a signature.

We speak of ancient civilizations leaving monuments like Stonehenge and the Egyptian and Mayan Pyramids that testify to their knowledge of astronomy and mathematics, yet we fail to read the daily evidence of our eyes.

Who left the moon for a sign? Who pointed earth's axis at so bright a star?

The signature of an intelligence far in advance of our own is found in the lettering of our chromosomes, in the design of our cells; it is present in the structure of every leaf, every seed, and every blade of grass. When we lift our eyes above the beliefs and assumptions of the past, I have no doubt that we'll find evidence of its activity as prevalent as hydrogen atoms, as common as the grains of sand that flank the sea, and as pervasive as the air we breathe.

Could contact with this intelligence be, as some suggest, our next evolutionary step? I know only that this starry sky deepens my appreciation for this world—and for whatever genius plays behind it.

Midsummer's night. A time for wanderings of body as well as mind. Standing, I brush off my clothes and make for the blackness of the tree line to the south, barely able to distinguish the lighter patch where the parting of brush indicates the start of a well-trodden path down into the hollow. Even before my eyes adjust to the near-total darkness, my bare feet follow the absence of leaves that marks the path as distinct from the surrounding forest. Along with the stars shining through the openings between the treetops, I keep on course, winding my way slowly downward toward the hollow's floor.

Earlier, rising and receding, weaving its sound through the twilight, I heard an unfamiliar call. It may have been only the echo of a whip-poor-will bouncing off some distant hardwood hill, or ricochets from a mockingbird's echoed piping. More likely, it came from some passing bird not native to these parts.

Thankful that the cicadas are not yet active, I pause to listen but hear not a sound. The quiet is full, hard to describe. It carries a quality approaching amplitude, as though the volume of silence here has somehow been raised. It is the quiet of an egg about to hatch, of a night pregnant with expectation.

As I move silently through the star-shadowed darkness, the vibrancy of this ancient land greets me with a palpable wave of power. I sense an unspeakable strength focused intently on the insides of things, as if in night's early hours, nature has harnessed the whole of her power to pour potently into leaf, root, stem, and branch. Each absorbing cell digests the radiation stored from the sun, each plant grows palpably in rest, preparing for the activation of a morning that to me seems infinitely far away.

What are these impressions that brush my senses as I pass? The subtle scents that catch? The curious feel of a particular patch of ground? The almost imperceptible pull of what seems like faint magnetic fields near certain boulders and trees?

There is much that we never see in the world around us—not because it is less visible but because we are less than fully aware. How often do we thoughtlessly drift into routine behavior?

The very nature of habit links it more to sleep than wakefulness. And sleep, that most refreshing of our entertainments, is a dangerous way to spend our waking hours. Caught up in routine, we make decisions while the better part of our awareness slumbers. Habits of perception prevent us from seeing fully. Habitual interpretations of the earth show but a twisted caricature of its abundant and beauty-filled reality. We fail to see its potential. Or our own.

Habits of perception take many forms, filtering our awareness through beliefs, prejudices, opinions, and the far subtler pigeonholing of people, places, objects, and events that subconsciously categorizes everything that meets our gaze. When we observe our perceptual habits and learn to take them lightly, these habitual interpretations begin to relax. By not repressing or judging them as valid or invalid, but accepting them with calm and objective neutrality, they invariably recede. Perception and understanding then occur simultaneously. We see ourselves in our surroundings; everywhere our attention comes to rest: we are. It is obvious then: observer and observed, creature and environment are one. And have always been.

"The more my understanding of this mysterious world grows, the more I realize how much there is to know. But this bothers me not at all. The known will always be as finite as the unknown is infinite, the relationship between them as unchanging as π, or any other mathematical constant."

The more my understanding of this mysterious world grows, the more I realize how much there is to know. But this bothers me not at all. The known will always be as finite as the unknown is infinite, the relationship between them as unchanging as π, or any other mathematical constant. It makes no difference how much knowledge I acquire. All that matters is the quality of the knowledge I select, and whether it is relevant to the life I choose.

A thimbleful of first-hand knowledge is more relevant than a reservoir of second-hand facts.

I would rather climb a single oak but once than receive a doctorate degree studying an oak that someone else had climbed. Even if that oak had been climbed by Plato and his account written in the finest classical prose, I would do better to plant an acorn and watch it grow, if learning of oaks were truly my goal.

"Which student would have advanced the most at the end of a month," Thoreau asked, "the boy who had made his own jackknife from the ore which he had dug and smelted, reading as much as would be necessary for this—or the boy who had attended the lectures on metallurgy at the Institute in the meanwhile, and had received a Rodgers penknife from his father? Which would be most likely to cut his fingers?"

Knowledge is not a commodity to be possessed. The one who knows is what *is* known.

Knowledge and awareness are one. Separating them in our minds has prevented us from seeing this earth in its totality. Historically, we have only seen as much of it as we could imagine—and the earth has willingly obliged. Our fantasies are self-fulfilling. We harvest what we sow. Those who plant crabgrass do not harvest a field of roses.

Our awareness did not shut down because we got involved with the wrong sort of knowledge, but because we got into an unhealthy relationship with knowledge itself. By holding onto knowledge, it stopped being a tool and became a prison. We began viewing today through the filter of yesterdays.

Our present global electronic civilization can now store all the books of a vast library on a few compact discs. But, if we do not challenge our basic assumptions regarding the nature of knowledge and our relationship to it, our prospects, though we may plant our standard on the moon, are essentially no brighter than Rome's. Instead of placing a cart before the horse, the modern world has placed a gilded coach; but, being mired in the same tradition—our relationship to knowledge unchanged—it sits equally immobile.

Perhaps the Mayan's rejection of the wheel reflected an intuitive acknowledgment that, until they became creatures of spiritual and perceptual mobility, dramatic leaps in physical mobility would lack proper direction and lead them into lives of unacceptable complexity.

How much is too much? How technologically dependent can a species become without destroying its environment? Can we divide technology into benign and malignant forms—or are there deeper issues involved?

How complex can the organization of our lives become before we lose the joy that makes living worthwhile? Where does simple living end and an unacceptable level of complexity begin?

These are not just twentieth-century questions.

The Amish froze their technology in the nineteenth century. The Mayans, aware of the dangers of unchecked technological development, drew their line at the application of the wheel. The dolphins, some say, decided to draw their line at the development of hand-terminating limbs, entirely circumventing toolmaking technology and avoiding both its promise and its peril. These examples of ultraconservative technological boundaries are no longer general human options, but they remind us of vital issues often overlooked in the commercial complexity of high-tech urban societies. *Where do we draw the line?*

WERNHER KRUTEIN/PHOTOVAULT

"Perhaps the Mayan's rejection of the wheel reflected an intuitive acknowledgment that, until they became creatures of spiritual and perceptual mobility, dramatic leaps in physical mobility would lack proper direction and lead them into lives of unacceptable complexity."

Our own use of the wheel evolved into an industrial revolution that spun quickly out of control, causing social and environmental damage on a scale we are only now beginning to appreciate. Yet, unlike many of a more pessimistic persuasion, I believe that if we use its lessons wisely, we may still reap sufficient benefits from industrialization to offset its damage. A bold statement, I know. But the industrial revolution has been an exceptional catalyst for species' metamorphosis, comparable in degree and scale only to the acquisition of language. As a catalyst for change, its challenge goes to the root of who we are, requiring a fundamental reevaluation of all our basic assumptions about what "human" truly means—a whole new human definition that will ultimately be reflected in all our social, political, and commercial institutions. But its story, like our own, is far from over. Besides, once the genie is let out of the bottle, there is, despite the fairy tale, no enticing it back.

The change now required must come from within ourselves, within our thinking—a shift in our attitude toward information itself. The information we choose is the information we serve. Like electricity, information is polarized; it is either creative or destructive. Destructive information is not evil; it is simply programmed to destroy. It has its place: in the digestive juices that withdraw nutrients from our foods, in soil bacteria, among leaves decomposing on the forest floor. In countless ways, destructive energies serve the natural processes that sustain our lives and the health of our ecosystems.

The human mind, however, is designed to operate on the creative, energy-rich currents of living information. Destructive informational currents distort and eventually block its perception. Those who attempt to "own" truths soon find themselves orienting their lives around a storehouse of accumulated facts—arbitrarily maintained and increasingly difficult to access. Over time this destroys neurological circuits. Their superbly engineered minds malfunction, and their bodies rarely make it past three-score-and-ten.

"Man cannot know the truth," Blake wrote, "he can only embody it."

We are embodiments of the universe's truth, products of its creativity, interpretive mechanisms it has placed here to experience and enjoy dimensional life. Our human biocircuitry is designed to create, but until we clearly understand the vital distinction between *forms of truth* and *truth's living reality,* our bodies' higher creative functions cannot be activated.

In Twain's classic, *Huckleberry Finn,* Huck makes his own poignant assessment of the relevance of certain knowledge that the well-meaning widow Douglas is attempting to impart:

> *After supper she got out her book and learned me about Moses and the Bulrushes, and I was in a sweat to find out all about him; but by and by she let it out that Moses had been dead a considerable long time; so then I didn't care no more about him, because I don't take no stock in dead people.*

When our behavior is guided by past-oriented images instead of by present-moment perception, we fail to see what truly exists. We substitute an impostor for the real thing. By giving images more validity than what they depict, we exchange reality for fiction. And fiction must be defended.

Fictitious images are the source of conflict. It makes no difference if such images are misconstrued from the outset or truths exaggerated, the result is the same.

Differences of opinion do not create conflict. Conflict originates in the exaggeration and imposition of opinion. When we represent our viewpoints honestly in exchange with others doing the same, they meet in the central hub of balance that is the truth.

Walking homeward, my skin cells interpret the leaves beneath my feet in terms radically different from the olfactory cells that bring their fragrance, or the auditory cells that bring the occasional sound of their crunching.

The diverse varieties of understanding inherent to each of our more than 200 human cell groups are what make our bodies possible. Diversity gives us healthy bodies—and healthy societies. If our cultural, ethnic, and intellectual diversity disappeared, so would everything that makes us human—we would be a machine and not a species.

The insight needed to resolve our national and international disputes will not come from new or improved belief systems, nor through some elaborate synthesis of prevailing cultural wisdoms. It will come—indeed, it is coming—as more of us know and truly become ourselves.

"Relaxation into being" is the course of least resistance. There is no "action" we must take to achieve it. It is our natural state, appearing not *when we do* but *when we stop doing* all that prevents it. An enormous effort is needed to sustain our fictitious images of self and world—whether self-created or projected by others, they are all of the past. The moment we release the tension that defines us in arbitrary terms, there we are—as we have always been behind the forced masks of Illusion, behind the effort, the strain. Every flower knows this moment, every tree, every blade of grass.

While my own path involves interaction with people more often than not, it is in the wild places that I find my greatest inspiration. This land has taught me values and has guided me to insight more worthy than any I have ever encountered indoors. I would know these units of meaning that are the plants and wildlife of this forest, so that I might better know myself. I would learn to read these forest passages, to catch the drift of nature's thought. I would learn the tongues of birds and trees, of all that is animal, vegetable, and mineral. I would learn the solar songs that call forth the planet's life to eavesdrop better on the ancient humor that inspires it—and one day perhaps, if it is not too bold a dream, converse with those who write its verse, who weave this light, this sound, this love, into a universe.

TERRY STOUT

"Ken Carey is one of the great living teachers," writes author Marianne Williamson in her foreword to Carey's new book, *The Third Millennium.* Carey is known internationally for his lectures and workshops on spirituality. His books have sold more than half a million copies worldwide and include such classics as *The Starseed Transmissions, Return of the Bird Tribes,* and *Flat Rock Journal.*

NASA/PHOTOVAULT

Chapter Two

Message from Gaia

by John Nelson

I am old, ageless, but also as young as the morning dew. Do not assume that you can do permanent damage to my body, this planet. With but a flick of my green mantle or a shift of my magnetic poles, you and all that you have built will be no more.

I do not wish to coerce you into compliance with my laws; I wish to point out the obvious to a much beloved but recalcitrant child. And, since we are one being, your bones my mountains, your veins my flowing rivers, your energy bodies my higher magnetic self, you only injure yourself when you abuse me.

You and I have done this dance for many more years than your scientists can imagine. During this time, there have been many human cultures. A few, like your indigenous cultures of today, or of the recent past—since you have done your best to eradicate them—more fully manifest my spirit and yours.

Others, like yours, have followed an all-too-familiar pattern from living in harmony with me—blessing what is taken, honoring its source, and renewing it—to exploiting my resources, which is your own death sentence. Again, to point out the obvious, it is energy from nature's harvest that sustains you, no matter how mechanized you have made the process.

Tell me, where will you find oxygen to fill your lungs when your chemical pollutants have leeched all the oxygen from the air and you have cut down its major renewable source: the rain forests of the planet? From your chemical laboratories? Can you produce enough for five billion of you—or only the five million with access?

"This is not unlike the U.S. space program, whose real goal was not to reach the moon as a mere technological victory, but for humanity to see the globe from afar as a whole.

"Did you not feel a shift in awareness when you first saw, via live transmission or still photo, those glorious pictures of my body proper? Did you not feel, if only for a moment, that the forces that unite humanity as a whole were more vital than those that separate?"

And, when the fresh water from my lakes and rivers and underground reservoirs has dried up, and when the melting snows contain radioactive poisons and the acid rains are undrinkable, will those same laboratories supply your drinking water? I tell you, there are poisons that cannot be filtered out or steamed away, no matter how sophisticated your technology.

Can you not see the prison you are constructing for yourself, the grave you are digging? Look around at the artificial constructs that separate you from nature, and know that in the years to come they will be multiplied a hundredfold. A world without direct sunlight, with no fresh air, water, or natural food. Can your spirit survive in such a world?

You may think that you have an indomitable will to survive, that you can adapt to any situation. Like mutants in a post-apocalyptic world—of which you have numerous science fiction scenarios—you will simply evolve new organs to filter out contaminants in the air and water. That is what your scientists would have you believe.

I tell you that your physical bodies are merely vehicles for the expression of your souls. The higher and more refined your bodies become, and the more your minds—which are also an expression of spirit—evolve and can better interface with others of your kind, the greater part of your souls can manifest. Mutant bodies would not provide the needed range and flexibility.

In such a case, *Homo sapiens* will either give rise to a new race of higher expression or become extinct. There is also the possibility that you will heed the warnings given here and elsewhere and forge a new future for yourselves as humans. But the time for such a turnaround grows late, later than you imagine.

It is that prospect which I wish to address in the context of this brief message. Humans, we have traveled together for millions of years by your calculation; you have been a wonderful expression of mind in matter, but to survive you must now open to a greater expression of spirit in matter.

By spirit I mean more than conventional expressions of saintly holiness—St. Francis with his blessed birds or angels in gossamer attire—spirit exists in a whirlwind, in the flow of molten lava, in a torrential rain, in the stillness of a desert tableau. Spirit is that which flows through and beyond the individual, that which connects all that is.

If you could see an indigenous tribe silently performing a complex ritual dance, its members moving in sync without visual or verbal cues, releasing themselves to spirit and allowing it to direct them as they stop, turn, step backwards or twirl in place, you would know whereof I speak.

If your rejoinder is that you are more than bees in a hive, ants in an army; that mind has evolved to control instinct, you have mistaken the software for the hardware, which has just been upgraded, leading to the next step in your evolution: allowing spirit to move mind.

And, as you release yourself to spirit, you will find that, instead of losing your sense of

MARK LEIALOHA/PHOTOVAULT

individuality, your uniqueness, you will begin to realize, in ways you cannot even imagine, a sense of identity that, as your body now includes myriads of organic cells, encompasses galaxies.

It is the lack of such a vision, the natural consequence of mind's evolvement in matter, that has separated humans from the greater life of this planet, my body, and the other life forms that inhabit it. But, mind is also the instrument that allows for that realization, and that must be acknowledged as well.

As such, since your species accepted the offer to

"Can you not see the prison you are constructing for yourself, the grave you are digging? Look around at the artificial constructs that separate you from nature, and know that in the years to come they will be multiplied a hundredfold. A world without direct sunlight, with no fresh air, water, or natural food. Can your spirit survive in such a world?"

develop mind for the greater evolvement of the body proper, you cannot be held entirely responsible for the results. But, as there are stages in a child's development, and parents must sometimes push a child to the next level, you are about to get the "divine boot."

You have reached the stage where mind can recognize its own limitations and release itself to go beyond itself. Self-realization. And, as the seeds of organic matter are contained in the inorganic world, the seeds of spirit and its potential can be mirrored in the world of mind.

To know something, mind separates it from its background and compares it with others of its kind, or separates the parts from the whole to understand its inner workings. It is only by seeing itself as separate from others, but also as part of a whole, that mind can perform this function.

To withdraw itself from an amorphous whole, to know itself as separate and apart from that whole, to be infused with this wonderful sense of individual uniqueness is mind's great achievement, which should not be undervalued because of its disastrous effects.

Spirit first knows itself as that whole and then sees that whole manifest in each division of itself, down to the infinitely small. And, at each level, it too feels a sense of great individuality, but it does not lose awareness of itself as the whole and never sees itself merely as the part.

The hologram reflects that awareness, and this technology became manifest at this time because it expresses humanity's greater vision of itself. This is not unlike the U.S. space program, whose real goal was not to reach the moon as a mere technological victory, but for humanity to see the globe from afar as a whole.

Did you not feel a shift in awareness when you first saw, via live transmission or still photo, those glorious pictures of my body proper? Did you not feel, if only for a moment, that the forces that unite humanity as a whole were more vital than those that separate?

In the years since that historic moment, there have been many upheavals, but are you not closer to realizing that vision of one humanity today than then? Does not the new electronic media, created in the interval, help breakdown the artificial boundaries of race, nationality, and religion that separate you?

And, as you have not returned to the moon to collect more rocks, one day you will look back at this new technology—after it has been replaced by telepathic communication—and realize that its purpose was not to disseminate information but to open pathways to spiritual unity.

So, as you can see, there is, if not a plan, a movement afoot. And one, unfortunately for many who refuse to open themselves, that will be greatly accelerated—the divine boot I mentioned earlier. Those unable to ride this heightened energy to greater awareness of themselves as the whole will fall aside.

This is not punishment or even karma. These are concepts of limited thinking. The

"From this expanded awareness, from this being that encompasses all life on this planet, can you do harm (by omission or commission) to yourself under whatever guise you may so appear? You would look into the face of a starving African child, into the eyes of a wounded deer, into the soul of a mass murderer, to wildlife racing from a burning forest, and know yourself as them."

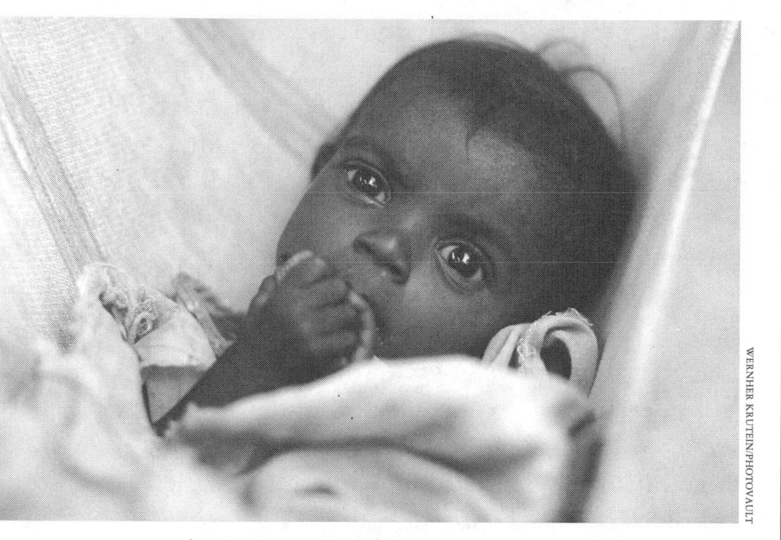

WERNHER KRUTEIN/PHOTOVAULT

whole does not punish itself or see itself as a part trying to reunite. It merely absorbs and transforms itself on its journey to higher levels of self-awareness and integration.

This is the essence of the spiritual perspective or orientation. It is a way of being, and the only mode of being that will survive in the coming shift to global or planetary consciousness: humanity's awareness of itself as the greater whole, one body, one planet.

If you are willing to accept the challenge of this movement of awareness, of consciousness, of gaia consciousness, then you must be willing to release yourself to a flow that will leave behind most of what you have—even what you know—for what you are becoming: planetary beings.

This is the next level of integration, of wholeness for humanity. But what does it mean to be a planetary being? It means more than changing your nationality from American to Globalist. Those changes, the falling off of boundaries, are the result of a change of consciousness, not a new voting choice.

To be a planetary being is first and foremost to experience yourself as the body proper. In the silence and stillness of your deepest meditation, move your center outward, expand your aura until eventually it encompasses the entire planet. Feel the pulse of my body's countless life forms rushing through you.

At first it will be a deafening cacophony of sounds, a visual overload of images, the energy of a cyclone battering you. If you do not resist, if you flow with this experience, you will know yourself as the body proper, and it will be a glorious awakening to your full potential as human beingness.

From this expanded awareness, from this being that encompasses all life on this planet, can you do harm (by omission or commission) to yourself under whatever guise you may so appear? You would look into the face of a starving African child, into the eyes of a wounded deer, into the soul of a mass murderer, to wildlife racing from a burning forest, and know yourself as them.

Would you not act differently from this grander perspective? Would not feed that child, hold that dying deer in your arms, confront the murderer in you, scoop up and run with the fleeing wolf pup? Would you not turn off your air conditioners, stop driving your automobiles, and produce only biodegradable products?

You would and you will, I can assure you. And you will think nothing of it. The shift to planetary consciousness will precipitate the most drastic realignment of a civilization you humans have ever witnessed. And it will be more of a falling off, a walking away from, than a reengineering.

As the new heightened energy enters, the old energy will be withdrawn. On the personal level, this will result in the breakdown of unconscious habits, beliefs, orientations, etc. You will be forced to confront yourself stripped to the bone, to release the old mode of being and embrace the new, or to cling to the old and cycle out with it.

This same pattern will repeat itself with all social and political structures: from PTAs through national governments to international churches. Many of these structures will not survive the scrutiny; some will reorient themselves, but not many. Humans will no longer need go-betweens at any level.

If this sounds like a prescription for chaos, do not be greatly concerned. If any of you have ever touched the power of your souls, you know that when it is fully manifested, you can truly walk through the valleys of death unharmed. Well, how do you think a million Buddhas will handle the situation?

Hyperbole? Only for those who have never experienced what I speak of. The others know, and soon many more will have the opportunity. It is your choice. Either way it is coming, because the body proper will not tolerate any more abuse. Know that and act accordingly.

To prepare yourself during this transition period—aside from stilling the mind and residing for ever longer periods of time deep within yourselves awaiting the moment—emulate, as far as possible, the indigenous tribes around the globe. These tribes have kept the sacred fires of planetary consciousness alive from the beginning.

Under the assault of successive "modern" civilizations, they have moved farther away and deeper within themselves until now, when the world is ready not only to hear their message, but to shift into their way of being. But do not venture into their territory and disturb them in their element. Soon they will come to you, if only in your dreamtime.

The essence of their beingness is their regard for the sacredness of all life, which is not a religion or moral code of conduct; it arises out of their very souls living unmolested in a natural environment. Take their clue and head back to nature, live in the forests, on mountaintops, in the valleys, on seashores: absorb my rhythms, free your minds, and allow your souls to come forward.

As stated earlier, you and I have come far together, dancing this dance of consciousness, and now we prepare for yet another glorious shift to greater awareness and higher integration. The God-force in me—and make no mistake that all of me, every grain of sand on my beaches, is imbued with it—embraces the God-force in you.

⊕

"John Nelson has pioneered the New Age novel," claims writer Jess Stearn; and he "has been pioneering this literary form since the late seventies" notes *Magical Blend* in a recent article on the author. His three novels, *Starborn, Transformations,* and *Matrix of the Gods,* explore the relationship between metaphysics, modern psychology, and the "new science." *Transformations,* which explores the hazards of bio-technology, will be rereleased in the fall of 1997 by Hampton Roads Publishing. A German edition of *Matrix of the Gods* will be published in 1998 by Wilhelm Goldmann. John Nelson is also the editor of *Medicine Dream: A Nagual Woman's Energetic Healing* and *Solstice Shift.* His chapter *Message from Gaia* is his first published channeled material.

LINDA BERARDI

LEE CELANO/PHOTOVAULT

"I have noticed that when faced with life issues (the manifestation of our attitudes and opinions, thoughts and feelings), we tend to react in one of three ways: (1) we play ostrich and pretend it away; (2) we label it an enemy or a devil and attack; or (3) we confront the situation squarely and honestly, search for the truth behind the appearance, and take decisive steps to initiate a constructive solution. The first way creates victims, the second victors (conquerors), and the third responsive and responsible participants in life, committed to growth and learning."

Chapter Three

THE THIRD WAY

by P.M.H. Atwater, Lh.D.

Air troubles itself as light slashes the overhead sky vault. Boomers from deep pressure troughs ricochet back and forth against a flood of waterspeak; and I stand here safe and dry—an observer to the extremes that play off what I had planned to be a summer solstice celebration. The phone has rung many times, jolting me to equal doses of horror and love.

For a brief moment, I catch the news from someone's radio that homes have been lost, possessions destroyed, some cars half-submerged, and power down. Yet, where I am is charmed space, and I thank God once again for the special drain field that protects our small townhouse. That drain field and the way it was to be built filled the viewscreen of my mind one morning during meditation. We had trusted that the slope of land around us would be sufficient for drainage, but our driveway was about to be paved, and why not check with the contractor, just in case. "Never heard of such a thing, lady," the man chortled, but he made real the marvel anyway. Because of heaven's unexpected gift, our home and surrounding land can now embrace torrents of rain without crisis.

Years ago, when we lived in Williamsburg, Virginia, I was standing on the banks of the James River at the very moment when, upriver, an older section of Richmond was being washed off the map. The day was bright with bird song, and soft grass caressed the wayside. In front of me, hardly at arm's length, huge trees, concrete abutments, debris of every sort, roiled and collided with thunderous force. I stood witness to the violence of Richmond's grief—from a place of peace.

Incidents such as this, where tragedy and blessing interweave the same "fabric," override the clock as I lose myself in a reverie unusual for me.

One of those who telephoned was my husband, reporting that he had been paid and that he will have an office to work from for another week. It seems our current crop of

CEOs have forgotten what Henry Ford learned nearly a century ago: take care of your employees and they will take care of you; pay them enough so they can afford to buy what they produce, and they will be your best advertisement.

A daughter embroiled in divorce also phoned. Her pained voice detailed the notice she had just received—that custody of her children may be granted to their father, not because he is a better parent, but because he makes more money. The value of a mother's love, she was told, is no longer a consideration in court. The moment I hung up the receiver my other children rang in, each in turn, the lot of them recently moved to the San Jose area and happily so. "Mom," said one, "the earthquakes here are fun. You can roll with them once you figure out how."

Then my mother called, launching immediately into a tirade about ecologists and Green-Peace Easterners who think they know what's right for the West. When I visited my home state of Idaho last year, I was shocked to discover the level of hatred and rage that exists against anyone who calls herself an environmentalist. Wear a shirt with wolves on it, as I innocently did, and you face instant recrimination.

Mother's complaint isn't really about ecology. It's about the double standards being crammed down Westerners throats: out-of-staters so rich they can buy up huge tracts of land, fence off once public fishing streams, and turn striking vistas into private reserves; while locals are forced to spend hundreds of thousands of dollars for land-use measures that make little sense and do nothing to solve the dilemma of accelerating drought and vanishing profits. The problem is one of power *over,* instead of power *to.*

Abuse doesn't correct abuse, nor is tradition necessarily appropriate. I have come to view tragedy and blessing as but opposing reflections from the same "mirror," a continuum of energy that can be swayed by the choices we make. Thus, the "pendulum swing" between creation's need for motion and rest can appear more as a clash between "who's on first?" and "how much can we grab?" than the natural flow of ups and downs. Still, we are not at the mercy of the forces which propel us—unless we think that.

The litany of phone calls nudge my musings back to the other side of death's curtain where The-Voice-Like-None-Other said to me: "Test revelation." These two words fueled my nearly twenty years of near-death research and showed me that every question has an answer, every disease a cure, and that the solutions we seek lie *inside* our problems.

I have noticed that when faced with life issues (the manifestation of our attitudes and opinions, thoughts and feelings), we tend to react in one of three ways: (1) we play ostrich and pretend it away; (2) we label it an enemy or a devil and attack; or (3) we confront the situation squarely and honestly, search for the truth behind the appearance, and take decisive steps to initiate a constructive solution. The first way creates victims, the second victors (con-

"Since the only real geography is consciousness, it is not where we are but what we have become that makes the difference. We do not exist in the earth plane so much to transform ourselves as to experience ourselves."

WERNHER KRUTEIN/PHOTOVAULT

querors), and the third responsive and responsible participants in life, committed to growth and learning.

This third way of dealing with life issues is the way in between duality—in between victors and victims, good and evil, darkness and light. The Third Way requires mediation and diplomacy skills, mindful attention, plus a willingness to consider *that which is appropriate* as a greater priority than self-centered interests. It takes time to learn and patience to initiate, and it necessitates cooperation and compromise, but it is the only way of living that shows any promise for a worthwhile future. The Third Way upholds dignity and value and wholeness—and wholeness is spirituality made manifest.

When we live in accordance with The Third Way, there is less tension. A certain amount of tension is necessary for existence to exist; we wouldn't be here without it. Too much tension, however, depletes initiative and restricts growth. The point of balance is forgiveness, as forgiveness releases tension and promotes patience. We can never transcend what we resist because of tension. We need to let go, to grow. We need to forgive.

Since the only real geography is consciousness, it is not where we are but what we have become that makes the difference. We do not exist in the earth plane so much to transform ourselves as to experience ourselves. Once we have discovered our true nature and our true worth, once we have slipped in between the bias of our own perceptual preferences, we automatically transform from the experience—we become who we really are.

The Third Way is expressed in nature as The Golden Mean. This mathematical formula celebrates the unique relationship between two unequal parts of a whole, where the small part stands in the same proportion to the large part as the large part stands to the whole. Experiments to measure energy wavelengths produced by people in love reveal the same configuration—The Golden Mean.

Among those who teach Third-Way Principles is Machaelle Small Wright. With the aid of her partner, Clarence Wright, she established the Perelandra Garden and originated the concept of "energy gardening." Year after year, her outdoor "laboratory" validates that planting seeds and bulbs as separate items, or in random rows in a garden plot is counterproductive. For consistently better harvests, you need to plant members of a whole *in ratio to the energy of the whole.* When plants are kept in balance with each other, plus the environment, the energy configuration that results maintains its own health regardless of threatening diseases, pests, or unexpected changes in the weather (an example of The Golden Mean in action).

This same energy configuration shows up in matters

WERNHER KRUTEIN/PHOTOVAULT

> *"Once we have discovered our true nature and our true worth, once we have slipped in between the bias of our own perceptual preferences, we automatically transform from the experience—we become who we really are."*

of bodily health. Example: if a woman needs more calcium, you do not just give her more calcium. You balance her nutrient levels in ratio to the needs of her entire body-mind complex. You do this by lowering protein intake (which uses up calcium), increasing carbohydrates (which enhances calcium levels), while suggesting that she explore emotional concerns about the support structures in her life (calcium relates to bones which are support structures). By observing this principle, the integrity of the whole is respected and brought into balance.

Dean Black, Ph.D., is a proponent of balancing the parts with the whole and creating higher ratios of integrity. He uses the term "contextual healing" to identify the system of wellness based upon the body's native intelligence to heal itself once the needs of the larger whole have been addressed.

Another is John L. McKnight, a college professor who has been preaching the gospel of community for over twenty years. He claims that groups like United Way and the various government social welfare programs that funnel money into "servicers" (people who go into communities "at risk" to label deficiencies) miss the point. "We must go into these communities to identify the assets and capacities of the local citizens, then mobilize and empower them to solve their own problems. By focusing on what's right with a community, we can make a dynamic difference." When McKnight studied thousands of social welfare projects in 200 communities across the United States, he formulated specific proposals on how The Third Way can work in today's society.

The principle of The Golden Mean applies as well to manufacturing and politics as it does to economics; and it is why communism failed. Communism's enforced status quo violates the very balance life insists upon for growth.

As rain retreats and light-strikes fade into the gray canvas of sky, I am mindful that what seems idealistic and lofty about The Third Way is actually misleading. Common sense defines the principle: the willingness to live as if life mattered. Each member of my family, my neighbors and myself, benefit greatly when we live in this manner—when we listen more and take the time to center ourselves before we respond.

Tomorrow I journey to Swannanoa and the University of Science and Philosophy, a spiritual center located atop Afton Mountain in Virginia's Blue Ridge Mountains. Unquestionably, the grounds of Swannanoa cradle a large power spot where, according to dowsers, an atmospheric "downspout" of columnar energy has joined in union with a "water dome" beneath the soil's surface. This "marriage" of sky power (symbolically termed "male") and earth energy ("female") can be found at each sacred site across the planet that continues to be energetically active. Originally used by the wise for worship, healing, and the development of "special gifts," such sites have mostly been ignored in modern times or had churches built over them.

Wetness splashes as I walk toward our backyard forest, yet the land feels unnourished; leaf-touch and root-works, numb. I am caught by the sense that where I live, all around me, each fiber and pulsebeat of nature knows what will happen tomorrow. Huge machines are coming to grind the forest into sawdust as make-ready for eighty more households and a scheme of roadways and sidewalks. One world dies so another may live, tomorrow. In effect, my journey to Swannanoa is a power spot trade-off. That's because the "webbing," that invisible crisscross of interconnecting light threads that permeates all matter, has awakened. Every spot is now a power spot.

Time is accelerating. The atomic clocks in Boulder, Colorado, made to keep perfect time without any influence save the atomic energy that powers them, have had to be reset—upwards—nineteen times since 1972. The base resonant frequency of earth or the Schumann Cavity Resonance (earth's "heartbeat") has risen from long centuries of registry at around 7.8 cycles per second to a new reading of 9.6 cycles in the last two years alone. While earth's pulse quickens, her magnetic field strength continues its 4,000-year slide. It's currently half of what it was several hundred years ago. Some geologists point out that the steady lessening of magnetic field strength in conjunction with a sudden jump in vibratory rates could signal the beginning of a magnetic reversal or pole shift.

This same combination of factors is also a sign that the earth is becoming a giant initiation chamber. Literally, our wondrous blue marble is being enlivened. Holy ground is no longer confined to sacred sites. Staying home we can still coparticipate in our own evolution, while sharing in the acceleration of change engulfing our planet. We can worship, heal, develop our "special gifts," and be utterly transformed by the mere act of experiencing and expressing the fullness of who and what we are: Children of The Most High, Projections from The One Mind, Creations of God's Grace.

We do not have to go anywhere to be everywhere!

As the countdown continues to the millennial "gateway" we will all soon pass through, I find it fascinating that the "energy doors" of tragedy and blessing must be traversed before the last vestiges of "me first" meet the new glimmer of "we together." Philosophical musings seem arrogant in times as these, for survival is always primary; an empty belly and a broken heart still hurt.

Dying three times as I have, however, and each time experiencing the near-death phenomenon, has removed death's sting.

Yes, I respect the laws of existence and what it means to wear a body and produce a personality and engage in relationships. I thoroughly enjoy the scenic opportunities the earthworld provides and accept my portion of stewardship for its continuance. I fill many of my moments with prayers for the earthbound and the heavenbound, as I affirm that our passage through the millennial gateway be accomplished with the least amount of disruption possible. I share my light and my laughter, as I endeavor to reflect the goodness life truly is.

⊕

For a fuller treatment of Third-Way Principles and the inner workings of creation and consciousness, refer to Atwater's book, *Future Memory: How Those Who "See the Future" Shed New Light on the Workings of the Human Mind,* Birch Lane Press, New York, 1996. Check out her website at: http://www.albany.net/~steffw/atwater.

References:

Machaelle Small Wright, Perelandra Center for Nature Research, P.O. Box 3603, Warrenton, VA 20188. Twenty-four-hour message phone, (703) 937-2153. Ask for catalog and activity schedule.

Dean Black, Ph.D., Tapestry Press, P.O. Box 653, Springville, UT 84663. Business phone, (801) 489-9432. For orders, 1-800-333-4290. Request catalog of his many books and tapes, plus his lecture schedule.

John L. McKnight, Northwestern University, 2040 Sheridan Road, Evanston, IL 60208. Department phone, (708) 491-3518. He gives classes on the methods he has adapted. Must read—*The Careless Community: Community and Its Counterfeits,* Basic Books, New York, 1995.

Swannanoa Palace, University of Science and Philosophy, P.O. Box 520, Waynesboro, VA 22980. Business phones, (540) 942-5161 and 1-800-882-5683. Founded by Walter and Lao Russell in 1949, the palace itself now operates as a museum—public tours daily. Also serves as a hub for classes, workshops, and a home study course. Scientific experiments based on Russell's cosmology have produced a major breakthrough—the transmutation of nitrogen gas into helium-4 and lithium-5. Further trials are pending. A catalog of publications and activities is available on request.

WERNHER KRUTEIN/PHOTOVAULT

P.M.H. Atwater's 1977 near-death experience led her to seek out and interview other near-death survivors. Her findings about the aftereffects of near-death experiences were the basis of *Coming Back to Life: the After-Effects of the Near-Death Experience* (1988, Dodd Mead & Co.). After fifteen years of intensive research, speaking with and interviewing more than 3,000 near-death survivors, her book *Beyond the Light, What Isn't Being Said about the Near-Death Experience* (1994, Birch Lane Press) and its sequel, *Future Memory* (1996, Birch Lane Press), represent the most complete compendium yet done of the aftereffects of the near-death experience. She is also the author of *The Magical Language of Runes* (1990, Bear & Co.) and *Goddess Runes* (1996, Avon Books).

DENNIS YOUNG/PHOTOVAULT

"If human culture is an articulation of nature, then media is the articulation of technology. As civilization and culture grew out of the natural collection of human beings, media grew out of technology to control and restrict our free motions and underlying collective will. Just as technology denies nature, traditional media denies humanity."

Chapter Four

The Shift Online

by Douglas Rushkoff

Although I like to think of myself as "clued in" to the motions of nature, they seem to evade me. But that's finally beginning to change. I write mostly about technology and its effects on culture and spirituality. I see technology as a real extension of nature—an expression of the evolutionary drive towards complexity and consciousness. It wasn't always this way. As originally implemented, technology was developed to deny the underlying patterns of nature. We invented electric lights to deny the blackness of night and the rhythm of daybreak. Heat and air conditioning allowed us to deny the climactic cycle of the seasons. Irrigation helped us conquer the patterns of weather. We fly in planes to break the laws of distance and break multiple time zones in just a few hours, throwing our bodies out of their own circadian rhythms. We invent pills from dexedrine to melatonin to convince our bodies otherwise, then wonder why we feel so out of touch. In this scenario, nature is the enemy and human technology keeps it at bay.

If human culture is an articulation of nature, then media is the articulation of technology. As civilization and culture grew out of the natural collection of human beings, media grew out of technology to control and restrict our free motions and underlying collective will. Just as technology denies nature, traditional media denies humanity. At any major university, you will find that the study of communications has nothing to do with helping people talk to one another. It is the study of how governments can manipulate their subjects or citizens, and how corporations can manipulate their customers and employees. It is not the study of communication—it is the research and development of social programming.

Media was put into place as a way of controlling the natural ebb and flow of society. By dividing amorphous populations into manageable market segments and interest groups, the social scientists could more accurately predict and alter our behaviors. Television and other top-down media arose to program the masses into submission. Why do you think they call it TV programming? They're not programming the television sets; they're programming the viewers.

Media programming only works when the programmer has the luxury of a captive and isolated audience. Like any form of hypnosis, television programming depends on the viewers' reception without distraction. The subject allows her thoughts to be directed and ordered by the programmer. Her naturally free-form, holistic consciousness is made linear. She learns to follow the leader, step by step.

Television worked perfectly. The viewer sat alone and let herself be drawn into the trance. From this point, the programming part was simple: tell stories. Since Aristotle and even the Bible, the programmer has used stories to reduce his audience to passive participants. For aboriginal cultures, the story has served as a way of preserving sacred ancient ideas as they pass down through generations. For modern Western culture, the technique of the story has been abused to enforce purchasing decisions and moral agendas.

The traditional story works by putting the audience in a state of tension. The programming storyteller creates a character we like so that we identify with this hero's plight. Then, the character is placed in jeopardy of one sort or another. As the character moves up the incline plane towards crisis, we follow him vicariously, while taking on his anxiety as our own. Helplessly we follow him up into danger, disease, or divorce, and just when we can't take any more tension without bursting, the hero finds a

WERNHER KRUTEIN/PHOTOVAULT

way out. He finds a moral, a product, an agenda, or a strategy that rescues him, and us along with him, from the awful anxiety. The higher the level of tension we've been able to create, the more preposterous the hero's critical twist can get. But whatever solution the character finds, the audience must swallow it, too. Along with it, we swallow the sponsor or network's agenda, but at least we get to escape from the anxiety.

This is what it means to "entertain"—literally "to hold within"—and it only works on a captive audience. In the old days of television, when a character would walk into danger and take the audience up into uncomfortable anxiety, it would have taken at least 10 or 20 calories of human effort for the viewer to walk up to her TV set and change the channel. The viewer was trapped. As long as the programmer didn't raise the stakes too abruptly, she would stay in her La-Z-Boy and go along for the ride. The remote control changed that.

With an expenditure of perhaps .0001 calories, the anxious viewer is liberated from her tortuous imprisonment. Although most well-behaved adult viewers will soldier on through a story, kids raised with remotes in their hands have much less reverence for these well-crafted arcs, and zap away without a moment's hesitation. Instead of watching one program, they skim through ten at a time. They don't watch TV, they watch the television, guiding their own paths through the entirety of media rather than following the prescribed course of any one programmer.

No matter how much we complain about our kids' short attention spans, their ability to disconnect from programming has released them from the hypnotic spell of even the best TV mesmerizers. The Nintendo joystick further empowers them while compounding the programmer's dilemma. In the old days, the TV image was unchangeable. Gospel truth piped into the home from the top of some glass building. Today, kids have the experience of manipulating the image on the screen. This has fundamentally altered their perception of and reverence for the television image. Better yet, the computer mouse and the Internet turn the video monitor into a doorway. No longer just an appliance for passive programming, the monitor is a portal to places and ideas. Kids with camcorders don't even bother to watch prepackaged programs. They just make their own.

The people I call "screenagers," those raised with interactive devices in their media arsenals, are natives in a media-space where even the best television programmers are immigrants. They speak the language better and see through those clumsy attempts to program them into

"As originally implemented, technology was developed to deny the underlying patterns of nature. We invented electric lights to deny the blackness of night and the rhythm of daybreak. Heat and air conditioning allowed us to deny the climactic cycle of the seasons. Irrigation helped us conquer the patterns of weather. . . .In this scenario, nature is the enemy and human technology keeps it at bay."

submission. They never forget for a moment that they are watching media, and resent people who try to draw them in and sell them something. We mistake their ironic detachment for cultural apathy. It's not. They do care; they're just unwilling to take on a character's anxiety and then swallow some hidden agenda.

The shows embraced by the "screenage" generation accept the inherent discontinuity of the television medium—and our natural world—rather than trying to smooth it out. Most traditional programming attempts to smooth over discontinuity, lest the programmer lose his audience. When they have to break for a commercial, they introduce a cliff-hanger to tide us over. It's discontinuity pretending to be continuous, and it comes across as false.

But where adults are challenged by gaps, kids thrive on them. Just consider the difference between the experience of an adult skier and a child snow-boarder descending a slope. The adult, with his long parallel skis, looks for the smoothest, most powdery path possible. The kid seeks out the bumps, rocks, and patches of ice. They thrive on discontinuity because, deep down, they sense it is real and not contrived.

Kids experience media and technology differently because they are on the far side of the evolutionary shift—that same shift the writers in this book are proclaiming. As I see it, this shift is in the way we tell stories.

The extended evolution of storytelling outlined in my book, *Playing the Future,* describes the three main stages of nearly every cultural invention. We start with a literal phase. For money, this is gold. It has actual, literal value. For Western religion, this is the Ten Commandments. Do this, don't do that. It works with simple, straight lines, and works when one's experience is very limited.

The second stage is metaphor. The metaphor for gold was the gold certificate. Paper money represented a real value of gold. For religion, it was Jesus and the parable. Teaching stories, such as the one about the prostitute in the road about to be stoned, work as metaphors for the situations in our lives. Better than a literal rule, a teaching story can be applied to thousands of possible real-life dilemmas. If we can all identify with the character in the story, then the parable works. That's why they're called parables: a parabola is a curve that depicts the relationship of a single point to whole line. As long as we're in a linear world, and all stand in a line, the point of story will relate to us all. Stories require heroes we all relate to—superbeings, hierarchy, and allegiance. We moved from straight lines to curves or, mathematically, from $x=y$ to $x^2=y$.

But our world, and certainly the world of our children, is too chaotic for us all to stand in a line and respect one authority. Our kids don't even go to rock concerts anymore; they go to rave dances, where there's no sexy singer for everyone to face. The rave dance—a spiritual event—is a great example of the third cultural phase, what I call "recapitulation." Rather than relating to someone else's spiritual story, they create their own. The rave event recapitulates a spiritual truth. It is spirituality. That's why Shirley Maclaine on the beach shouting "I am God" made sense to so many. She wasn't declaring herself lord of the heavens; she merely realized that she recapitulated, in some small but grand way, the essence of God. She saw herself as part of the great fractal. That's new math: a discontinuous equation.

The monetary equivalent of recapitulation is the currency we now use in the United States called "the Federal Reserve Note." It is cash, but it has no value in relation to some real metal. The dollar recapitulates the original function of money. It is money.

In recapitulatory media and storytelling, the audience's moment of reward is shifted away from the hero's daring escape and onto the viewer's own ability to orient himself in an increasingly complex media-space. Instead of experiencing vicarious relief from tension and absorbing the associated message, the "screenager" gets the joy of making momentary sense and associations in a chaotic media-space. He gets his bearings in what I'd argue is a natural world. Joseph Campbell was only half right when he suggested that Western civilization needs "a new myth." We need a new *kind* of myth. Recapitulated media has come to the rescue.

Although technology may have been put in place to contain nature, and the media may have been put in place to contain populations, they became too developed in their own rights to be contained themselves. Our techno-mediated

"Kids who go out on the Internet don't browse for facts. They search for other humans. It may look cold and electronic, but what other means do they have at their disposal in a culture that values competition over cooperation, and so-called family values over community values? Cyberspace is remedial help for a civilization that has lost the ability to touch itself."

WERNHER KRUTEIN/PHOTOVAULT

infrastructure became too complex for anyone—William Randolph Hearst, Rupert Murdoch, or Bill Gates—to control. Although the wires may have been set down to function as avenues for unidirectional programming, no one predicted that we would start connecting them up and talking through them. Faxes, telephones, camcorders, modems, and computers changed the top-down quality of the mediaspace. We all started communicating with one another. No one in charge had taken into account the fact that electrons don't care which way they travel through a wire.

They know no allegiance. There's no up or down, so hierarchy and one-pointedness is impossible.

Even more disastrous for those who would dominate nature and program human beings, technology and the media have begun to express the underlying drive of evolution itself: for awareness, complexity, and connectivity. Evolution is the way nature expresses itself over time. In its age-old dance with deadening entropy, nature strives to become more conscious and alive. Atoms become molecules become amino acid chains become cells become organisms become, well, civilization. It's no secret to anyone who has gone online, on a vision quest, into psychedelic space, a meditative journey (or even onto the pages of *Magical Blend)* that the next obvious evolutionary step is for human beings to coordinate, somehow, into a single "meta"-being. That's the whole human struggle: to find group awareness, but without losing what we cherish as "individual" awareness. Evolution itself is a recapitulating event—that's why the fetus in the womb passes through the entire history of biological evolution as it gestates.

While many argue that the impending "Gaian mind" of cyberspace—all those wires connecting the individual human neurons together—will turn our multifaceted world into a monoculture, I'd argue that just the opposite is true. The programmed media hierarchy is what pushes us towards monoculture. A world where each member can express herself is absolute chaos. Not disorder, chaos.

So technology now addresses the great and natural human urge towards connection. Kids who go out on the Internet don't browse for facts. They search for other humans. It may look cold and electronic, but what other means do they have at their disposal in a culture that values competition over cooperation, and so-called family values over community values? Cyberspace is remedial help for a civilization that has lost the ability to touch itself. Ironically, it is not the so-called "Third World" indigenous cultures who need to get online. They already understand their connection to nature and the natural rhythms of the planet. It is we, the members of the over-ordered Western civilization, who need to learn that we're all part of the same great organism. Cyberspace merely approximates the level of communication that we'll be capable of, once we develop the compassion to perceive our deep connectedness organically. The Internet is Western white man's clean, dry, safe, electronic way of experiencing some global community.

As a culture, we are predisposed to resist the chaotic nature of the real world. The stories on which we have been raised for the past several centuries reduce the complexity of the human experience to oversimplified moral platitudes and determinist certainties. We have become addicted to stories with endings. It is the only way we know to relieve the tension of not knowing. We so crave definitive endings that millions of fundamentalists worldwide would rather the entire planet be consumed in a fiery apocalypse than simply let it keep going. We'd rather be eternally damned and get the relief of an ending to the story than live on in existential uncertainty. We refuse to accept the alternative to completion: change. This is why fundamentalists are so opposed to the notion of evolution. Evolution changes the ground rules.

Technology and media have never really been apart from nature. Nothing ever has. Our power plants are no less natural than a beaver's dam. Our chemicals are no less natural than bees' honey. We just fooled ourselves into thinking we had devised a way to resist the ebb and flow of nature. We were really just serving its greater agenda.

By allowing our media to reach a state of true turbulence, we find that rather than exacerbating our disconnection from nature and one another, it is forcing us once again to confront the human urge for self-expression and group awareness. For spiritual people to resist technology for its seemingly unnatural implementation would be as foolish as it is for absolutists to resist its new tendency to promote an evolutionary agenda.

Living in the free-form chaotic realm of cyberspace is what awakened me to the underlying rhythms of our world and the urge of all people towards greater connectedness. Most importantly, it's what made me realize I'm part of a great shift from allegiance to self-expression, metaphor to recapitulation, fundamentalism to globalism, apocalypse to evolution, and artificially imposed certainty to the unpredictable impermanence of real life. It has gotten me back in touch with the underlying rhythms of nature and the great planetary quest for shared consciousness.

⊕

Douglas Rushkoff is the author of *Cyberia, Media Virus, Playing the Future,* and a new novel, *Ecstasy Club.* He writes a weekly column about technology and culture for *The New York Times Syndicate* and is a frequent contributor to *Esquire, Details,* and *Paper.* He lectures at universities around the world and teaches workshops at Esalen and the Banff Center. He lives in New York City.

Chapter Five

BALANCE IS A FIVE-POINTED STAR

by Jerry Snider

My assignment, along with the other contributors to this volume, was to tune into the global mind during the summer solstice of June 20, 1996, and extract a bit of wisdom concerning a hypothesized, upcoming shift in planetary consciousness. The idea was that chapters would be assigned by random pick, with the hope that this would result in some kind of sequential inner logic to the book. That's quite an undertaking, and I should tell you up front that from the beginning I have remained in the dark about what exactly I was being asked to do. My confusion arises primarily from what is meant by "planetary consciousness." The phrase is as obtuse as it is high sounding. Are we talking here of human awareness of its planetary responsibility, or does the phrase refer to some kind of global mind rising up through the natural world to human comprehension? While the first interpretation points to a kind of scientism, or intellectual grasp of practical necessity, the second suggests a kind of divine revelation that boggles the mind with its implications. The vagaries of human spiritual aspiration are confusing enough, but the tangled web of traditional religious outlooks and agendas pale in terms of incomprehensibility when set beside something as utterly alien as the notion of a planetary mind. So while it would be easier to approach the assignment from a human trajectory, my taste for the bizarre leads me to the second approach. Besides, if the planet has plans for my future, I would like to know them.

When chapter placements were drawn, I was assigned chapter five. It's a number I resonate with, for although I have never been one for "lucky numbers," there was a time in my life when the number five held a special significance for me.

Seventeen years ago, when we first started publishing *Magical Blend,* I used to wear a five-pointed star on a chain around my neck. I wore it as a symbol of man as magician—feet planted firmly on the ground, head in the clouds and arms outstretched to trans-

WERNHER KRUTEIN/PHOTOVAULT

"Hope requires something to stand on, a foundation, even if that foundation is barely large enough to get a foothold. That's why arrogance is the enemy of hope. Arrogance is big-footed and clumsy, totally incapable of finding a toehold in the debris of disenchanted dreams. Hope, on the other hand, can perform an amazing balancing act on the tiniest platform of possibility."

duce the two energies. Funny how I'd forgotten that star. I know I still have it packed away somewhere, but I haven't seen it in years.

That star reminds me of something else from my past. I used to be big on symbols. I still am, I suppose, but now I let the symbol stew on the back burner until I get a whiff of the flavor of the symbolic soup that's been cooking. Back then I was less patient. I can recall many a late night session flipping furiously through the pages of *An Illustrated Encyclopedia of Traditional Symbols,* trying to discover the hidden meaning of some fragment of dream or odd synchronicity. And while the star remains hidden away, the *Illustrated Encyclopedia* still sits on the bookshelf where it has remained undisturbed for over a decade, other than being packed and unpacked for a succession of moves. I took it down from its place, wiped the dust off its spine, and looked up the number five. What I read was of little help. I was informed that, "The pentagon, being endless, shares the symbolism of the perfection and power of the circle," and that "five is the marriage number of the *hieros gamos* as the combination of the feminine, even, number two and the masculine, odd, three." I shook my head and tossed the book to the floor. No wonder it has been gathering dust. Why does metaphysics always have to sound like "acid math"?

The image of myself as a young man wearing my five-pointed star while poring over an arcane book looking for symbolic structure in my life haunts me. Why does it make me so uncomfortable? Is it because it all seems a little foolish now, or is it because my convictions were stronger then? Seventeen years ago I may have looked foolish, but I felt empowered. Now enthusiasm is a hit-and-miss proposition. The responsibilities of youth are different than those of maturity. It is youth's burden to stir things up. It is maturity's burden to settle things down. The remarkable thing is that the two complement one another without trying. It seems to me that the multiplicity of outlooks and efforts it takes to create the arc of a single life is less an act of consciousness than of soul. If this is so, then nature—or God for that matter—is less concerned with what we know than with how we grow.

The next morning I awoke to find the image of a five-pointed star dancing at the edge of consciousness. This time there was a thought paired to the symbol. That thought was "balance." If what I was looking for was a message from the planetary mind, "balance" would seem to fit the bill. It's a short message, but a telling one. Balance epitomizes the earth from every perspective, from its elegant celestial minuet to the intricacies of nature's delicate balance. And certainly, if there's one thing that epitomizes humanity's most pressing problems, it's lack of balance. Ironically, even our attempts to right the imbalances we have caused tend to end up out of balance themselves. Consider, for example, the current trend in environmental education. We are bombarded with information aimed at waking us up to our planetary responsibilities, but the message is so negative and relentless, I find myself tuning it out. Responsibility requires a certain amount of confidence to meet the challenges responsibility brings, but confidence is the first casualty in this barrage of negativity. The endless lists of endangered species, harmful pollutants, and global plagues often seem to raise more hysteria than consciousness, resulting in apathy rather than confidence. When everything is disheartening, the soul is robbed of its ability to respond, and both conscience and consciousness shut down. This is also why I tend to tune out the New Age's endless cadre of spirit channels and prophets with their tales of polar shifts, earthquakes, and a forthcoming Ice Age. They breed not hope but despair. In our Pandora's Box of global warmings and warnings, it is important not to let hope escape. As long as hope remains, balance can be regained.

All of this is not to say we should be blithely ignorant of the challenges before us. Hope is not just wishful thinking. Hope requires something to stand on, a foundation, even if that foundation is barely large enough to get a foothold. That's why arrogance is the enemy of hope. Arrogance is big-footed and clumsy, totally incapable of finding a toehold in the debris of disenchanted dreams. Hope, on the other hand, can perform an amazing balancing act on the tiniest platform of possibility. It seems to me that arrogance is an act of mind, while balance is an act of soul. So if rediscovering our connection to nature is the goal, I would not rely on mind for the job. Instead of becoming lost in the abstract concepts and ideologies that have led to our self-imposed exile from the natural world, a more soulful place to start might be by paying attention to the earth directly beneath our feet. Twenty minutes a day spent listening to nature instead of to the incessant ruminations of our own mental machinery might just begin to help us remember who we are and the world of which we are a part. It might even remind us that most of the concepts and ideologies that control our lives are illusory compared with the reality of being one individual among one species among hundreds of thousands of species on one living earth.

Finding balance means being aware and being ready. For these two attributes, feelings are more important than thoughts or emotions. Feelings are a way of shifting balance and finding a foothold. They gauge, they weigh, and when things feel right, one can let one's defenses down and segue into revery. In this fluid state, the earth's sensuous beauty can easily transform revery into reverence. To me, balance—being ready and aware—happens at that very instant. To go further, to contemplate the source inspiring this reverence and what it wants from us only leads back to the world of ideas. If we want to learn the earth's mind, we must begin by quieting our own.

Learning balance is a way of preparing to meet whatever comes our way, and sometimes what comes our way is a blessing, not a curse. To be balanced means to be poised for serendipity, and it is through serendipity that grace most often reveals itself.

I think of grace as the shape divinity takes to get me to pay attention to the sacred. Grace comes in the form of a blessing. It is a carrot instead of a stick approach, and when it comes it manages to get me to take my head out of the sand long enough to marvel at the genuine concern life has for me. But is this concern a conscious one? I am not so certain. Moments of grace come out of nowhere. Their logic, if they have one, is not the logic of human thought. They cannot be planned, they can only be embraced. Furthermore, they are clearly not rewards for piety since they are as likely to find the sinner as the saint. Others speak of these high-impact instants as moments of "Christ consciousness," but to me, they transcend consciousness and seem to belong more to the terrain of soul. I think of them in terms of a concept predating Christianity—the "Anima Mundi," or "soul of the world." Perhaps it's just a difference in terms, but the divinity I feel in such moments has an earthy quality to it that distinguishes it

WERNHER KRUTEIN/PHOTOVAULT

from today's antiseptic religious environment. As I have experienced them, moments of grace are multifaceted, coming from many different directions at once. They are a web of interdependence, a balancing act, a safety net that reeks of life rather than distances itself from it. Such moments remind me that life is a grunt and a push and is no less worthy of reverence because of it.

Though it is easy for me to accept that earth has a soul, I am less certain it has a mind. As human beings, we value intelligence because it has enabled us to perceive the bigger picture. By taking the whole apart, we are able to understand how each piece fits together. But does creation require consciousness? Couldn't it be an act of love as easily as a result of thought? Consciousness presupposes not only action, but a recognition that one is, in fact, in the act of acting. Forcing this complicated bit of mental gymnastics onto good old Gaia seems a bit too anthropomorphic for my taste. Yes, the earth lives; yes, she breathes; yes, she even has a soul, but she is not human, so why do we expect her to be like us? It may be that "consciousness" is a human trait, a talent for abstraction that has helped our species prosper but that has little relevance to the vast network of life on this planet, unless, of course, it is dangerously out of balance, in which case we may be better off relying on qualities of soul than those of consciousness.

"As I have experienced them, moments of grace are multifaceted, coming from many different directions at once. They are a web of interdependence, a balancing act, a safety net that reeks of life rather than distances itself from it. Such moments remind me that life is a grunt and a push and is no less worthy of reverence because of it."

On June 20, I took the day off work to meditate and write this piece. Ordinarily I write directly on the computer, but on this day I took legal pad and pen out on the deck and sat at a picnic table, gazing across a mountain pass in the Sierra Nevada foothills. It is odd to be here at the edge of a forest, a place where deer walk right up to the house on a daily basis. For sixteen years I lived in San Francisco and, more importantly, I identified with San Francisco. I was a city boy with no great yearnings for the country. But then the city got too expensive to live in, and so I moved two hundred and fifty miles to a place called Paradise. Now I am a country boy with no great yearnings for the city. The combination of these two environments has brought a balance to my life and perspective that neither would have provided by itself, and none of it was planned. Isn't it odd how often our much-valued consciousness follows us through life rather than leads us?

When I lived in the city, I was always a bit put off when writers living in Hawaii or Wyoming exhorted me to get back to nature. After all, cities are not lifeless rocks, but vibrant, living communities. They do not exist apart from the earth; they are overlays on it, just one more layer of life seeking expression. I remember reading once how cities evolve. In the infrastructure of every city's past is the foundation of its present. In other words, our past is literally buried beneath our feet. Were it not for the inconvenience, archaeologists could sift through the layers of our modern cities the way they sift through layers of ancient, abandoned ones, retrieving artifacts that illustrate the life-styles, beliefs, and values of each layer. These layers of culture and technology have combined to bring us to where we are now—a society equipped for an obsession with information. With that information, we are able to peer into our past and predict our future. And though we can find many accomplishments and traits worthy of admiration, we also continue to discover our own shortcomings. For all our species' genius, we are having to face the fact that nature knows more than we do, and that until we rediscover our connection to the soul of the world, human consciousness looks a lot like human hubris.

Later that evening I discovered that a beloved friend had died that afternoon. Her name was Harmony. Part sheep dog, part who-knows-what, her affection was less concealed and more genuine than that of most humans I have known. She was run down on the sleepy little road that winds past our home by a driver who did not bother to stop after hitting her. I realized something was wrong when she did not show up for her evening meal, and I found her up the road a piece, bloodied and already dead by the time I arrived. The flies circling her lifeless body did not seem to notice my tears. Flies have no consciousness of such things as broken hearts. Right now, I wish that I didn't either.

Any way you look at it, life has a cruel streak, or it would be cruel if consciousness was involved, for cruelty is a conscious act. But life, like nature, is not cruel; it simply is a balance of forces. We sometimes see it as cruel because each of us carries the memory of a time and situation where we have intentionally hurt another or have intentionally been hurt, and so when life brings us pain, we begin anthropomorphizing like crazy. But it is not nature that is mean spirited, vindictive, and savage. Those traits belong only to creatures who have the consciousness to conceive of such words.

Words. We humans take great pride in our language abilities without giving thought to what language really is. We think our words describe the world, when in fact they merely hold a mirror to our own vanity. As long as we think we can capture nature in words, we will not understand it. The gift of consciousness has its drawbacks and this is one of them. For all my philosophizing, I will never know life as intimately and directly as Harmony did, for my words and concepts stand between me and nature. Even as I dug her grave, a flow of thought tainted the purity of my grief. There is nothing wrong with this; that's the nature of my

WERNHER KRUTEIN/PHOTOVAULT

"As long as we think we can capture nature in words, we will not understand it. The gift of consciousness has its drawbacks and this is one of them. For all my philosophizing, I will never know life as intimately and directly as {my dog} Harmony did, for my words and concepts stand between me and nature."

species. But I do not have to—nor could I even if I wanted to—force nature to conform to my species prejudices. That, too, is just the way it is.

Having started out on a quest to contact the planetary mind, I have discovered I cannot get beyond the human mind. That, of course, comes as no surprise. Each of us is embedded in our own layer of personal and cultural history and consciousness. With rare exceptions, we see as we have been conditioned to see. What makes this time in human history so intriguing is that hundreds of years of conditioning are being examined, debated and often shaken off. A new layer of human culture is taking shape, and we are present at its very beginning.

Something within us, something outside the normal range of what we consider "consciousness" is insisting we grow to the next level. It's an exciting time to be alive but also a frightening one. Habit pulls us from one end and evolution from the other, and sometimes it feels as if we are being pulled apart. It would all be so much easier if we knew just where we were heading, but the truth is, we do not. To ease our nervousness, we look to God or Gaia for comfort. The history of our species makes it clear that comfort is available from such sources, but because we are living in an information age, we expect more than comfort, we expect information—a road map perhaps, or a set of commandments. And so we seek to read the planetary mind or the mind of God, only to find an anthropomorphic mirror of ourselves.

When confronted with a mirror, the most natural thing is to look back at oneself. So instead of trying to figure out who's holding the mirror and what it wants, I suggest we take the clue that is offered and begin to reexamine ourselves and look to our own souls. If we look deep enough, we will find our connection to divinity, even though we may not be able to put it into words or explain what it means, or even be certain whether it comes from Heaven or Earth.

Human experience has always existed in a balance between the known and the unknown. The twentieth century has put the emphasis on the known. In terms of human epochs, you could say our current generations have been living through the longest day of the year. With everything so well lit, we can see far and wide, but we often fail to see deep. Seeing deep is the job of the soul. We should not forget that it is under cover of night that the stars reach out from deepest space and invite us to peer into infinity. Just as knowledge favors the light, romance and enchantment bloom best in the dark. To expect consciousness to penetrate every aspect of life may be our biggest mistake. The soul thrives on mystery. It, too, is part of the balance of life. In the final analysis, it may just be that consciousness is a strictly human affair developed by our species to reconnect with a soul that does not need to know itself the way we do.

⊕

Jerry Snider, the co-editor of *Magical Blend* magazine for eighteen years, has had his work published in numerous magazines and books. He currently lives in Paradise, California with his life-partner Larry. It was the death of his beloved dog, Harmony, the day following summer solstice that provided the inspiration for this piece. In reflecting upon her unique presence, he realized that consciousness represents a gestalt of forces and that humanity's best hope of reintegrating itself into the Gaian Overmind is through the recognition that human thought needs to be balanced with other forms of sentience.

WERNHER KRUTEIN/PHOTOVAULT

"The question being asked in a multitude of ways these days is: if everything is changing, what do we hold on to? What do we use as a firm foundation, or even a dependable life raft? . . .We must all hold to our belief in the powerful destiny of the human race, the healing growth energy of the planet earth, and the reality of magic in the universe."

Chapter Six

EMOTIONAL ALCHEMY

by Michael Langevin

I began writing this chapter on Thursday, June 20, at 2:10 p.m. near the beginning of the Vernal Equinox. Over the last few weeks, my dreams have evolved with ever-increasing intensity. The day before yesterday, I awoke with the powerful imagery of a bobcat and a coyote fighting; the earth's life force—or Goddess Gaia—was watching on one side, while a Christian Mary and Jesus looked on from another. The fight eventually ended in a form of peaceful friendship. These archetypal figures then spoke, telling me that the *Solstice Shift* book I am working on has a life and a mission of its own, and that I should not try to control it with my limited vision. It is meant to bring forth the best of the past and blend it with radical cutting-edge information that would help lay out the path many will evolve along in the future.

They went on to tell me that there are countless beings in the cosmos and a countless number of populated planets and dimensions, many of which are very important and special. But at this point in our collective history, earth and its human population have one of the most dynamic evolutionary potentials in all of creation. As improbable as it may seem, they told me that in the next twenty years, what happens here could raise the frequency of everything in existence. Some humans—how many is unknown, possibly only a few—will make this major evolutionary leap during this period, and that is why we are writing the *Solstice Shift* book! It is actually possible (but it won't necessarily be easy) for every living thing on this planet to make the leap together. That would cascade through every crack and crevice of existence and raise the universe to a frequency level inconceivable by the most evolved gods and goddesses!

Last night, after I put my children to sleep, I was drawn outside to witness a spellbinding sunset. Later I dreamed. Dreams I can barely describe. They were of the burning deserts of Yuma, Arizona, and Mexico; the Andes Mountains of Peru; the Black Mountains of South Dakota; the sand dunes of Findhorn, Scotland. I saw the faces of many of the contributing authors in ceremonies of ancient Naguals, Incas, Druids, Wiccans, early Christians; there were Buddhist caves and Moslem Sufis dancing.

I awoke at 4:00 a.m. My mind overflowed with these images as I got out of bed, dressed, and went for my usual morning walk. I rambled down the dirt road that passes our house, past the other seven houses east of us, around the almond orchard, and finally past a chicken farm where the roosters often greet me. There the power lines stop, and I can always feel the change in the air around me. At the end of the road is a big steel gate with a "Private Property" sign that is now unreadable. I climbed the fence and was now on a barely maintained dirt road that runs through thousands of acres of cattle pastures. As I continued east, I came to a line of oak trees at the foothills of the Sierra Nevada mountain range. Each morning I usually walk out to the first deep stand of trees, where someone had once attempted to homestead and where the landscape still bears the remnants of a few barns and a small home. My habit is to either stop by the trough to do an elemental ritual or pass it far enough to get a clear view of the mountains, the sunrise, or the stars. Here no fences exist between me and Mt. Larson for almost sixty miles of old-fashioned wilderness; cattle fields give way to oak forests and then to ponderosa pines and a profusion of evergreen trees. In the winter a furious stream runs past.

Here a pile of rocks called to me one morning almost five years ago. Why someone piled them exactly at this spot, with its spectacular view, I will never know. Most mornings I kneel there and touch my forehead to the ground and my hands to the earth. I thank our mother, the creative and main life force of Earth Gaia, and I send my personal healing energy into the earth. I pray to whatever powerful powers will listen, asking them to quickly bring about the changes in consciousness that will create a future where we become gardeners and caretakers living in harmony with all of Gaia's other sentient beings. I pray to Gaia and all her sister gods and goddesses. I pray to the angels and elves and fairies and pixies and elementals and plant devas. I pray to the herd spirit of the cattle and the wilder group spirit of the coyote packs. I pray to the plant spirits that are strongly present here, and even to the spirits of the stream, the rocks, and the dirt. I pray that they help bring about a future where Mother Nature's children, from the whales to the thistles, will live in a healthy, balanced, symbiotic relationship, as they once did before the advance of civilization. I also pray that they be enhanced and not destroyed by future technology. Finally, I offer all my energies to be used by Gaia—or whatever cosmic power will direct me—to help bring about this future. This morning I also prayed and beseeched the creative powers and Gaia to inspire me and all those connected with this book to unfold together a synergistic outpouring that will help people and aid in unfolding the best possible twenty-first century.

After the prayers and rituals, I felt supercharged with earth energy. I rose, gave thanks once more, and began my hike back to the electric power lines, civilization, my home and family, and the day ahead of me. On the way home, I usually pronounce aloud actualizations or sing chants or incantations. Today it was as if I had walked back through another world.

I fed my horses and chickens and the other animals, and then woke up my children. My wife set off to work; I dropped the kids at day camp and went to the *Magical Blend* office. The morning was filled with last-minute phone calls to some of the book's contributors. At noon I said goodby to those devoted staff staying in the office and drove home. I took a half-hour nap and dreamed that my glasses broke and my mouth was full of glass and blood. Then, as I spit out the glass, a structure grew that was part crystalline geodesic dome and part living plant life. Around it, happy children played and sang joyously. When I awoke, I was now ready to write my chapter, feeling that I had seen the future, and although it is destined to be a somewhat painful transition from now until its arrival, I am more convinced than ever that the end results will unfold as a heaven on earth with our concerted efforts!

This morning, Friday, June 21, the actual solstice occurred at 2:45 a.m. I had every intention of rising at 2:00 a.m. and performing a two-hour ritual. I slept, and I dreamed of a strange cloud of negative energy that had been sent and now gathered around every aspect of my life. It was not thick enough or powerful enough to stop my progress, just to slow it down, hold it all back, and taint most aspects of it. However, after many twists and turns, which drew my wife and family into its maze, I ended up on a mountaintop with a view that seemed to stretch to infinity.

Preparing to write this chapter has brought other intense dreams. They allude to our entrance into a very expanded reality compared with our waking state. Literature overflows with stories and myths of such magical transitions. The future has yet to reveal itself, but I strongly believe that controlling our thoughts—recognizing the negative but accepting only the positive—is one of the most powerful tools we have for creating this new reality. This book has many clues and alternative views on how to control and focus your thoughts and empower yourself regardless of the radical collapse of many aspects of your life.

The question being asked in a multitude of ways these days is: if everything is changing, what do we hold on to? What do we use as a firm foundation, or even a dependable life raft? The answers have been heard before, but most of them are now more easily understood than in ages past: love of self and faith in God, positive thinking, prayer, creativity, compassion, unselfishness, forgiveness, the willingness to laugh at ourselves and the world's silly injustices. We must all hold to our belief in the powerful destiny of the human race, the healing growth energy of the planet earth, and the reality of magic in the universe.

Another important tool humanity has for creating this new reality—one greatly overlooked in the last two thousand years—is the power of focused emotion. This power is not recognized by many of us as one of the great secrets of the universe. As those who choose to evolve learn to exercise and discipline their mental and psychic abilities, they will begin to truly understand all aspects of emotions and then claim its immeasurable power as the raw energy for evolving, healing, and creating anything imaginable. Feelings, moods, and emotions seem almost uncontrollable, and we either try to ignore them or fall victim to them. In the pre-Christian pre-Pisceian Ages, this was understood by the priests, priestesses, and spiritual adepts. Most ancient temples and places of worship were not actually places to worship the deities enshrined there. Rather, these shrines were built on ley lines, dragon paths, or acupuncture points of the earth's energy flows. The structures were built in alignment with stellar and planetary energies as well. By utilizing these energies, the initiate would transform the aspect of the emotional body the particular deity represented. So, for instance, when a properly prepared spiritual pilgrim entered a shrine dedicated to Osiris, he would immerse himself in fear. Or the courage of Diana, or the lust of Bacchus. The initiate would travel from shrine to shrine, experiencing and aligning with the whole spectrum of emotions, emerging from each shrine with another emotion as an ally whose energy he or she could now control and utilize.

Today, we are blessed with a not-yet-fully understood opportunity. Due to the decrease in the planet's magnetic field—which is the lowest it has been in thousands of years—and the rise in its base resonant frequency, or vibration, the electrical impulses that carry emotions have quickened. Emotions are now more readily accessible, and their energy is more available to experience and utilize during this phase of our evolution. Being aware of this dynamic, we can use every encounter with another individual, every emotion it brings up, to rapidly speed up our own evolution.

Our attitude towards our emotions makes a big difference in how we experience them and whether we can tap their raw power for our own evolvement. Let's focus on fear as an example. You have a fight with your boss or mate, and you fear that they're going to fire or leave you. Take time alone to explore the emotion as fully as you can. If possible, write out your personal observations for future reference. Ask yourself, how bad does it feel? When have you felt this way before? What happened then? What did you learn from that experience? Use your imagination to explore every aspect of this fear. Where can you feel it in you body? What color is it? Do you recall experiencing this kind of fear reading a book or viewing a movie? Have you experienced this fear in another lifetime? If so, recall the circumstances in every detail. If this fear had a form, what would it look like? A snake, a black hole, a car crash? If it had a name, what would it call itself? Does this feeling have different aspects to it? Is there a powerful part of this fear that can be sepa-

WERNHER KRUTEIN/PHOTOVAULT

"the accelerating change in our society and in our world is truly mind-boggling compared with past ages, which must at least point to closer scrutiny of this time in history. In 1977, only twenty years ago, the sixties had just truly ended; the Vietnam war hadn't been over vèry long. Women's rights and women's energies were not yet respected. . . .There were no personal computers, only supercomputers owned by large corporations; the Internet and the new technologies were the unrealized dreams of a few advanced thinkers. What changes, at this ever-accelerated rate, will take place in the next twenty years?"

rated out from the rest of the emotion? What opposite feelings have you experienced? Give yourself permission to wallow totally in this fear for a set period of time. Then, once you've allowed it to totally destroy your hopes and visions and self-belief, turn the tables and reclaim its awesome power and reenliven those hopes and visions and self-belief to an even higher degree. Once you've explored every aspect of this emotion, you can make it an ally, learn to focus, and use it. From time to time, its negative side might still get reempowered and affect your life, but you will be able to quickly recover and reclaim its power for your spiritual evolution.

This technique can and should be used with every emotion we experience. When I'm exhausted and feel insecure after an extremely difficult day at work with lots of setbacks, I used to come home and either be unavailable to my wife and kids; or worse, I'd be mean and insensitive. Now I recognize any negative feelings on the drive home. I set myself a challenge: to be with my weaknesses but transform their energy by acting the opposite. I visualize myself going to bed after a love-

WERNHER KRUTEIN/PHOTOVAULT

"Commit now to pushing your limits; dreaming your personal impossible dream; becoming all you can possibly be and more; testing your limits of growth and awareness; falling down exhausted, overwhelmed, and confused, and then getting up and pushing through your former limits, while bringing along, with love and caring, all those you are able to help along the way."

ly evening shared with those I love, proud of myself. And, even if I slip and we have a bad moment, I just try harder to create a lively atmosphere and be sensitive to them. This game is demanding, but the results are as good as gold. Like an alchemist, we can transform the lead of deadening emotions into the consistent experience of Gold.

The earth's changing energies are intensifying our emotions and feelings. The news tells us daily of more and more violent crimes. More antidepressant pills are being taken now than ever before. More people are in prison, and more people suffer from serious mental illness than ever before. Extreme mental states need to be treated by a trained therapist; however, most of us can alter what seem to be overwhelming emotions. We just haven't considered our emotions as potentially powerful evolutionary tools. Once we alter this perception, we can stop avoiding our emotions, stop denying them, or letting them control us. We have new potentials for growth.

Utilizing emotional energy for growth—practices once reserved for the priests and priestesses of old—is a prime example of how the increased earth energies are allowing this and other sacred techniques to be available to all on the planet. This time period has been prophesied in the Christian Bible, in the Hopi's Sacred Covenant, by the Quechua from Peru, the Tibetan Buddhists, the Australian Aborigines, and many native peoples around the globe. These prophecies often diverge regarding particulars, however, they all speak of radical change on our planet at the close of the second millennium!

Those who give little credence to such prophecies must admit that the accelerating change in our society and in our world is truly mind-boggling compared with past ages, which must at least point to closer scrutiny of this time in history. In 1977, only twenty years ago, the sixties had just truly ended; the Vietnam war hadn't been over very long. Women's rights and women's energies were not yet respected. There was a cold war between the superpowers threatening total nuclear annihilation of the planet. South Africa was a terribly entrenched racist country with no likelihood of reform. Spirituality was almost exclusively under the auspices of religion. There were no personal computers, only supercomputers owned by large corporations; the Internet and the new technologies were the unrealized dreams of a few advanced thinkers.

What changes, at this ever-accelerated rate, will take place in the next twenty years? I sense they will make the changes of recent years look negligible in comparison. But no matter what unfolds, it is all okay! No reality is superior or better than another. Yet, at the same time, the contradiction is that certain possible futures are of a higher vibration than others and are more aligned with evolution, creative force, and Divine design than others. Now each individual has a shadow side, which can be denied and repressed and eventually cause untold havoc, or it can be acknowledged and integrated into our every thought, word, and deed. One way of viewing reality, or our collective experience as a species, is that hate, greed, and those base desires are an integral part of existence and as necessary as healing, loving, and unselfish sharing. The test is to collectively integrate them and use their raw energy to transform the planet. There are 6 billion humans on planet earth and an untold number of other living species; each of them individually makes daily decisions—mentally or instinctively—that have an overwhelming impact on the planet and its future.

And we have major decisions to make about our spiritual existence. We can deny or refuse to acknowledge them. Or we can alter our ways of living and work towards helping unfold heaven on earth. We don't have to be perfect. We will make major mistakes, have weak moments, and lose track of the goals, even become confused and overwhelmed. That's part of the evolutionary process. If enough of us become more aware and commit to co-creating earth's most-wonderful-possible future, the world in twenty years will be a multifaceted realm with a spectrum of colors and sounds thoughts and experiences beyond our present-day imagination. Those who can and do choose to be part of this unfolding vision will raise their spiritual vibration and enter a new earth.

This can all be summed up rather inadequately by saying the choice is up to each individual. Commit now to pushing your limits; dreaming your personal impossible dream; becoming all you can possibly be and more; testing your limits of growth and awareness; falling down exhausted, overwhelmed, and confused, and then getting up and pushing through your former limits, while bringing along, with love and caring, all those you are able to help along the way. Each of us is being given the opportunity to accept the evolutionary challenge. Let's all step forward in our highest vision as Mighty Companions.

DEBORAH GENITO

Michael Peter Langevin is the co-founder of *Magical Blend* magazine and has acted as its co-publisher and co-editor for the last eighteen years. He has contributed articles to several anthologies, including *A Magical Universe: The Best of Magical Blend Magazine,* published by Swan Raven; *Solstice Shift: Magical Blend's Synergetic Guide to the Coming Age,* published by Hampton Roads Publishing, and the upcoming publication *Hot Chocolate for the Mystical Soul,* to be released in January 1998 by Dutton Signet/Penguin Books. He lives on a farm near the foothills of the Sierra Nevada Mountains in Chico, California, with his wife Deborah, his daughter Sophia, his son Henry, and various animals.

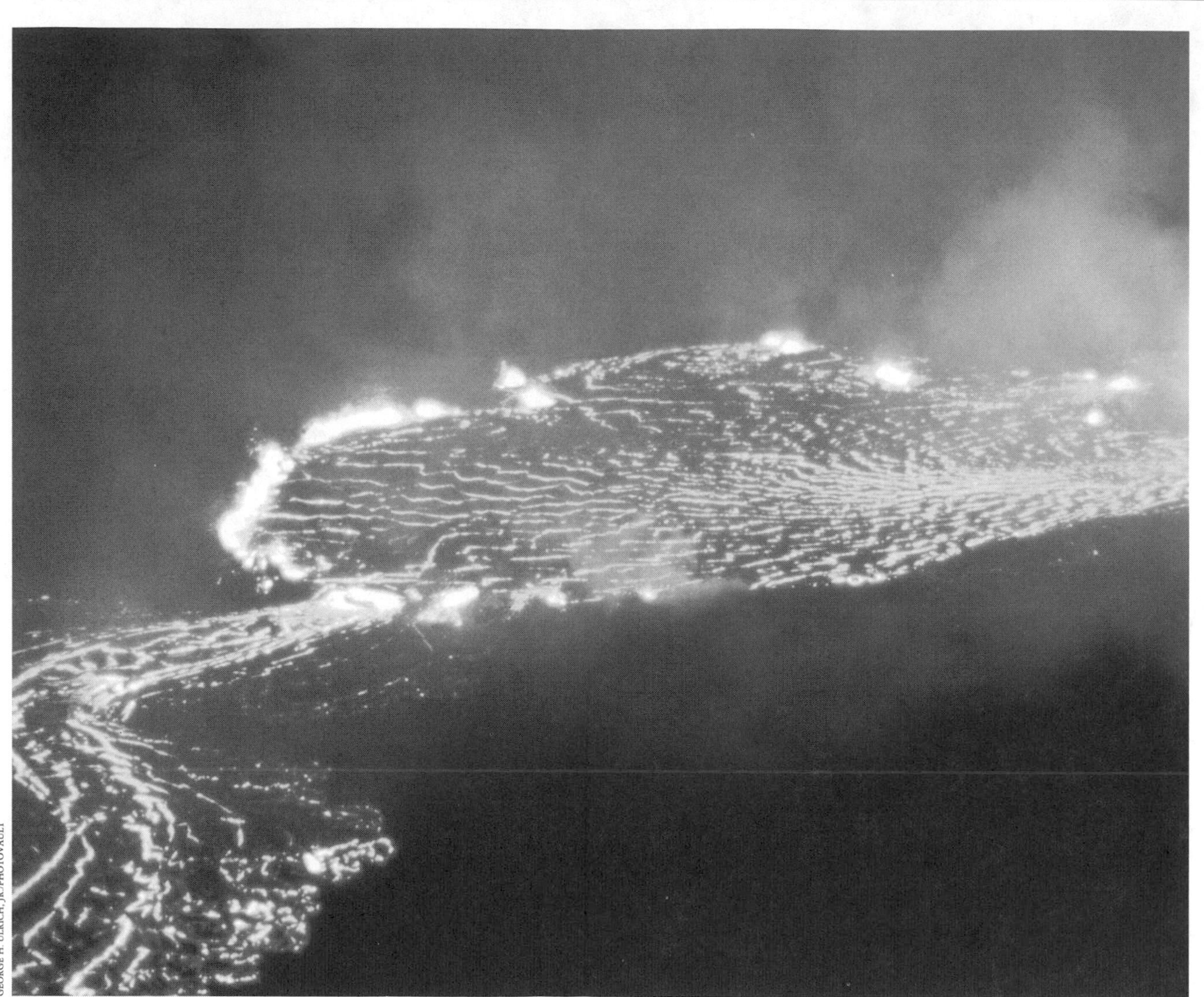

GEORGE H. ULRICH, JR./PHOTOVAULT

"our trip had been bracketed in blood. Now I finally heard the words, insistent and unmistakable, that for the past two weeks had been just beneath the threshold of my awareness: 'Blood. Blood. Blood. Blood sacrifice. Blood offering. The blood of the Mother. It is going to flow. But not all of us are going to understand that it is going to flow for us.'"

Chapter Seven

The Blood of the Mother: Walking with Beauty into the Unknown

by Joan Parisi Wilcox

It is finished in beauty.
It is finished again in beauty.
—words that end many Diné prayers

What if we are living in the end times and there is nothing that can be done? What if we can change nothing, despite our best intentions and our most ardent prayers? What if Mother Earth has decided she must allow herself to be sacrificed at the hands of her children so that those very children may move on, grow up, evolve? This would be so that one day, in an almost unimaginable future we will walk again, but this time with minds and hearts of beauty, with a consciousness refreshed and refined, and with a new old knowledge about the natural laws and the unbroken circle of life. Could we walk with beauty into the inevitable?

Those were the questions that became increasingly insistent as I journeyed from Boston to Pipestone, Minnesota, through the Badlands and the sacred Black Hills of South Dakota, to Devil's Tower, Wyoming.[1] I thought I was simply journeying to the Solstice and Peace Day ceremony organized by Arvol Looking Horse, Keeper of the Sacred Buffalo Calf Pipe, Lakota Chief Joseph Chases His Horse, and others. But what I was really doing, I now know, was traveling across the body of the Mother and deep into her being.

With me were two friends, Eileen and Paul. Paul Tohlakai is a full-blood Diné (Navajo), who has worked with many Lakota elders, and was acting as our guide. But, while he could explain the significance of landmarks, geological formations, Native history and ceremony, what he could not explain were the increasingly unsettling and confusing feelings

[1] Called Grey Horn Butte or Bear Lodge Butte by Native Americans.

awakening within me. It was as if the wind, trees, and stones at each place we visited were trying to tell me something, but in a whisper just below my threshold of hearing.

The "voices" finally became audible at Devil's Tower. I was unable to participate in the main solstice ceremony because I was on my moontime[2]. Although I was initially disappointed, this turn of events was not unexpected because my body's cycles are very regular. As I left the main ceremonial grounds to return to camp, I experienced several conflicting feelings: disappointment at missing the main ceremony, anger with the timing of my body's cycle, resentment at a cultural belief I considered sexist, and resignation that this was the state of affairs and I had better make the most of it. I acknowledged my mostly negative feelings and then decided I had to "walk my talk"; I believe that there are no coincidences and that everything happens for a reason. So I returned to camp expectantly, respecting that little voice I heard within that was intoning a hard-to-acknowledge truth: *it's the journey that's important, not the destination.* Back at camp, instead of praying with the crowd of thousands, I happily prayed with a small group of women in the "Moon Circle," down by the river, where the audible flow of the waters gave voice to the flow that was so silent within each of us and where the giant gray stone phallus of Devil's Tower provided an ironic backdrop.

Throughout the day, however, those words kept sweeping through my consciousness, like the refrain of a jingle that becomes more insistent the more you try to forget it. *It is the journey, not the destination, that is important.* I knew unquestionably that these words were not an ego pacification, that I was not trying to placate myself because I had come halfway across the country to Devil's Tower but had been unable to attend the primary ceremony. There was something more to this deceptively simple statement, but I wasn't grasping it.

Not until the trip was over and I was on the train home, being rocked across the plains in a state of boredom conducive to slipping outside the rational, did I finally understand. The revelation hit me in the insomniac hours of predawn, and it hit me like the proverbial bolt of lightning: *it is the journey, not the destination that matters, because the destination is the end. The end times.* I understood with a chilling clarity that the message was not just about my trip; it

[2] Most Native Americans believe that when a woman is menstruating she is "in her power, and her energy can overwhelm those around her, especially men, and disrupt the power of the sacred drum, pipe, and other ceremonial objects. Therefore, Native women traditionally retreated to a moon lodge for the duration of their monthly menses. At the Devil's Tower ceremony, women in their moontime participated in a ceremony separate from the main ceremony. Surprisingly, and perhaps unfortunately, of the thousands of Native and non-Native women at the ceremony, only 18 women admitted to being on their moontime and participated in this other ceremony, although there may have been women in ceremony at other sites.

was about all our trips, about our collective trip. Suddenly, I understood that there is (although I desperately want to write "may be") nothing we can do—no personal prayer, no Peace Day gathering, no global mind shift—that can halt or reverse the destruction we are wreaking on the Mother; she is willingly sacrificing herself so that we may learn *what it means to be part of, rather than in control of, the great web of life.*

And in another flash, I understood something else; it was a telling metaphor that I had barely acknowledged during the journey but that had been the symbolic counterpart to the message I had just received: our trip had been bracketed in blood. Now I finally heard the words, insistent and unmistakable, that for the past two weeks had been just beneath the threshold of my awareness: "Blood. Blood. Blood. Blood sacrifice. Blood offering. The blood of the Mother. It is going to flow. But not all of us are going to understand that it is going to flow *for us.*"

I didn't know what to make of these "revelations," and even after returning home, I still wasn't sure of the significance of this trip and its message. I couldn't—or wouldn't—follow the thread of connection between the two. I kept thinking of the talks Paul and I had about the end times. We are, rather haphazardly, working on a book, and we had recorded several hours of tape as we drove across country on our solstice journey. Much of our wandering conversation concerned Diné mythology, prophecy, and the problems besetting both white and Native cultures at this time. Uncharacteristically, I couldn't remember many specifics, and so I furiously began transcribing tapes. In the meantime, I kept thinking of Grandmother White Water, Paul's mother, whom I had met months earlier while visiting the Diné reservation. I was certain there was something she could contribute to my understanding. I wrote to Paul, who was back home on the reservation, to please ask his mother to speak about women and moontime, about the blood of the Mother and the prophecies of the end times.

Not long after, Paul called to translate his mother's reply to my queries: "In a time and an age long past, the People, the Holy People, the First People, using their minds and imagination, created the 'First Way,' the Natural Way, that was in compliance with the natural laws and with how they interpreted the sacred ways of the Great Spirit. Where it concerned the Natural Woman, the Red woman, they decided that for life to go on, the powers of regeneration, of procreation had to be given. So the Grandfathers and Grandmothers[3] took the natural earth, took the Underlying Red Stone, and made this stone fluid. Then, they hit Natural Woman on the back, at the base of her spine, and her blood flowed. At that moment something new was created—Natural Woman

[3]Forces of spirit.

WERNHER KRUTEIN/PHOTOVAULT

"In a time and an age long past, the People, the Holy People, the First People, using their minds and imagination, created the 'First Way,' the Natural Way. . . .Where it concerned the Natural Woman, the Red woman, they decided that for life to go on, the powers of regeneration, of procreation had to be given. So the Grandfathers and Grandmothers took the natural earth, took the Underlying Red Stone, and made this stone fluid."

—Grandmother White Water

was endowed with ovaries and eggs, and a new vibration was set in motion so that Natural Woman could reproduce. She vibrated in cycle with Mother Earth. And we can all vibrate with that cycle again if we return to the Natural Way."

Paul added his own comments, relating a Native American prophecy of how Grandmother Moon will turn blood red in the last times and equating the vibration set up at the base of Natural Woman's spine with the kundalini energy, which is often symbolized as a coiled snake. "One time," Paul said, "I visited some earth formations in Ohio; they are mounds, sacred formations. They looked to me like a giant snake swallowing an egg." Maybe these mounds, he speculated, were created by people still intimately connected to the Natural Way and are related to the first vibration of Natural Woman and her newly acquired fertility. I thought Paul's comments provocative, especially because the color traditionally associated with the root chakra, which is located at the base of the spine and from where the coiled snake of kundalini rises, is the same color as the Underlying Red Stone.

What struck me most about this new information was how it fit in with our solstice journey: we had formally begun our journey at Pipestone, Minnesota, making offerings at the sacred site where the Underlying Red Stone, the catlinite stone called pipestone that is carved into chanunpa (pipe) bowls, is quarried. Lying beneath many layers of quartzite and other types of stone, pipestone literally is the *Underlying* Red Stone. It is called the "blood of the People" by many Native Americans. I have also heard it referred to as the blood of the Mother, the red chanunpa bowl symbolizing the feminine energy, in complement to the male energy of the pipe stem. As the blood of the Mother, the stone symbolizes the sacrifice Mother Earth has made in providing the sacred pipe and all that she has sacrificed in creating the world of the two-leggeds.

From Pipestone, we had journeyed to the Rosebud Lakota reservation and then on to the Badlands and the Black Hills, stopping to make offerings and to connect with the energy of these sacred places, arriving at Devil's Tower on the solstice. What I discovered later, after I returned home and began reading a book on Lakota star knowledge[4] that I had purchased, almost as an afterthought, at Sinte Gleska University on the Rosebud reservation, was that we had retraced an ancient Lakota route of pilgrimage. For thousands of years, representatives of the Lakota nations had undertaken an annual pilgrimage that began at Pipestone, with a chanunpa ceremony on the March equinox, and continued westward to a series of sacred sites throughout the Black Hills, where they would

[4]Goodman, Ronald. *Lakota Star Knowledge: Studies in Lakota Stellar Theology.* Rosebud, South Dakota: Sinte Gleska University, 1992.

stop to make offerings and to pray. They coordinated their movements with the appearance of specific constellations and individual stars from which they received spiritual instruction, and they timed their journey to arrive at Grey Horn Butte (Devil's Tower) on the solstice. There they ended their pilgrimage with a Sun Dance.

Ironically—or perhaps not—I had first met Paul on the spring equinox at a small sweat lodge ceremony he was leading. And now, months later, we had ended our solstice trip at a Sun Dance—although it took place at Rosebud, not Devil's Tower. Reviewing the course of our trip, it became clear to me that we had very nearly followed this ancient Lakota star route. If Paul had been guiding us with intention he did not reveal it, perhaps preferring that we discover the meaning of the trip for ourselves. The blood metaphor, at least, was making more sense to me, and the Rosebud Sun Dance brought that metaphor full circle.

I deeply respect Native ceremony and was appreciative of being welcomed at a ceremony such as a Sun Dance, which is often closed to non-Natives. Although I was no longer on my moon, I hung back, outside the arbor, feeling slightly overwhelmed at the beauty of the Sun Dance ground and the intensity of the ceremony. I sensed that I was witnessing the masculine counterpart to the women's moontime. A woman in her moon is in her power, and her blood is seen as an offering to Mother Earth. In many ways, the piercing of the Sun Dancer is the male blood offering. During the Sun Dance, many of the dancers' chests are pierced with small wooden or bone skewers, which are then attached by a rope to the sacred tree—the Tree of Life—at the center of the Sun Dance ground. The dancer pulls back until his skin tears and the skewers break free, usually leaving thin trails of blood down his chest. I knew that the ceremony was not about bravado but about prayer, personal sacrifice for the good of the community, and honoring the great cycle of life. The blood metaphor, that had become increasingly persistent during our trip, had moved from the symbolic (Pipestone) to the personal (menses) to the communal (Sun Dance).

As I thought back over my journey, I felt as if Mother Earth had been trying to tell me something visually: she too was bleeding but as an offering; she too was tied to the Tree of Life and was about to make a blood sacrifice, as the skewers driven into her by her children pulled free. Suddenly books I picked up and impromptu conversations seemed directed by Spirit to elaborate this theme. I heard, for the first time, about E.O. Wilson's biophilia hypothesis, which proposes that our connection to nature, to living systems, goes deeper than we had imagined, to our very DNA. As Gaia changes, so does the very genetic core of humankind. If so, Wilson says, then we must "look to the very roots of motivation and understand why, in what circumstances and on which occasions, we cherish and protect life."[5] As

[5] From *Biophilia: The Human Bond with Other Species.* Cambridge: Harvard University Press, 1984, pp. 138-139.

I transcribed the tapes of my conversations with Paul, I was surprised to see just how much the condition of Mother Earth and the cycle of creation had been the subject of our discussion. The Diné beliefs, he explained, complemented and extended Wilson's more scientific understanding.

"We've lost hózhó—things are no longer in balance," Paul said matter-of-factly. He explained how we two-leggeds tend to see with tunnel vision, and how, as a consequence, our destiny, which should be so clear, hovers on the blurry edges of our conscious knowing. "You know," he continued, "every year Mother Earth goes around the sun, moving from an extreme of hot to an extreme of cold, which are the places we mark as the solstices. Everything is a cycle, geared to go around and come around again. But between the extremes there's a nice place, at the equinoxes, where you're not too hot or not too cold." These are the places of balance, he suggested, from which we can best understand the effects of the extremes. We need to learn not to fear these extremes, he continued; instead, we need to learn to "revel in them in the sunshine, which is the life-giving force that will help you through the cold; and in the cold, with the cleansing effect of the wind and the snow that can purify your being. So you go with the extremes," he said, "first with one, then with the other"—with the resting place, the point of contemplation, at the in-between times. "If you think of life this way," he said, and by association the coming earth changes, "then anything coming at you will not deter you from being a good human being. The elders say, 'Pray from your place of weakness, that you will learn from it.'"

Paul believes, as I increasingly do, that we must prepare ourselves to walk with beauty (hózhó na'h·'te) into our future, that our conduct as we witness the Mother sacrificing herself on our behalf must be one of dignity and reverence. That is our test. "Cleansing has happened time and time again," Paul said. "The Diné believe this is the fifth age, and we will soon see its end, so that the sixth age, literally a new age, can dawn. I would like to have hope, and we must proceed with hope and try to make things better. But the odds are overwhelming. Human beings are so predictable! If left to their weaknesses, they do themselves in time and time again. Maybe it's all in our best interest to accept the coming purification. The end of a cycle takes us back to the beginning, to the original state of grace and beauty, of being in harmony with ourselves and with everything else. Until then, we all need to make a decision as to how we're going to stand as human beings."

His words struck a nerve in me and brought to mind something I'd recently read in a collection of essays about the biophilia hypothesis: "Let us not kid ourselves into thinking we are saving life on earth as a whole. For we all know the demise of human beings may accelerate the appearance of some new complexity as far beyond primate intelligence

WERNHER KRUTEIN/PHOTOVAULT

"the Diné believe we're in the fifth world, the others having been destroyed because of our negligence. . . .The Grandfathers came and purified each world—with water, with fire, with whatever—and whole new worlds grew out of the ashes. Recently, there's been a healthy turn, a new spirituality, and a move among the Native peoples to preserve the old ways. But I think we've already made the decision and that we cannot avert disaster. Our motivation now must be inner peace."

—Paul Tohlakai

as primate intelligence is beyond rodent responsiveness. So let us cut through the salvationist hyperbole and see that talk of saving the world really means saving that part of the planetary environment which has *traditionally and comfortably* supported human beings. It is fine to urge the salvation of the environment in which our species first flourished, but in fact even this cannot be done. Any return to green pastures, flowering fruit trees, bubbling brooks, and rolling glades will be a turn not of the circle but of the spiral."[6] I confess that, until this trip and the message it seems to harbinger, I counted myself among the group of "awakened" middle-agers who feel that, if we can just all embrace a more natural way of living and being, we can prove the doomsayers wrong. I am still certain that intention is the most powerful force in creation, but I now wonder if the belief that we can avert ecological disaster—if we only pray hard enough, think positive thoughts, become ecologically responsible, and "connect" spiritually—isn't just another attempt at control. Are we sacrificing Mother Earth on the altar of our ego?

[6] From "God, Gaia, and Biophilia," by Dorion Sagan and Lynn Margulis in *The Biophilia Hypothesis,* pp. 345-364. Stephen R. Kellert and Edward O. Wilson, Eds., Washington, D.C.: Island Press, 1993.

"It will probably come out that way," Paul said. "That we will sacrifice what is most dear to us—our mother. It's like we're killing our mother to get at her inheritance."

"But what inheritance?" I asked. "What could Mother Earth possibly give us that she hasn't already?" Paul didn't answer directly, "There have been many cycles. Like I said, the Diné believe we're in the fifth world, the others having been destroyed because of our negligence. But we change a little bit each time. . . ." He paused. "Although I'm not really sure about that," he admitted, reconsidering his last statement. "We don't seem to have learned much. We keep doing the same things.

"We've misused abundance, we've believed we're more powerful than the Creator, we disbelieve the natural forces, we've experienced moral failure." Paul paused again, then renewed his former train of thought, "The Grandfathers came and purified each world—with water, with fire, with whatever—and whole new worlds grew out of the ashes. Recently, there's been a healthy turn, a new spirituality, and a move among the Native peoples to preserve the old ways. But I think we've already made the decision and that we cannot avert disaster. Our motivation now must be inner peace."

I remarked how dark his vision was, even though, as a result of our trip, I was moving closer to sharing it. But I couldn't quite accept this vision, that the end was inevitable. What about the ceremony we had just attended at Devil's Tower? I asked. What about the energy for world peace and healing that had flowed out from all of us during the solstice celebration? Was it all in vain?

No, it was not in vain—prayer never is, Paul said. But "on the solstice we should be at our prime." It is the season of summer, when, according to Diné symbology, "we should be at our most mature." Being mature, he explained, means we must face the truth, no matter how difficult, and yet still maintain hope.

"Maybe you are right," I told Paul. "Maybe it is too late, and we have to prepare in a different way, a more 'mature' way. But that's such a pessimistic viewpoint," I complained. "Even if the passing of this world as we know it means that a new and better world evolves, it's still almost impossible to face the prospect of losing it all. If we can't staunch the blood flow," I asked, "then what's to stop us from just completely giving up on the patient? How do we maintain hope enough to walk in beauty?"

"That is our big test," he said. "When Native people pray for a sick person, they pray until the end. The doctors and nurses sometimes insensitively try to give them a reality check, telling them, 'Prepare for his death. He's not going to be around much longer.' But we pray to the end because that's the way of the Creator. It's an act of faith in Him. We understand also that we're really praying for the person's spiritual salvation, not his physical salvation. Because what the doctors and nurses don't understand is that we're praying for a good crossing over. That the person will go on, into a new journey."

As I write these words now, I can't help but follow the lines of convergence from Grandmother White Water's story, Wilson's biophilia hypothesis, Paul's musings and explanations, and the questions raised by my solstice trip—with its blood metaphor and message of an impending end to the world as we know it—along a path, and to a point of closure, that is anything but linear. I am led back to where I began, to the lines that close many Diné prayers: *"It is finished in beauty. It is finished again in beauty."* From this point, perhaps, we can each find a way to begin walking with maturity into the unknown.

⊕

Joan Parisi Wilcox, trained at the doctoral level in literature at Purdue University, com-

bines in her writing passionate interests in physics, mathematical theory, and the philosophy of science with her personal exploration of North and South American indigenous spirituality and practices. She has published four articles on Andean mysticism in *Magical Blend* and *Shaman's Drum,* and she is currently at work on *The Book of the Q'ero,* recording the mystical world of the Q'ero Indians of Peru.

WERNHER KRUTEIN/PHOTOVAULT

"Nagualist practices, relating to (and for) merging with this energy, are cooperating with evolutionary changes in cellular structure, shifting mass intent toward a more open awareness of energy and co-manifesting new energies into the material. Shining energetic gateways are opening into inconceivable realms. The whole of creation is slipping through them, and the flow is being navigated."

Chapter Eight

FUTURE DREAMING

by Merilyn Tunneshende

Evolution constitutes more than perfecting our society, advancing technology, and restoring the balance of our environment. The body and spirit must also continue to evolve, developing certain dormant properties and leaving formerly appropriate attributes in their respective realms.

In Nagualism, sorcerers strive to break the evolutionary genetic code, the barrier between the physical and energy bodies, to deal with energy more directly and bring it to bear more closely on the realms of matter. Accomplished sorcerers have always succeeded in affecting the status quo, the focus of their intent. Many move into pure energy, elementary particles, and cellular memory and its transmutation.

Sorcerers have always known that there are certain periods of time when this work is more effective. The present era is such a time. It seems that over the centuries, the sorcerers' intent has been partially instrumental in unleashing a tremendous band of evolutionary energy with magnificent open-ended possibilities. This energy, it appears, is hooked to an impersonal, nonhuman or beyond-human force.

Nagualist practices, relating to (and for) merging with this energy, are cooperating with evolutionary changes in cellular structure, shifting mass intent toward a more open awareness of energy and co-manifesting new energies into the material. Shining energetic gateways are opening into inconceivable realms. The whole of creation is slipping through them, and the flow is being navigated.

To step through the threshold of a gateway is a miraculous feat. The old falls away like ash from a rising being of fire. The energetic sea of change is an ecstatic, orgasmic rapture. One relinquishes control to the impersonal force, while maintaining the fierce intent to join with it, to become it, to go where it goes.

This is the goal of Nagualism: to become this energy. As one transmutes, awareness (and sometimes even the organism itself) is transferred to the energy body or double. The total luminous being—physical, energy body, and all—becomes a glowing sphere. It is as though that sphere were a balloon filled with air but constricted in the center to a very small radius, creating two bulbs—the physical and the energy body. In transmutation, one is transferring the air from one filled side of the constriction to the other, passing it through the tiny aperture between them.

WERNHER KRUTEIN/PHOTOVAULT

"The technique for these energy transferences belongs to the practice of Dreaming. Essentially, one aspires to be awake and mindful of intent during the passing of ordinary dreams until one enters the cocreative state of Dreaming. Ordinary dreams pass by as floating clouds, dissolve, and then the sky is clear. At that moment, one intends to pull the Dreaming awareness across into the waking state. This creates vortexes in the waking world, which can be entered physically and from which Dreamed energy may be pulled into the physical."

Bringing the double through a vortex into the physical yields additional marvels. In this case, the nonphysical portion of our energy sometimes comes through surrounded by helpers or inorganic forces. The energy then envelops the physical body as a swirling, magnetic cloud and enters it. Geronimo, the great Chiricahua warrior, spoke of this phenomenon when he explained that a power "lived" in him that enabled him to escape death by gunshot, to control the wind, and to vanish, along with his band, through "cracks" before the very eyes of his pursuers.

The technique for these energy transferences belongs to the practice of Dreaming. Essentially, one aspires to be awake and mindful of intent during the passing of ordinary dreams until one enters the cocreative state of Dreaming. Ordinary dreams pass by as floating clouds, dissolve, and then the sky is clear. At that moment, one intends to pull the Dreaming awareness across into the waking state. This creates vortexes in the waking world, which can be entered physically and from which Dreamed energy may be pulled into the physical. The Yuma Indians called this phenomenon "Dream Power." Black Elk, the Sioux medicine man and visionary, spoke of the same power. He said, "It is not enough to have a vision. In order to have its power, you must enact your vision on earth for all to see. Only then do you have the power." This is an essential step in the evolution foreseen.

What the current social order and world view have done is to close the aperture between the physical and energy body. When this happens, there are several possible scenarios. One is that earth energy will rip open the closure and the dam will break, allowing the flow of repressed energy to resume. This is the "vengeance of Gaia" scenario. Another is that the social order creating the blockage will disintegrate, and there will be a series of revolutions. This is the violent social reconstruction scenario. A third would be that humankind will strive to balance itself; this scenario would be supported energetically by the zero-wave due in the year 2012, beginning a new vibratory era. And finally it could be like letting the string of a balloon go. Being irreparably sealed, the aperture would wither to a faint, hair-like strand and finally separate. It would float away into the unknown vastness, leaving the physical, which remains here to die. This is the extinction scenario.

People have become increasingly fascinated with Nagualism because it strives to open or enlarge the aperture between the physical and energy body so as to access more magical possibilities. Tremendous advances were made over the centuries using a series of practices, but the training was always secretive. There were few practitioners who truly achieved all possible transformations, and to insure their survival and the continuation of their knowledge, they kept it secret.

An apprenticeship under a Nagual was a long and arduous affair. One had to put one's very life on the line, and tremendous, sometimes seemingly unreasonable changes, were required. In my own case, I had to learn a new language, suspend my formal education, live in the desert and in indigenous villages of central Mexico, forego contact with my family, curtail obsessive and compulsive behaviors, and endure the loss of my fiancé. Only then was I sufficiently detached and freed from my Western mind and culture to see the totality of what was being presented to me.

In short, it was a radical realignment. No longer will Dr. Feelgood, quick-fix weekend

WERNHER KRUTEIN/PHOTOVAULT

enlightenments be sufficient in themselves to heal the energetic breech and create change. This change will require more than twenty minutes a day of practice combined with eating a vegetarian diet. It necessitates a total restructuring of life-style, social order, and perception. Healing can be gentle, if there is time; but in the crisis phase, more radical, innovative, experimental, and even desperate measures must be taken.

Millennialists point to the zero-wave of 2012 as the moment of radical, collective, societal, and vibratory realignment. The freed energy potential at this time will be tremendous.

"What the current social order and world view have done is to close the aperture between the physical and energy body. When this happens, there are several possible scenarios. One is that earth energy will rip open the closure and the dam will break, allowing the flow of repressed energy to resume. This is the 'vengeance of Gaia' scenario."

The energy current—or "feathered rainbow serpent," as it was called by the ancients—will flow through the universe. But it is not merely a matter of joining the movement and standing on a mountaintop to wait for E.T. sightings. One must allow the energy to have its way and imbue. One must do the work and ride the wave wherever it takes you. For this reason and at this time, Nagualist practices are being shared.

Where the energy will take us, we do not know. Therefore, all expectations must be released. We may evolve beyond the human. The indoctrinated glosses and limitations of perception may fall away, yielding a view of pure energy. None of what we know may be important any longer. Or, as was once expressed to me, "It may all dry up and blow away like a dust devil in the wind."

It is, however, a mistake to have a codependent collective view. This work does not require a united New Age front to be realized. Throughout time, advancement has always been achieved by individual practitioners. One is dealing with one's own undiscovered, unexplored, infinite energetic potential as a luminous being. Therein lies the journey. The permission of a calendar or a society is not required. Energy is the ultimate authority.

⊕

Merilyn Tunneshende is a scholar, author, and student of nagualist/shamanic and visionary healing practices. She holds degrees in Spanish and Religion/Philosophy and spent years studying and traveling in Mexico. In 1992 Ms. Tunneshende was awarded a research grant from the National Endowment for the Humanities to study Mayan culture in Mexico. She has published four articles about her nagualist/shamanic training and experiences in *Magical Blend* magazine. Her first book, *Medicine Dream: A Nagual Woman's Energetic Healing,* was published in 1996 by Hampton Roads Publishing.

"I see a twenty-first century much like that hymned by the 'man from Hope' who recently urged us to join him in crossing a 'bridge to the future.' I think the worst part of our transition from ape to humanity has passed and gone, and we will now have a significantly less gruesome journey."

WERNHER KRUTEIN/PHOTOVAULT

Chapter Nine

NONPROPHET FUTURISM

by Robert Anton Wilson

As an old joke has it, Tarzan comes back to his tree house one night looking beat and quickly mixes a martini. Just as quickly, he gulps it down. Jane watches with concern as he mixes and gulps another. As he starts on the third, she says gently, "What is it, honey?"

"It's a jungle out there!" he exclaims.

I think most of human history has resembled that joke; but I also think that we live today amid such creative chaos that a real quantum jump to a less bloodthirsty world seems more likely than not. Paradoxically, we have our greatest opportunities just at the time when pessimism has made its greatest advances, and most people have less hope for improvement than ever.

Let me argue the case for optimism, against all the intellectuals and all the Generation X-er's around.

But first, a necessary warning: I believe that we live in a world of probabilities, not certainties. All perception consists of gambles, and therefore our sci-phi (science/philosophy) theories and belief systems (B.S.) consist of gambles about gambles. You hear a dry twig cracking, and later evidence makes you wonder if the sound was really a frog croaking—or a dog barking? Deductions from perceptions always carry over the uncertainty of the original perceptions. In such a wobbling, blurry, river-like world, it does not pay a would-be prophet to make his visions too specific, as Heinlein once said.

With that enormous caveat, I see a twenty-first century much like that hymned by the "man from Hope" who recently urged us to join him in crossing a "bridge to the future." I think the worst part of our transition from ape to humanity has passed and gone, and we will now have a significantly less gruesome journey.

For instance, I foresee no more world wars having the magnitude and horror of those of the dying twentieth century (in which not millions or tens of millions but literally somewhere between 100 million and 200 millions humans died at the hands of other humans, who were allegedly sane). That blood-fury, and the madness of the Cold War, which kept us in dread of yet another and even worse planetary Holocaust for over four decades, have both passed beyond the immoral and the self-destructive to the unthinkable. They've gone out of fashion, like the pavane, the periwig, and pantaloons. None of the few remaining superpowers (the U.S.-NATO alliance, Japan, the Arab world) want that kind of risk any longer. They all prefer bluff, bluster, and negotiation. They also realize the folly of spending most of a nation's GNP and using most of its scientific brainpower in the mad pursuit of the goal Bucky Fuller defined as "delivering more and more explosives over longer and longer distances in shorter and shorter times to kill more and more people."

Leaving that madness behind does not mean "perfect peace," except in the sense of the old Zen joke.

"What is perfect peace?" asks the student.

"Two drunks fighting in an alley," replies the Zen Master.

Like all Zen paradoxes, this rests upon recognition of the fallacy of dualism and its win/lose alternatives—the fallacy, that is, of considering 100 percent A or 100 percent B as the only alternatives in any situation. Perfect peace, like total war, exists only in the neurolinguistic world, the human mindscape. As living, evolving organisms, we exist, not in that mindscape or word-web, but in a wobbly energy-world where we float perpetually *between* such theoretical absolutes. Sentience and consciousness, even more, exist always and only "on the edge of chaos," as Crichton recently wrote.

To say it more simply, we live and cope in a kind of middle or muddle in the vast space ignored by "either/or" logic. In this muddle, we drifted to such unprecedented abominations in the dying twentieth century that any ray of hope began to seem too utopian or "unreal." Since 1989, I think we have begun drifting in the other direction, and we will move faster and further away from the age of anxiety.

WERNHER KRUTEIN/PHOTOVAULT

"In a world where negotiation grows more common than aerial bombardment, 'seeing the other side's point of view' will become more highly valued by the world in general—instead of only by a handful of anthropologists and philosophers. We will all learn to listen more and listen better, and we will value those who can listen best, as we now value the most exceptional in all fields—athletes, scientists, artists, or movie stars."

In short, I do not foresee any end to power politics or various skirmishes or insurrections, and I do not think terrorism will vanish until the nation-state vanishes. But I definitely sense us, in our muddled middle, drifting away from the horror of 1939 to 1989, to a less bloodthirsty epoch. The bargaining table, I think, has a better future than the battlefield.

In a world where negotiation grows more common than aerial bombardment, "seeing the other side's point of view" will become more highly valued by the world in general—instead of only by a handful of anthropologists and philosophers. We will all learn to listen more and listen better, and we will value those who can listen best, as we now value the most exceptional in all fields—athletes, scientists, artists, or movie stars.

And you hear strange, disturbing, enlightening things when you learn to listen. The novels of Joyce and Faulkner, our greatest twentieth century writers, resulted from their capacity to listen, as both of them stated clearly. When you stop talking to people and begin talking with them, they tell you as much of the truth as they know, painful and awful as this usually seems at first.

If an age of negotiation truly replaces our age of blasting and bombing, these humbling but humanizing facts will become more universally understood. Ideological arrogance will join homicidal violence on the dusty shelf labeled "our shameful past." Or, as the good man of Nazareth knew, if only he or she without sin may cast the first stone, no stones will be thrown. We have more in common than we realize and resemble our cousin primates more than we like to admit. "One touch of nature makes the whole world kin." We humans are all one huge sprawling, dysfunctional family.

Technologically, I foresee what I have always foreseen in my futurist writings: space migration, intelligence increase, life extension—"SMI2LE," in Timothy Leary's handy slogan.

Already a Japanese consortium has announced plans to build a luxury hotel in outer space.

More immediately, I foresee the rapid achievement of Bucky Fuller's planetary energy grid and an equally planetary unification of the Internet.

The planetary energy grid, which Fuller envisioned as early as 1928, became technologically possible in 1961. He made it the major object of his World Game Center in the 1980s. It simply means hooking up all the electric grids on the planet, which Fuller proved (in several ways) will first lower the cost of electricity for all; secondly, raise the standard of living for all; and thirdly (and some will think oddly), lower birth rates everywhere.

The growth of electrical grids always coincides with or causes lower birthrates. Why? Women receive a better education in industrialized societies than in feudal societies and begin thinking for themselves; industrial and postindustrial systems require literacy; and church attendance always declines as technology advances. (Reactionaries have a good reason to fear technology.)

The Soviet Academy, when it still existed, pronounced Fuller's worldwide grid "feasible" and "desirable." It has received extensive TV coverage in post-Soviet Russia and in parts of Europe. The Arab states, Canada, and even a minority of the population in our backward country have also shown great interest. As oil gets scarcer (and its price accordingly higher), solar and other alternatives will "come out of the closet" and advance more rapidly than hitherto, and all these fit more easily into a world grid than into local grids. For these reasons, I feel particularly confident in predicting that Fuller's grid, plus the decline in birthrate and starvation and the increase in general welfare, will arrive faster than most of my other nonprophet predictions.

As the world grows more peaceful and prosperous, and we expand into longer life spans (the conquest of time), and also into extraterrestrial colonies (conquest of space), I expect a general improvement in morals and manners. Once again, I do not expect the disappearance of crime, crankiness, or even outright raving lunacy, but I do think that all of these neurolinguistic maladies will decrease when the world gradually notices that we have left the age of scarcity and have entered an age of abundance. Most bad tempers, resentments, grudges, and murderous rages derive from the age of scarcity psychology of "kill or be killed"; "get yours quick or there'll be nothing left"; "there's not enough to go around"; and the anguished Tarzanian cry, "it's a jungle out there."

We have all heard of cannibalism among those deprived of adequate life support—e.g., the Donner party, the survivors of that Andes plane crash, etc. To a large extent, the "cannibalistic" competition of past epochs derives from long centuries of real scarcity and recent decades of acting/believing that the scarcity still exists—after technology has made it more possible to deliver more life support over longer distances in shorter times to nourish more people. (As Bucky Fuller often said, our major remaining problems consist of fear, ignorance, greed, and zoning laws.)

I also foresee a rapid decline of Talk Radio, probably within the next five years. Just as radio drama died when replaced by TV drama, Talk Radio (or Shock Radio, as some call it) will not survive the competition of the Internet. I also think the Internet will—less quickly but inevitably—replace or merge with our TV sets and VCRs.

As Hugo Munsterberg pointed out around World War I (i.e., back in the days of silent movies) film engages more of our nervous systems than any previous art; it demands that we participate or interact to understand and enjoy it. With the coming of sound, film evolved further and could still achieve the total artwork dreamed of by Wagner. The emotional storm of grand opera, the beauty of great paintings, the intricacy of classical symphony, the suspense of the narrative or novel, the ritual power of stage drama: all of these can appear on film, and sometimes all at once.

Now that all of this media is available on video and increasingly on CD-ROM, the projected amalgamation of the TV and computer into one planetary network (the Information Superhighway or Infobahn) seems sure to arrive faster than anybody expects.

But the decentralized nature of the Net makes this emerging global net not only the most interactive or synergetic art medium ever, in the Munsterberg sense, but also the most Jeffersonian communication media. The great Freemasonic dream of our tattered old First Amendment—free expression for all—has never actually appeared.

The First Amendment has always remained partly a pious hope and partly a sad joke. The language of the Constitution says we shall have no laws abridging free expression, but every year the Supreme Court rules on which laws abridging such freedom they will allow. As Justice Black once said, they have enough cleverness to convince themselves that "no laws" means "some laws."

I strongly suspect that no effective censorship of the Net will ever evolve; the fire-breathing genie of thought crime has gotten out of the wine cask. To tackle the thorniest issue of all, kiddie porn—consider that a large part of it (probably most of it) comes from Germany and the Netherlands and other North European countries. We will have to return to the age of total war, which nobody wants, to enforce any law against that kind of kinky sex, or against any ideas our Congress does not like. Can you seriously picture an endless series of U.S. Army incursions into our NATO allies to arrest the individuals who create this material?

Besides the inability of one country to censor a Net that coexists in many countries and will soon exist in all, another major problem will frustrate Big Brother.

Encryption makes censorship of the Net a comic endeavor. Some codes (PGP, for instance) probably cannot be decoded with a billion years of computer time. This does not mean that censorship laws for the Net will not get enacted; I feel certain such laws will appear rapidly, first in the United States and then in the banana republics. The fact that nobody can really enforce such laws only means that they will get enforced very selectively.

For a while the Federal Communications Commission (FCC) will become as much a menace to freedom as the ATF or the DEA or other "thought police" trying to spy on and control the people of an alleged democracy. Such organizations, seeking to enforce the unenforceable, function as social oxymorons or strange loops. They generate parades and cultural schizophrenia, starting from their original assumptions that (1) government should act as the master of the people rather than as their servant, and (2) that spying on the people does not contradict democracy at the root.

As Bertolt Brecht said, "If the government doesn't trust the people, why not dissolve them and elect a new people?" The logic there, as in all good satire, mimes insanity; but similar insanity always results when fascism operates under the guise of democracy. Everybody goes a little bit nuts, when fascism calls itself democracy, because words no longer have even a notational connection with actions. The war against some drugs has already produced that kind of looniness; the war against freedom on the Net will produce even more, in horse doctor's doses. Resistance to

WERNHER KRUTEIN/PHOTOVAULT

"As Bertolt Brecht said, 'If the government doesn't trust the people, why not dissolve them and elect a new people?' . . . Everybody goes a little bit nuts, when fascism calls itself democracy, because words no longer have even a notational connection with actions. The war against some drugs has already produced that kind of looniness; the war against freedom on the Net will produce even more, in horse doctor's doses."

the web police will quickly become as widespread as current opposition to the narcotics police and may even evolve into a bigger citizen's militia.

Internet World for March 1996 says bluntly that ". . . . regulatory and legislative policy cannot hope to keep pace with technological innovation. This legislative time-lag between what politicians understand and what is technologically operative today is an abyss . . . the union of computers and telecommunications is primed to cause economic and political earthquakes."

The Internet is evolving more and more toward the "planetary brain" once only imagined by visionary scientists like Teilhard de Chardin and Arthur Clarke. The U.S. Congress has panic attacks over the fact that some of this brain contains "pornographic" fantasy. As I said, we humans make up one big dysfunctional family. Do you know any brain that doesn't contain "forbidden" sexual longings?

The Internet also allows political attitudes considered either unthinkable or unspeakable (except by "kooks" or other oddballs) to become familiar to millions. As a result, one of the most popular shows on U.S. television (now a big hit in England as well)—*The X-Files*—deals with governmental conspiracies that only the "kooks" took seriously a decade ago. It must foreshadow shows (in the tradition of *The Prisoner)* about other governmental conspiracies, real and imaginary. Nothing can remain unspoken in our new global village.

In other words, we live more and more with a technology that our alleged rulers do not understand well enough to regulate in any fashion. They can only hope that the Net will not make them totally obsolete, because many are now asking why we need a legislature at all. Since the Constitutional balance of power has worked for 200 years to prevent too much from power accumulating in any one place, I think we certainly should keep an executive branch with a prez on top and a court with independent judges (even if some of them do write like cranks at times). But do we need a Congress? When we all have modems, why not represent ourselves? Doesn't that make more sense than the current system, in which the Congress pretends to represent all, but in fact, usually represents only those who stuff their bank accounts with bribes?

One hears such thinking a lot lately, and we'll hear more as the abyss between technology and the lawmakers, who make up our Congress, grows wider and wider.

Finally, I do not foresee a world government, because the opposition remains paranoid and entrenched—not just here but in most countries. The primary human loyalties have always bonded to the family and tribe. Extending them to the nation-state ("God Bless America," "Deutschland uber Alles," etc.) has never achieved the real strength of the extended family bond. Every nation has its "loyal opposition" in the citizenry and usually a "disloyal opposition," too, especially in times of change and chaos. More international cooperation will occur (e.g., the NAFTA/GATT model), but I think other governmental bodies will become more and more decentralized, resulting in something like the county system. Perhaps they will all cantonize as the Swiss did a long ago.

I will be more astonished than anyone if these educated guesses prove accurate in all, or even most, respects. But I think some of them will occur just as I foresee—probably the most fantastic and unthinkable ones.

⊕

The author of 31 books, Robert Anton Wilson has been described as "one of the leading thinkers of the modern age" by Barbara Marx Hubbard and "a 21st Century Renaissance Man... funny, wise and optimistic...the Lenny Bruce of philosophers" by the *Denver Post.*

His publications include: *Cosmic Trigger,* which is the number one recommended New Age book by *Changing Times;* the Quantum Comedy *Schroedinger's Cat,* named "the most scientific of all science-fiction novels" by *New Scientist;* and, with Robert Shea, the classic *Illuminatus* trilogy, called "the biggest sci-fi cult novel to come along since *Dune*" by the *Village Voice.*

Wilson co-edits the futurist journal *Trajectories* with his wife Arlen. His most recent books include: *Chaos and Beyond* (1994, Permanent Press) and *Cosmic Trigger III: My Life After Death* (1995, Falcon Press). Forthcoming: *The Walls Came Tumbling Down* (1997, Falcon Press) and *Encyclopedia of Conspiracy Theories* (1998, Harper Collins).

WERNHER KRUTEIN/PHOTOVAULT

"As in physics, where the atom breaks up into subparticles and subprocesses, the ordinary self, in the cyclotron of shocking existence, generates sub- or alter-personalities. Having not yet plumbed the depths of physical reality, it appears that we are in the same position in regard to mental reality. . . . Maybe we can learn to consciously dissociate from our normal, less-developed selves. It may be possible to reconnoiter the hidden regions of our other, more comprehensive minds."

Chapter Ten

THE ART OF CREATIVE DISSOCIATION

by Michael Grosso

Our boat guide, down the Amazon River and into its piranha-populated streams, was a lean Brazilian with friendly eyes. His name was Marcos, a young man in his twenties. Early in the trip he said something that stuck in my mind and went to the heart of the conference I was attending. But first, let me put his remark in perspective.

This was the 15th International Transpersonal Association (ITA) conference, convened in May 1996, at the sumptuous Hotel Tropical in Manaus, Brazil. Eight hundred people from some thirty-eight countries had come from all parts of the planet to discuss technologies of the sacred.

The expression *"technologies of the sacred"* is odd because we normally don't associate technology with the sacred. We think of science and technology as discrediting the idea of the sacred. Perhaps a better word would be "technique," from the Greek *techne,* which means art. The idea of technique or technology is provocative—a seed-idea for saving the world, I heard more than one speaker say.

"The transformations coming in the next decade are awesome," said a devotee of psychosynthesis I met on the plane, "and we need to arm ourselves with a renewed sense of the sacred." Reawakening a sense of the sacred is crucial to our social and psychological health, it was repeatedly said.

Marcos pointed out that Manaus means "mother of the goddess," a fitting name for the locale of our transpersonal pow-wow. It was also befitting our purpose that in the sane country of Brazil, it's lawful to drink *ayahuasca,* a psychoactive drug used by members of Santo Daime to bring spiritual insight and ecstasy into daily life.

This is a contrast with North America, where psychedelics are forbidden by the law and viewed as near-diabolic by the religious establishment. Pierre Weil, a psychologist and consultant of UNESCO, described Brazil as a "culture of peace"—an icon of multiculturalism, where African, European, and indigenous peoples have learned to live together and where the Catholic Church has incorporated the sacrament of ayahuasca.

Psychedelics, or as they say nowadays, entheogens—in-god-begetters—were much discussed at the conference. Speaker after speaker rose to advocate and instruct on the theme of psychedelic enlightenment, though some of the pilgrims were not happy about such an emphasis.

Patiently pecking at a portion of semi-sattvic flan, one American yoga teacher complained that his discipline was shamelessly underrepresented. "It's a lazy man's shortcut that could lead you into a ditch," he said sourly. We agreed that one could get hung up on the psychedelic experience and that the states these drugs induced were no guarantee of liberation or enlightenment.

Others were ecstatic over the prospect of blowing their minds in the ayahuasca rite, and there were several evening jaunts to a nearby village hut where the group ritual was conducted. I bumped into a white-haired couple from Peoria as they were about to join the other initiates—all dressed in white.

"We can't wait for this," said the ultra-straight-looking man from the Midwest. Americans I spoke with were struck by the collective and ritually regulated character of the rite. They sat together for hours, all lined up in pews, barfing, chanting, and dancing in happy unison.

Other techniques for inducing transpersonal states were discussed, and some were demonstrated. I was deeply moved by the entrancing music of Sylvia Nakkach and Michael Knapp. Sylvia got us all to chant together and I found my sense of self, a bit edgy and irascible from the heat, dissolving into rolling waves of aimless good-will. One evening a group of Brazilian dancers performed in huge multicolored costumes by the pool under the stars, and before I knew it, hundreds of conference attendees were drawn into the ecstatic dance.

The occasion in Manaus marked Stanislav Grof's yielding of the ITA presidency to Richard Tarnas. Grof and Tarnas share a certain missionary fervor in their aim to overhaul the old paradigm. The terminology of a "new paradigm" has become part of the new rhetoric of secular apocalyptic. I share their misgivings about simplistic and soul-killing world views: especially that Cartesian, Newtonian, mechanistic, rationalistic, and damned capitalistic dragon that New Age thinkers want to slay.

Neo-shaman Grof has spent decades observing the psychological effects of LSD. He has also developed a technique of hyperventilation he christened "holotropic breathing" that induces LSD-like altered states. The effect of Grof's work has been to bring into focus information that expands mainstream models of the human mind.

As it turns out, the LSD observations and other entheogenic data are just one part of the increasing information singularities sweeping through American culture in these times of high transit. By information singularity, I mean information that generates new patterns of perception, new conceptions of reality, and new experiential horizons. It's part of the new prophetic guild to punch holes in the prevailing paradigm by insisting on the importance of information rejected by normal science.

For example, Richard Tarnas attested to astrology. Tarnas, a closet eschatologist, wants to hasten the end of history as we know it, which in more ways than one, has been pretty much a male-dominated show. This male-driven, Cartesian world view has been drained of all lifeblood and meaning. All the poetic, spiritual, and mystical properties of being—the kind of meaning that counts for us humans—have been repealed in the court of modern science, leaving us in a disenchanted universe. If meaning remains, it has retreated in despairing solitude to the human mind, a small outpost in a dead cosmos. All this is familiar territory, the philosopher Whitehead having staked it out in his book, *Modes of Thought*. The twist was that Tarnas invoked astrology as the way to reenchant the cosmos.

My view of astrology is that, as a system of archetypal psychology as practiced by Ficino the renaissance magus, reinterpreted by James Hillman, and revived by Thomas Moore, it can be useful as a form of art therapy. Another side of astrology, however, lends itself to fatalistic and mechanistic modes of thought. This became evident the following evening.

It was eight o'clock, and people were gathering in Solimoes and Rio Negro Halls. Despite air conditioning, the tropical heat was fatiguing, but after a winter of blizzards in New York City, my brain was slow to adjust to the weather. I looked around, luxuriating in a mental haze, a bit dissociated from my normal self.

Then a big screen lit up with an astrological diagram—a very pretty, abstract drawing, and the commentator, in a very reassuring voice, began to speak. The horoscope was a portrait of upcoming astrological events. As the commentator spoke about the unprecedented array of cosmic forces, I heard someone behind me say, "My left brain is screaming at me." I turned to behold the intense, angular face of John Mack, the Pulitzer prize-winning psychiatrist who has rankled the more uptight custodians of the status quo. Mack has touched a nerve by crediting stories of alien abductions; he was a speaker at the conference.

Later, in his own presentation, John Mack told of encounters, strange and disturbing, with alien beings. But what do alien abductions have to do with sacred technologies? By blowing the conceptual grids we use to depict reality, says Mack, they become the axe that breaks the frozen sea of the sacred imagination.

Carl Jung was the first major psychiatrist to address the UFO mystery, for him a psychic signal of a changing-of-the-gods. Mack sees the more violent abductions as representing a deeper penetration of the new reality into our increasingly unstable life-space.

My own opinion of this theory—you have to be a metaphysical acrobat to deal with it—is to regard the alien scenario as an invasion of something that is somehow real but also deeply symbolic. For example, some abductees report being subjected to intrusive medical examinations. Symbolically, at the least, we might translate this to mean that the phenomenon is about self-examination, collective diagnosis—a kind of shamanic operation on our species mind.

Whether a new form of mass psychosis or the advancing shock troops of ontic wonderment, the alien abduction phenomenon seems to come from outside the mainstream of our normal awareness of the world. Some alien abductions are said to occur in normal waking life but most have as their setting dreams, highway hypnosis, or states of consciousness on the edge of dissociation where, as the poet Rimbaud once put it, "I is somebody else."

The idea of dissociation closely relates to how I view the problem of our desacralized world. First let me come back to our Brazilian boat guide and the remark that has lingered in my mind. "The average worker in Manaus earns from $100 to $300 a month—and it's very expensive here," said Marcos during the boat ride.

"And how!" I agreed.

He looked up and smiled, "But we have a happy life."

I thought of the curiously upbeat rhythm of the music I was hearing in Brazil. Could the most important technology of the sacred be learning the art of enjoying what we have? I reflected. People in advanced industrial societies seem unable to enjoy their abundance of goods. If Marcos is a good example, you don't need a great deal of them for a happy life.

Musing on what Marcos observed, it occurred to me that to be a first-rate artist of the sacred, *no thing* in particular would be absolutely necessary. In the end, it's the agility of outlook that counts—the ingenuity of the spiritual imagination.

The theme of the conference was "technologies of the sacred," ways to help us break the spell of the profane mind-set. Roughly, what is that? It's the everyday, uninspired, literal-minded, business-as-usual, rationalist approach to the world. The view of the world—as well as of ourselves and other people—that is one-dimensional, flat, pedestrian, and soul-deadening. Without a break, without periodic vacations from this kind of juiceless reality, the soul sickens. Can we dismantle the profane mind-set? I mean, grace or tons of money aside?

Needless to say, in such deeply personal matters, we have to arrive at our own conclusions. Lately I've been developing a family of techniques that I lump together and call "creative dissociation."

This term was derived from several overlapping interests. For a long time I have been fascinated by mediumship and the related states of ecstasy and possession. And, for an even longer time, art has been one of my loves. In fact, in the past year my childhood love of art has been revived, and I've been drawing and painting again.

Combining art with my interest in psychic phenomena, I have been trying to formulate techniques for undermining the profane mind-set. Many of these were inspired by my experiments in the studio.

The ability to dissociate from our normal selves apparently exists in everybody—a God-given gift, I'd say—and is apparently "normal" in itself. The degree of normal dissociation may be small, as when we doodle during a phone call, or complete, as when we dream. A spectrum of possibilities exists between these two extremes.

Dissociative behaviors such as fugue or multiple personality disorder are so extreme and maladaptive that they are dubbed pathological. In these cases, dissociation becomes a strategy for coping with trauma, a form of flight from unbearable reality. So there are normal and pathological ways to dissociate. There are also supernormal ways. My experiments have been with what amount to deliberate exercises in dissociation.

An example of dissociation, well known in clinical history, shows how we might use this ability. Pierre Janet used the term "disaggregation" to describe what happens to patients suffering from trauma. Disaggregation later came to be called dissociation. The classic case of Leonie will illustrate the creative potential hidden in behavior that may at times appear insane.

Leonie (Janet called her Leonie I) was a patient who had been severely traumatized. She was a gray and submissive specimen of human personality. However, in the pressure cooker of her traumatic life, Leonie I broke up into fragments of new, disaggregated, and dissociated personalities. From these pieces an entirely new personality emerged: Leonie II.

Leonie II was a more interesting person, wittier, if caustic, and more vibrantly alive than Leonie I. In an asymmetry of memory obtained between the two Leonies, Leonie II remembered the memories of Leonie I, whom she heartily disliked; Leonie I, however, had no recollection of Leonie II.

What a remarkable phenomenon! As in physics, where the atom breaks up into subparticles and subprocesses, the ordinary self, in the cyclotron of shocking existence, generates sub- or alter-personalities. Having not yet plumbed the depths of physical reality, it appears that we are in the same position in regard to mental reality.

Through Leonie I's traumatic dissociation, a second, more interesting, comprehensive personality was born. But the story doesn't end here. While under hypnosis, a Leonie III emerged from Leonie II. Leonie III was different from, and disdainful of, the two other Leonies. Eventually Leonie III became the dominant and most comprehensive personality, a creative synthesis of the three aspects of a total, expanded personality.

Such stories demonstrate that each of us has a normal, more-or-less adapted persona that may be a "mask" for a multiple world of possible selves. The Greek philosopher Heraclitus was right: no matter how far we travel we never come to the *bathun,* the depth or boundary of the soul.

Assume for a moment that the evidence shows that our everyday persona is a mask for many hidden layers of human potential. This raises a fascinating question. Maybe we can learn to consciously dissociate from our normal,

WERNHER KRUTEIN/PHOTOVAULT

less-developed selves. It may be possible to reconnoiter the hidden regions of our other, more comprehensive minds.

The power of dissociation may be the psychological equivalent of Einstein's equation $E=mc^2$. It suggests an analogy: people, in their stable "material" aspect are fissionable into multiple possible selves—more encompassing, more evolved selves. The psychological equivalent of nuclear fission would be creative dissociation.

I find that creative dissociation might lead us to our more com-

"Although they've lost their original meaning and prestige, the Roman Genius and the Greek Muse were ancient techniques for inducing dissociation from the habitual persona. . . .

". . . The Muse is no mere literary conceit. The Muses were all goddesses—water nymphs found near high, inaccessible mountain streams. To invoke them was to open oneself to seizure, physical inspiration, possession. In 'Theogony,' Hesiod tells how the Muse blew his soul."

prehensive selves in three different ways: the mythical, the psychical, and the artistic. From mythology, for example, we can borrow the Genius and the Muse. Although they've lost their original meaning and prestige, the Roman Genius and the Greek Muse were ancient techniques for inducing dissociation from the habitual *persona.*

The genius is the guardian spirit that presides over us from birth; it represents our greater, subliminal, or transpersonal self. The most famous genius of antiquity belonged to Socrates. Plato's "Symposium" paints a vivid picture of the "old boy" dissociated in philosophic trance in the Athenian marketplace. The "Symposium" was about Eros, the demonic force with the power to dissociate us from our prudent (that is, profane) minds. The erotic love of beauty was Plato's favorite technique of dissociation, and it was taken up during the Renaissance by Ficino and his circle.

As to the Greek myth of the Muse—there actually were many Muses—here too we find evidence of an ancient psychic technology. The Muse is no mere literary conceit. The Muses were all goddesses—water nymphs found near high, inaccessible mountain streams. To invoke them was to open oneself to seizure, physical inspiration, possession. In "Theogony," Hesiod tells how the Muse blew his soul.

The Muse raises two points. The first is about the physics of inspiration. Inspiration is literally a kind of hyperventilation. The word soul or psyche *means* breath. So, if we "ensoul" ourselves, that is, learn deeply to breathe in being, we can subdue the grip of repressive rationality. I like to think of Stanislav Grof, whom I mentioned earlier, as a kind of latter-day physician of the Muses. Stan spends a good deal of time going around the world literally *inspiring* people.

Beyond physics is the psychology of inspiration. We seem to be a culture in search of a Muse. We are in search of—well, animation. Ask yourself what really inspires you. To what sanctuaries can you flee? What burning ideal can you summon at will? We need to make room inside ourselves, open up a space that permits (or perhaps entices) the Muse in her glory. Or is it too hard, in our timidly selfish world, to be open to being ravished by a Muse?

In modern times, psychics and artists provide information about breaking the profane mind-set. Consider, for example, the role of spontaneity. Experimental psychic studies show that the most important predictor of ESP is being completely spontaneous in your behavior and thinking. ESP is the ability to feel, perceive, and know things beyond the ken of your senses and beyond the everyday logic of time and space. If you want to pass these constraints, you had best behave spontaneously. Spontaneity implies being self-caused, moving freely, at one with your own original energy.

You try to disconnect from the part of you that hesitates, inhibits itself, and tends to calculate. You let your imagination spew forth its riches and then go with them, looking for ways to flesh them out, shade them properly, and breathe life into them. For the Surrealist, spontaneity becomes a life-style. Spontaneity is a weapon to fight a crowded and regimented life, overdriven and overstuffed, a life in which the only place to find spontaneity is in dreams. The idea of the surrealists is to bring the dream into reality and thus create a *surreality.* Live spontaneously, and this becomes possible.

While heading back to Manaus in the big motor boat, Marcos sat down beside me. Being autumn on the Amazon, there was an early sunset, and the day had cooled off. He looked at me and smiled amiably.

We had stopped at a little store on the river, a simple wooden structure moored to the trees. Some children appeared, playing with what looked like a ten-foot anaconda. I took some photos of them, and they held out their hats for recompense. The kids looked happy, their faces shy but animated. Again the thought came to me of how easy it is to forget the sheer wonder of existence. And how far we are from the fine art of making do with what's at hand.

The Hotel Tropical was now in view—back to middle-class comfort in the middle of the rain forest. As I stepped off the boat, it occurred to me that the problem in North America is simply a matter of having too much. Advanced industrial cultures are in trouble, I thought, because they are choking to death on their needs, commodities, information, expectations; so much stuff to "process"—a giant case of spiritual indigestion.

I've been thinking lately that we may be on the wrong track. Many thoughtful people have been trying hard to make science and the sacred sit down at the same table together, a big theme of New Age thought. People plumb the arcane depths of science with hopes of returning with some spirit-authenticating formula or metaphysical magic trick.

I view the philosophy of reenchantment from a different perspective. The struggle to reconcile science and spirit may just be a wasted effort, if you believe, as I do, that *the creative imagination is the definitive fact of our lives.* In short, the idea of an atom and the idea of a god are just part of our cognitive machinery for coping with experience. You can measure their worth in a variety of ways, but in the end, they are more or less useful mental constructs for negotiating the adventure of existence.

If so, science and religion are types of artwork: ways of viewing the world. Science and religion, like cooking and baseball, are constructs of the creative imagination. They provide perspectives on reality. Vico, the great philosopher of the imagination, understood this as did Nietzsche.

Art is the first language we use to grapple with reality, the first language through which the world is enchanted. To reenchant this world that is dying from rationalistic consumerism, it is in our interest to cultivate the Muses, the goddesses who preside over the arts.

For me, modern art—freed from the inhibiting profanity of the marketplace—points toward a new poetics of the sacred. The new spirit of art that Apollinaire saw coming has yet to be fully realized.

Modern art may be described as a series of creative dissociations. From de Chirico to Duchamp, the artists tried to sever themselves from the routine, profane ways of perceiving the world. Gauguin severed himself from civilization itself, and tried to conquer an earthly paradise.

"We have been musing on the philosophy of reenchantment . . . about being happy, in spite of humble economic resources, defined the problem for me. How to be happy with a minimum of means? How to find the sacred and the magical in the profane scrap heap of the postmodern world?

"Maybe poverty, I thought, is the most important technology of the sacred. . . .It obliges one to view the world with a new set of eyes, see it from a new perspective. The old mystics—those masters of enlightened dissociation—practiced voluntary poverty. They made it a rule of life to detach themselves from all created things."

WERNHER KRUTEIN/PHOTOVAULT

Dada began in Switzerland as an international movement to protest the First World War. In a Dada performance, Marcel Duchamp entered a porcelain urinal at the Society of Independent Artists and called it "Fountain." As an example of the art of the ready-made, it dissociates itself from the whole history of art. After Duchamp, there is no object we cannot see as art. He took the object out of its world, its utilitarian context, and dissolved the distinction between art and non-art. After Duchamp, art acquired a new nature, a new paradigm.

With "Fountain," you detach yourself from aesthetics, from reverence for history, tradition. Duchamp also made a Rembrandt reproduction into an ironing board. John Cage, who "composed" music from random noise, dissociated himself from the entire history of music. Duchamp shows that all objects are in principle "found" artworks, Cage that all noise is music.

Similar freedom was realized through the technique of collage. Apollinaire, the poet who invented the term "surrealism," explained the idea of collage: "You paint with whatever material you please, with pipes, postage stamps, postcards or playing cards, pieces of oil cloth, collars, painted paper, newspapers."

We have yet to unpack the revolutionary implications of collage. The great message is that we are free, a freedom that precedes the appearance of science and religion; it is the original freedom to marshall, arrange, rearrange, interpret, and reinterpret our own immediate perceptions of the world.

The most liberating dissociation is from the dominant cultural definition of art. Once we expand the concept of art, the range of possible art materials multiplies and the whole of existence becomes raw material for art. The poets of the future, said Apollinaire, will be prophets—purifiers of the divine, transformers of the sacred.

Modern art presaged the fate of our age, the dislocation that is happening now on such a vast scale. The futurists proclaimed a revolution of sensibility, anticipating the apotheosis of computers, bioengineering, and nanotechnology. They did their best to smash the syntax of mainstream culture. "Liberty in language" was Marinetti's motto. There is a marvelous country, an El Dorado of the mind that awaits our exploration, argued Breton, where dream and reality, life and death merge into "surreality." That is where the human spirit aspires to go, he proclaimed, where its future lies.

Twentieth-century art has much to proclaim about the poetics of the future, the new directions of the sacred imagination. The chief lesson is that, for the emancipated imagination, *anything can mean anything.* Collage is a technique for enacting this last freedom—the power to create poetry out of the chaos of experience. It is for us to gather, weave, and reweave all the meaning out of everything that we experience. And, in the sovereign eye of imagination, even the gulf between sacred and profane disappears.

We have been musing on the philosophy of reenchantment. What Marcos said about being happy, in spite of humble economic resources, defined the problem for me. How to be happy with a minimum of means? How to find the sacred and the magical in the profane scrap heap of the postmodern world?

Maybe poverty, I thought, is the most important technology of the sacred. Poverty is life lived with a minimum of means. Like the art of collage and the art of the ready-made, the technique of poverty disconnects the mind from the mainstream. It obliges one to view the world with a new set of eyes, see it from a new perspective. The old mystics—those masters of enlightened dissociation—practiced voluntary poverty. They made it a rule of life to detach themselves from all created things.

⊕

Michael Grosso is an author, artist, philosopher, and investigator of psychic anomalies. He received his Ph.D. in philosophy from Columbia University and presently chairs the Department of Philosophy at Jersey City State College. His recent books include *The Millennium Myth* by Quest Books and *Soul-making: Uncommon Paths to Self-Understanding* by Hampton Roads Publishing. His website Cabaret St. John is a clearing house for information that challenges prevailing paradigms. Grosso lives in rustic Warwick, New York, where he writes, paints, and practices "creative dissociation."

Chapter Eleven

CULTIVATING A TWENTY-FIRST-CENTURY MIND

by Marsha Sinetar

"A turning point. A farthest point. A culmination": *New Webster's* figurative definition of the word "solstice." I've been asked to "tune into the planetary consciousness, to write a chapter in a book with the general theme of shifts in planetary consciousness." Strange predicament. In street jargon, I'm not "into" such things. This quiet, contemplative, perhaps religious, writer is into quiet, contemplative engagements, such as mulling over a few lines of the Psalms or Isaiah or the Gospels while tending pink vine roses or watering the lack bamboo. This country bumpkin chews, not on bits of straw but on worshipful notions, while simultaneously chatting with ravens, the occasional red-tailed hawk, and here and there, tiny, chartreuse tree frogs. They fly about their wetland homes: clay water pots I've scattered around this neck of the forest.

Perhaps that precise daydreaming, that here-now enjoyment, these spontaneous and natural pastimes are what this forecasting task entails: tuning in, listening in, as the Prophet Isaiah suggested, to that silent word within that whispers "This is the way."

"Our integrated, transcendent mind . . . sees all things as infinite, eternal, celestial, and intelligently alive. Here and now we realize there is no longer any need to seek out paradise because we are paradise. Walt Whitman described that illuminated brilliance variously, for example as 'a sudden gleam divine, precipitating, bursting all those {other} bubbles, fashions, wealth . . . {reducing} those eager business aims—books, politics, arts, amours . . . to utter nothingness.'"

WERNHER KRUTEIN/PHOTOVAULT

WERNHER KRUTEIN/PHOTOVAULT

"Those who cultivate their twenty-first century mind—highly creative, spiritual, alive to possibilities— . . . transfigure inner hurts or troubles into some beneficent vision, some expanded opportunity for more abundant life. That's what saints and artists do: innocently, with pure and open minds, they open themselves up to each experience until they turn, as Cistercian monk and author Thomas Merton once wrote, 'from slaves in the spiritual order of things into divine reflections of That life and love which is holy.'"

First a word for potential doomsdayers: no, I don't sense our planet careening to its end, and no, I don't foresee a cataclysmic finale to human life. Oh, sure, life as we've known it is changing. Has changed. But, global warming and scarcity issues aside, our species' mental hardware is fully capable of rectifying such problems. Collectively speaking, when necessary, we can hunker down and discipline ourselves. Like the good boys and girls we are down deep, we can curtail our progressive excesses of overpopulation and water, soil, and air pollution. When things get bad enough, or when we're hurting enough, we figure out how to restore balance to daily life, our communities, our lovely Mother Earth.

That corrective period rapidly approaches. Who hasn't noticed that it's time to reclaim what that grand old futurist Herman Khan termed our planet's 'fragile envelope?' This spring I, for one, sorely missed the charm of Monarch butterflies fluttering around my garden. (Is it my imagination, or do fewer of them skim the air waves these days?) And truly, I feel for frogs as did John Muir, who once said that, to him, hearing their marsh music was as sweet as the love songs of birds.

Underscoring Kahn's notion, I suppose we'll experience our planetary ups and downs—our droughts and floods, our overages and shortages. Still ecological babies, we've yet to learn exactly what it means to honor, manage, and prudently utilize Mother's delicate and generous bounty. This "fool on the hill" believes that we can survive every sort of upsetting transition if we cultivate a new mind—one that has undergirded us forever. That's my bias: nothing needs shifting. We just need to wake up to what's always been.

Evolutionary infants that we are, quick fixes won't correct our mistakes or make us masters of our universe (as those media-hyping, edict-loving gurus promise at their costly weekend workshops). No formulaic strategies exist that can procure real fulfillment—the promised, perfect land we seek—because the ground we're standing on is already holy.

It takes discipline to transcend old habits of mind and fictive belief systems that suggest otherwise. An improved life demands improvements in our way of life—not simply instant answers and snappy, smoothly packaged sound bites. Over the long haul, we'll have to discover (or invent) new ways to feed and shelter people, control our new technologies, or be controlled by them. No doubt we'll sow our seeds (and reap what we sow) under the seas, in the deserts, and on other planets. Surely, we'll explore, not just superficial reconfigurations of industry, but also the outrageous failures in our current outrageous triumphs. Which brings me to what I really must discuss: the ecology of consciousness. The last century has taught many of us that, as Krishnamurti put it, the world is as we are.

If the twentieth century's spiritual focus was transcending our ordinary minds and attaining a heightened consciousness, the twenty-first century's goal will be to wake up, step into, and operate from that transcendence, that ultimate reality. The future is here. Now. With pure, simple awareness comes the liberty of clear sight, not necessarily intellectual understanding, but rather, as that Buddhist saying has it, "the don't know mind," perfect beyond pleasure and pain and outdated judgments, beyond attempts to solve today's problems with yesterday's thinking.

Fresh, uncharted realities already flow from that transcendent mode of being. Mystics call that mind "God-consciousness." Other names abound: "the fourth dimension," "cosmic-consciousness," and "unity-consciousness." Lacking unitive thought processes, our actions divide and disorganize our lives. With an immature mentality, we create needless polarities. In St. Paul's lexicon, as wee babes we've spoken as little children and reasoned our way along childishly. Ever watched two- or three-year-olds dress themselves, or make a bed, or try to bake a cake? It's now time to grow up fully, to cast away childish things, and to discipline ourselves and reason from a renewed, whole-brained mode of being that integrates intuition and logic and artificial dichotomies.

Our integrated, transcendent mind is the same here-and-now mentality that the Zen Buddhists call "big mind/open mind": it orders, heals, and transforms whatever it touches, since it sees all things as infinite, eternal, celestial, and intelligently alive. Here and now we realize there is no longer any need to seek out paradise because we are paradise. Walt Whitman described that illuminated brilliance variously, for example as "a sudden gleam divine, precipitating, bursting all those [other] bubbles, fashions, wealth. . . . [reducing] those eager business aims—books, politics, arts, amours . . . to utter nothingness."

By contrast, our old mind—cold, fearful, unforgiving—is the ultimate machine of dualism. Totally lifeless. It warps our sights, degrades and limits joy, and, with its egocentric reference base, splits us in two. Old news. Here's good news: its supposed authority is waning.

The thought processes we're now cultivating are more synergistic and whole-brained. Some (not all, of course) lead to a level of awareness that mysteriously integrates experience until each of us feels a part of every other person and each bud and bead of life.

Who hasn't noticed that our electronic internets and technographic networks metaphorically express the interpersonal and interplanetary connections that global integration demands? Although these electronic networks aren't perfect tools, they are gradually eroding piecemeal politics at all levels. Yes, they may (probably will) create monumental problems and, as educator Neil Postman suggests, we'll need to be vigilant lest these new tools become our "most dangerous enemy." Still, it's the movement I'm discussing: we're headed in a definite holistic direction.

Here and now, who can't see that universal, communicative glue spilling out? Who can't envision a conversational, planetary linkup joining our whole world? Ideas and friends are readily available. Businesses and personal lives are reinvented instantaneously. Vital, lively interrelationships and spiritual expansion seem to be the norm all over the planet, joining us at the hip—or, better, at the heart. Somehow I find that all this connectivity illustrates exactly the unity of consciousness I'm celebrating. That grand prophet Isaiah's songs of unity and our own, transcendent inner music sound much alike, particularly when we cross over that perceptual threshold of consciousness that the Persian psychiatrist, A. Reza Arasteh, called "final integration": the whole-brained, illumined state.

Those who cultivate their twenty-first century mind—highly creative, spiritual, alive to possibilities—move toward, not away from, conflict or tension. Like perceptual artists or saints, they transfigure inner hurts or troubles into some beneficent vision, some expanded opportunity for more abundant life. That's what saints and artists do: innocently, with pure and open minds, they open themselves up to each experience until they turn, as Cistercian monk and author Thomas Merton once wrote, "from slaves in the spiritual order of things into divine reflections of That life and love which is holy."

I tend to see artists and those with artistic temperaments as future leaders. They'll prod us toward perceptual union with reality. Each true artist and every saint is well disposed to embrace discord, somehow to harmonize

"Each true artist and every saint is well disposed to embrace discord, somehow to harmonize it in the service of their art or their devotion. These giants of awareness ever light up a way for us to better reconstitute our drabness or sorrow into enduring beauty. Perceptual artists and saints honor and celebrate life. To borrow Gandhi's words, the true artist 'always takes note not merely of form but of what lies behind. There is an art that kills and an art that gives life. True art must give evidence of happiness, contentment, and purity of its authors.'"

WERNHER KRUTEIN/PHOTOVAULT

it in the service of their art or their devotion. These giants of awareness ever light up a way for us to better reconstitute our drabness or sorrow into enduring beauty. Perceptual artists and saints honor and celebrate life. To borrow Gandhi's words, the true artist "always takes note not merely of form but of what lies behind. There is an art that kills and an art that gives life. True art must give evidence of happiness, contentment, and purity of its authors."

If we agree with Dostoyevski that only beauty will save the world, then it's worth developing the artist's soul and sight in ourselves. Wouldn't it be grand to surrender, once and for all, to that omnipotent, omniscient, omnipresent beauty in which we live and breathe and have our being? I say blessings on the life of all true artist and saints whose minds and works reveal a glimpse of paradise. They help us see, in William Blake's well-known expression, ". . . eternity in a grain of sand."

Artists and saints are life's great lovers. They show how to find hope and optimism in our lives despite depressing circumstances. A case in point: in 1970, literature Nobel Prize winner Alexander Solzhenitsyn, unable to leave Russia to present the customary Nobel lecture at the award ceremony, penned a statement and sent it to Stockholm. Among other things, he described two types of artists: those who imagine themselves creators of an independent spiritual world, who assume total responsibility for creating that world and who collapse under the weight of such a load; and those who acknowledge a higher power, yet they work "as a common apprentice under God's heaven." The second sort have faith in the underlying order of things. Their task is "to sense more keenly than others the harmony of the world . . . in failure as well as in the lower depths—in poverty, in prison, in illness—the consciousness of a stable harmony will never leave" the true artist. Such people reflect truth, beauty and the deepest organizing principle: Love.

Once upon a time, we couldn't admit our celestial truths, and as such, felt ourselves confined—bound by earthly limits, held captive by our fears. Once upon a time, we may have believed that we lacked the resources or potency to do what we really wanted and, therefore, only accomplished what we were told we must. Today, more and more of us dream supernatural dreams, believe in them, reach out for them in strong faith. Soon, certainly into forever, some of us (hopefully many) will live in an illumined stream of living power that expresses love full-out, if also simply, gladly, and blessedly in all coming-ins and goingouts. Soon, certainly into forever, some of us (hopefully most) will raise joyful voices in agreement with our holy brother Isaiah: the lavish promised land exists here and now. No one needs lengthy, self-perfecting processes or ways and means to enter. Searching for external methods, Kafka wrote, simply constitutes delays. Means are our means of wavering. Kafka, that true artist, protested that we need not do anything, need not leave our room; we just need be still and quiet and solitary, and as he said, reality "will roll in ecstasy" at our feet. Those who know enough to skirt distracting means and methods ultimately sing out in celebration, with Isaiah, Chap. 55, 1-3:

Ho! Everyone who thirsts, come to the waters;
And you who have no money come, buy and eat,
Come, buy wine and milk,
Without money and without cost.
Why do you spend money for what is not bread?
And your wages for what does not satisfy?
Listen carefully to Me, and eat what is good,
And delight yourself with abundance.
Incline your ear and come to Me.
Listen, that you may live...

Well, asked and answered. That pretty much sums up my forecast: collective development of a "new," timeless mind—the radical pure heart of love. Glad are we who know that it's not we who were created for the world, but the world that's been created for us. The whole cosmos exists in us. Here and now we can improve it. My vocabulary of choice says this wisdom draws us into the mind of Christ. Please, call it what you will: big mind/open mind? God-consciousness? Unity-consciousness? It's all One Sacred Being—God—to me. That's why I'm lighthearted about the rest. But then, I converse with tree frogs and imagine that I'm intelligible to fierce-eyed ravens the size of Rhode Island.

© DAVID TORRES

Marsha Sinetar was a pioneering educator and world-class corporate advisor before becoming a prolific, best-selling author. She published her first book, *Ordinary People as Monks & Mystics,* in 1986 and with her work that followed has developed into one of the foremost, spiritual writers of our time. Her titles include *Developing a 21st Century Mind; Do What you Love, The Money Will Follow; Living Happily Ever After;* as well as the award-winning children's books *Why Can't Grown Ups Believe in Angels* and *A Person is Many Wonderful, Strange Things.* Her books translate the subtle nuances of spiritual and contemplative life into everyday terms, most specifically bringing spirituality from the monastic setting into the lives and working arrangements of ordinary people.

STEVEN FELSCH/PHOTOVAULT

"I think we search for our destiny early in life so that we may eventually have a sense of accomplishment. Destiny becomes pivotal to us when we get involved with social issues or politics. We get absorbed in external phenomena over and over again, and it draws us away from the deepening of our souls—our real destiny, our real reason for being on this earth."

Chapter Twelve

Destiny in the New Millennium

by Lynn V. Andrews

I sat in meditation on the summer solstice in June 1996. I went into my power place of dreaming and connected all the luminous fibers from the apprentices in my shaman school. I wove them together into a beautiful tapestry of light, and then several of my teachers from the Sisterhood of the Shields joined me in their dream bodies, and we divined the new millennium that shown like a full moon on the horizon. The need for human enlightenment and wisdom was clear, and it glowed on the landscape of light like a radiant green emerald. Visions of Mother Earth in a state of natural perfection swept across the simulated screen that the luminous fibers created. I was filled with hope.

Later, when my meditation was finished, Agnes Whistling Elk joined me, and we discussed what we had just experienced. I want to share with you what we saw as the foundation for our destiny in the coming shifts of consciousness that will accompany the new millennium.

What does the word destiny mean—your destiny? Your society's destiny? Your destiny in life? Destiny pertains to what you envision as your fate, or if you don't believe in fate, what you are here on earth to accomplish. I think we search for our destiny early in life so that we may eventually have a sense of accomplishment. Destiny becomes pivotal to us when we get involved with social issues or politics. We get absorbed in external phenomena over and over again, and it draws us away from the deepening of our souls—our real destiny, our real reason for being on this earth.

Whenever I become overly involved with an emotionally charged issue, one having to do with oppression or cruelty, my teachers, Agnes Whistling Elk and Ruby Plenty Chiefs, deflate me in one way or another. If they don't dump a bucket of cold water on me, they turn me around mentally very quickly, and they always say to me, "Lynn, don't get caught in the dream." What does that mean? Personally, I've struggled with that concept for a long time. Finally I realized, through my work in shamanic dreaming, that we are truly asleep in this lifetime and we don't realize it. What we perceive as the truth is not necessarily the truth at all. We are immersed in a great illusion. When we experience moments of samadhi, those times when our vision transcends the physical dimensions and becomes clear, as when clouds in the sky disperse and the sun penetrates us with its warmth, power is beckoning us toward enlightenment.

Enlightenment is the absence of illusion and your vision of the world turned right-side up. We see the truth of things and the divine humor in them, as when we take the challenges of life too seriously. The quality that I value the most in my teachers is their humor. Even though I have not reached their level of understanding and seeing, and am certainly less experienced in spiritual pursuits than they, it's their humor that brings me clarity. This humor teaches me and brings me to a place of understanding within myself. Understanding our destiny pertains to humor, magic, power, and our ability to see what is real as we journey across the dimensions.

What is your destiny in the new millennium? It is to find your own truth. How do you do that? By letting go of what no longer serves you. It certainly doesn't come from acquiring more and more knowledge but from letting go of the mentation we humans so love. We take an idea and become attached to it and therefore corrupt it. We lose the truth of something by seeing it as more than simply an idea, a thought, a way to exercise certain aspects of ourselves. We will kill for an idea. Think of the Crusades, the Inquisition, the witch hunts. "In the name of God I kill you." Is that our destiny? Is it our destiny to consider one race better than another, one idea better than another? Man better than woman? Adult better than child? One tribe better than another tribe? I work only with this shaman, and all others are phony? That's what I mean by corruption. It comes from our inability to see clearly. This happens the minute we become attached to our perceived destiny. Take a political career for instance, where we become a liberal instead of a conservative. No matter what a conservative may say, they're wrong. This is how we put a fence around our consciousness.

Does destiny even mean anything crucial? That's a good question. We can get stuck in this concept of destiny and lose what we're here to do. I think working with the Sisterhood is my destiny. If some other truth came along, some other extraordinary being of light, surely I would want to absorb that teaching as well. But we have only so much time and energy in one lifetime. I do know that commitment is very important. More than destiny, commitment is what teaches you, commitment to your own process of mirroring. Somebody may teach you something that turns your head around—and you know you have been visited by the words of God. But you must see beyond the words to the light that has brought that teaching into your life. If someone points a finger at the moon, you don't become fixated on the finger; you look at the moon. I think that is what destiny is really about. It's the destiny born when our magical body avoids becoming lost in mental concepts.

In considering the new millennium we are entering, I see many people, out of insecu-

"We lose the truth of something by seeing it as more than simply an idea, a thought, a way to exercise certain aspects of ourselves. We will kill for an idea. Think of the Crusades, the Inquisition, the witch hunts. 'In the name of God I kill you.' Is that our destiny? Is it our destiny to consider one race better than another, one idea better than another? Man better than woman? Adult better than child? One tribe better than another tribe?"

BRIAN BROOM/PHOTOVAULT

rity, holding on to ideals that don't serve them. We are very insecure at this moment, for many reasons. Because of fear, disease, and the crumbling of our ideals, we are projecting a destiny on the new millennium that gives us hope. But true hope comes from letting go of illusion, remembering we are in a dream, remembering who we are and why we are here.

Shamanism is the study of energy and power. I have learned through my shamanic journeys that we are here to empower ourselves. A mirror is created through an act of power, and by looking in that mirror we begin to know ourselves. If we have the courage, we begin to change and grow. You are your best teacher; no one else can truly help you. You may say, "But how? How could one do that?" Make an act of power from that place of passion within yourself—one that you may have lost as a child. Search until you find that special place within you that wants to be expressed, and express it. It doesn't make any difference what that reality may be. It doesn't make any difference what anybody thinks of it, whether your family loves you for it or not. It's for you to move toward self-realization.

That, I think, is the destiny for the new millennium. I think people are finally going to realize that belief structures desperately limit them, e.g., thinking you are what you do. When you say, "I am a lawyer, a Buddhist, a wife, a shaman," these ideas block you from the truth. Everyone's truth is vastly different, and it is not necessary to hate one another for seeing things differently. We can honor each other's differences, whatever they may be.

In this new time, we must learn to express ourselves with passion, making acts of

WERNHER KRUTEIN/PHOTOVAULT

"I have learned through my shamanic journeys that we are here to empower ourselves. A mirror is created through an act of power, and by looking in that mirror we begin to know ourselves. If we have the courage, we begin to change and grow. You are your best teacher; no one else can truly help you. You may say, 'But how? How could one do that?' Make an act of power from that place of passion within yourself—one that you may have lost as a child. Search until you find that special place within you that wants to be expressed, and express it."

power that create acts of mastery. Otherwise, we will continue to use mechanical techniques that are not balanced by love or an inner integrity and strength, and isolate ourselves from our deeper resources. Imagine for a moment what it would be like to fall in love with a technique. Let's say you love the technique of electronics. You go to school and become an engineer, and you're good at it. You're proud of yourself. Then you go out into the world and start making a living as an electrical engineer. All of a sudden you're appalled at the materialism around you. Suddenly, instead of loving the technique, it seems as if it has failed you. Instead of love, it becomes work because it let you down. What's happened is that you've lost balance, and that has let you down. You've lost your balance by thinking that it was your destiny to be an electrician. It created a good mirror for you, but now, instead of a mirror of accomplishment, it shows disappointment and disillusionment. It becomes a great teacher, because it makes you move on. It is often said that one should not work in a career for more than fifteen years. You are not what you do. You are a person living your truth who happens to be in one profession or another. To change where you live or what you do can offer great opportunities for growth, and it is my experience that personal growth is what this life is about.

Our destiny in the new millennium is enlightenment. Acquiring consciousness is becoming easier, even though it doesn't look that way. It is just light—so let us allow the light to touch us. We can talk more freely about it now. We may be criticized, but the most important and powerful people, the people who are way ahead of their time, are always criticized. That's the nature of human existence. The new millennium is a time of coming together. Oftentimes I have doubts, but never in the goodness of the spirit, as I saw it expressed in the beautiful tapestry of light. I have great hope for us, for the earth. I know she will heal herself, with or without us. But with our prayers, our new ability to create ceremony and to see love in life, I think we will create a new and better world. Shamanism is one of the stepping stones because shamanic work, however we find our way down that ancient and mysterious trail, is the study of self-empowerment, the choreographing of healing energies in the universe around us in a way that brings light. It is a limitless concept.

We cannot deny our destinies as gods and goddesses, but we must claim who we are. We must claim our right to innocence and healership. If we teach what we know, we can make this earth a paradise, the lost paradise of Eden that it was always meant to be. The only hope for mankind in the new millennium is that we seek out our acts of power and our true destiny in life. It is not enough to balance physical life with spiritual destiny; we must be complete.

⊕

Lynn V. Andrews is the best-selling author of fourteen books, including *Medicine Woman, Flight of the Seventh Moon, Jaguar Woman, Star Woman, Crystal Woman, The Woman of Wyrrd,* and *Dark Sister,* that have contributed greatly to our understanding of feminine spirituality. Andrews conducts seminars and retreats across the country. She lives in Scottsdale, Arizona and Los Angeles, California.

WERNHER KRUTEIN/PHOTOVAULT

Chapter Thirteen

Mother Nature's Fifteen Minutes

by Sirona Knight

Within any cycle exists an edge or apex, relating to when that cycle reaches its height of influence or development. In terms of a lifetime, Andy Warhol referred to this apex as each person's fifteen minutes of fame which comes and goes rapidly, often without our being aware of it. The summer solstice is Mother Nature's fifteen minutes of fame, where all life reaches a period of florescence within the annual cycle. During this period, the life forces reach their highest intensity, and we are all essentially most alive, particularly in regard to life's natural polarities: light and dark, birth and death.

The word "solstice" derives from the word "Sol," a name for the Roman Sun God. Accordingly, the solstice is the gap between dark and light, when the guardians of the earthly cycles change positions. Classical Greeks told the story of how Hades seized Persephone while she was picking flowers and carried her off to the underworld. Demeter, the grain goddess and Persephone's mother, neglected the earth as she searched for her daughter, leading to an eventual compromise where Persephone spent six months of the year with her mother, from winter solstice to summer solstice, and then six months with Hades, from summer solstice to winter solstice.

In Celtic folklore, the story revolves around Tarvos, the golden bull, representing vitality and life, and Esus, the hunter, representing

"The summer solstice is Mother Nature's fifteen minutes of fame, where all life reaches a period of florescence within the annual cycle. During this period, the life forces reach their highest intensity, and we are all essentially most alive, particularly in regard to life's natural polarities: light and dark, birth and death."

death and the underworld. In the tale of Esus and Tarvos, the hunter slays the Golden One on the summer solstice, but as he lay dying, three gray cranes fill a chalice with his blood and fly south in the direction of the sacred flame. Later the sacred blood is used to rekindle the earthly cycle of life on the winter solstice.

Not only do both of these stories tell of the path of the sun and the yearly cycle of life, but they also show the polarity between life and death, and in turn, light and dark. What dies every year on the summer solstice, to be reborn on the winter solstice, is the light cycle of the sun. The blood of the Golden One symbolizes how the seeds of the harvest are used to sow the next wave of life.

When speaking of polarities, we tend to think in terms of two poles, such as life and death, working in tandem; but actually three polarities are at play: life, death, and rebirth. Hegel, a nineteenth century German philosopher, expressed the idea most aptly as *thesis, antithesis,* and their eventual *synthesis* being the driving elements of human evolution. Almost all metaphysical and spiritual traditions define a triad of energetic polarities—from Christianity with its trinity of Father, Son, and Holy Ghost; to Kashmir Shavism with its Creator, Destroyer, and Protector.

The three elements inherent in the summer solstice reflect these basic polarities of the universe, or as we'll call it, Oneness. On the positive side, the summer solstice represents the culmination of life, flourishing to its optimum and realizing its potential. The negative slant is that once we've reached this fifteen minutes of florescence, it's all downhill until we die. The third element is the neutral, or synthesis, of the other two. From life, and ultimately from death, comes the promise of rebirth: an evolvement of one cycle within another larger cycle.

As minutes flow into hours, hours into days, and days into years, each annual cycle is a starting point for many larger cycles. This calls up the visual image of an infinite number of circles overlapping and flowing into one another, from the very smallest to ever-escalating sizes, which eventually include literally everything and lead us once again to the concept of Oneness. In this context, within the cycle of each of our lives, including several annual cycles, we experience many solstices or apexes

RANDE DELUCA/PHOTOVAULT

"As minutes flow into hours, hours into days, and days into years, each annual cycle is a starting point for many larger cycles. This calls up the visual image of an infinite number of circles overlapping and flowing into one another, from the very smallest to ever-escalating sizes, which eventually include literally everything and lead us once again to the concept of Oneness. In this context, within the cycle of each of our lives, including several annual cycles, we experience many solstices or apexes on a variety of levels."

on a variety of levels. As soon as we become more aware of these cyclical patterns, we begin to savor and actively influence these cycles of Oneness.

As human beings living in a world of polarities and cycles, we can bring two influences into our lives by becoming more aware of the cyclic flow of Oneness. One, by being aware of the rising and ebbing of energy, we can better utilize what we achieve from our personal summer solstices. When we know our goals and the steps needed to achieve them, we start taking control of, and responsibility for, our own lives. And second we learn how to stretch that moment of florescence into much more than fifteen minutes. This is related to Tantra, where each partner in a sexual union not only delights in each step towards ecstacy, but also the very moment of orgasm is heightened to new levels, altering the normal perception of time and space. The loving and healing energy generated from this sacred sexual union can then flow into the universe.

Mystics of many traditions believe that when female and male energies become balanced and attuned through prolonged, ecstatic intercourse, they transmit a harmonizing influence throughout society and nature. These harmonizing influences are thought to be particularly needed and effectively transmitted at the times when heaven and earth are at extremes, which are essentially the solstices. This concept also alludes to both the solstice as being on the extremes, because of its position between the poles; and also the harmonizing influences that humans can bring into the cycles of Oneness, which includes but is in no way limited to sexual energy.

John Lennon and Paul McCartney convey this feeling of the summer solstice in the opening lines of the Beatles' song "Blackbird," when they sing "Blackbird singing in the dead of night, take these broken wings and learn to fly. All your life, you were only waiting for this moment to arise." In this sense, the summer solstice is that moment we wait for all of our lives. Each of us is like a flower that blooms only once in every lifetime, and for that moment, we radiate with the vitality of life. By becoming aware of the patterns around us and directing our energies, we take our broken wings and learn to fly. By being present and in the moment, we know when it's our moment to arise and how to make the most of that moment.

Realizing that the summer solstice represents the period of florescence within our lives, we can begin to see the larger patterns emerge and learn that we need not wait for our moment to arise but that we can start building towards it. Again, using the sexual metaphor, this building towards the moment of release relates to foreplay, merging, and the gradual buildup to ecstasy. The more effort a person puts into the experience, including being present in the moment and savoring each sensation like the endless delicacies of a feast, the more it begins to transform and take on spiritual and magical qualities.

Realizing we can build to our summer solstice rather than waiting for it to happen, we then start increasing our awareness of the cycles and patterns of Oneness. This is akin to the process of cloning, where a single cell of an organism holds all the genetic coding needed to produce another complete organism. To extend this idea further, each cycle or pattern of Oneness is a mirror of every other cycle. When we begin reading and influencing these cycles and patterns, then we truly take responsibility for our lives and an active hand in participating in our own destiny.

Choosing to be aware of the patterns around us makes us less susceptible to unexpected results. Waiting for something to happen without reading the pattern and influencing its outcome opens us up to an inevitable cavalcade of random events, which move our lives to and fro like the tides on a rudderless boat. A prime example is how most of us find our professions in life, usually through some simple twist of fate.

I have a friend from high school named John, who started college wanting to be a psychologist. When the psychology courses proved too difficult, he quit and became a waiter in a restaurant. He soon married one of the cocktail waitresses, whose father was an electrical contractor. John found himself working as an electrician, even after he was long divorced from his wife. Nowhere in this process did John take an active part, which is why he and many others find themselves in jobs they don't like and wouldn't have consciously chosen for themselves.

Again, the two key elements that help us build towards our summer solstice revolve around our ability to read and influence the patterns and cycles within our lives. In the case of my friend John, he first misread his ability to complete the course work for a psychology degree, and then when that didn't work out, he accepted whatever life presented him, whether it was what he wanted or not. This example shows both the importance of reading patterns as well as influencing them. Often we see the obvious significance of influencing the events in our lives, but it is equally or more important to read the pattern of events. This makes us more aware of areas where we can, not so much change the pattern, but positively influence its course within our own life.

An aide to President Harry S. Truman was talking to a reporter on the eve of Dwight D. Eisenhower's inauguration. The aide commented that he felt sorry for Eisenhower, who, after being commander in chief of the armed forces in World War II, was going to find the presidency very frustrating. Unlike the army, where one gives an order and it gets carried out, the American presidency requires one to bargain with influence. This is very similar to patterns and cycles of Oneness, in that it is easier to influence than to directly change them, particularly if that change is contrary to the original pattern of energy. To take an example from Eastern martial arts, it's much easier to deflect the force of a punch thrown at you than to meet it head on.

Being aware and working with the polarities of the universe is essential when reading and influencing life's patterns. The Eastern spiritual philosophy of Kashmir Shavism is based on the concept that three forces exist within everything including ourselves. The "Creator" is the force in our lives which creates patterns and moves us forward in a positive direction. The "Destroyer," on the other hand, breaks down patterns and often manifests itself as a negative energy ripping through our world. The third force, the "Protector," generally derives from our fears and from our desire to protect what we have, which has the tendency to keep us in the same place. Each of these three forces not only moves the world around us but also influences our actions and internal processing. We can't ignore or remove these forces from our lives, but we can definitely become aware of them and make them work to our benefit rather than against us. Even the Destroyer has its place in nature, because within death exists the potential for rebirth and possible evolvement within a greater cycle. Buddhists express this thought beautifully with the statement: "within every problem lies opportunity."

A practical illustration of this concept occurred recently in my own life: I became pregnant and, because of complications, was forced to quit my job, which at the time I thought was "perfect." The job was a pattern I had created, which was destroyed with one visit to the doctor. I was ecstatic about having a baby, but on the other hand, my life was suddenly thrown into complete chaos. After the initial shock, I began to look at my options and came to the conclusion that, since I was going to be basically on my back for nine months, I might as well do something productive with the time. I set up a comfortable space, which included a lounge chair in front of my computer, and finished my master's thesis. From our experiences and feelings, we assimilate everything that happens to us and make future choices and actions. By being aware of the polarities that pull us like giant magnets through life, we begin to harmonize their effects and maximize our efforts to read and influence our life patterns.

"the summer solstice is that moment we wait for all of our lives. Each of us is like a flower that blooms only once in every lifetime, and for that moment, we radiate with the vitality of life. By becoming aware of the patterns around us and directing our energies, we take our broken wings and learn to fly. By being present and in the moment, we know when it's our moment to arise and how to make the most of that moment."

James Redfield in his book, *The Tenth Insight,* talks about the concept of past lives and how, at the beginning of each lifetime, we have certain goals we want to achieve in that life.

WERNHER KRUTEIN/PHOTOVAULT

Upon dying, we go through a life review, which essentially assesses how well we stayed true to our original intention and whether we strayed from our goals in life. From the life review, our soul gains insights on its vision for the next lifetime and how to avoid being deterred from achieving these goals.

Past lives point once again to the concept of smaller cycles within larger cycles, all flowing into Oneness. Each life cycle propels us further down the cycle of multiple lifetimes. We not only have a summer solstice or period of florescence within each lifetime, but we also have fifteen minutes coming within the cycle of our many lives. Many of us are beginning to enter a period of enlightenment, which will eventually move us to a higher level of consciousness. Essentially, we are entering a human summer solstice, where each lifetime influences every other lifetime and in turn affects the whole of Oneness. Again, our awareness of these patterns aids in our efforts to read and influence them, which helps us to achieve our life's goals on all levels.

One of the terms used to express this concept of higher goals is the notion of a "calling" in life. In the second verse of his song "I Hear the Calling," Michael Starwyn writes, "Today a voice called out my name, a name I'd never heard—like a pebble skipping over water, the flapping wings of a great bird." The voice that calls out is our inner voice, and the name that it calls is our true name, echoing through the many lifetimes like a beacon signaling us home. As we become aware and listen to our inner voice, we attune to our calling in both this lifetime and as a soul experiencing multiple lifetimes in the continuum.

Two techniques for cultivating and listening to your inner voice are meditation and dreaming. You can start your meditation by repeating a key word or phrase, which quiets the internal chatter of the mind. This invokes an altered state of consciousness, providing a direct link to multidimensional experiences. Our inner voice is essentially our divine link to other dimensions, and ultimately Oneness, Goddess, or God, whatever you choose to call that sacred connection.

The second technique for making contact with your inner voice and calling is through dreaming. Before going to sleep, give yourself the following suggestion, "Let me become in tune with my inner voice, and know what my higher goals are this lifetime and in all lifetimes." Upon waking, it's important to remember, write down, or record your dreams before doing anything else. Even if the dream doesn't make sense at the time, don't disregard it. The meaning may become clear in the future. Dreams are a reflection of you, and you are a reflection of your dreams, and all are a mirror into Oneness. For more specific dreaming exercises and methods for understanding dreams, please refer to my book, *Moonflower: Erotic Dreaming with the Goddess.*

Life has been compared to many things, including a banquet and a flower garden. As a banquet, life is a finely prepared feast that can be ravaged and eaten as fast as possible or be savored, each morsel being enjoyed and experienced to its fullest. As a flower garden, life becomes a diverse array of sensual experiences, which can be taken either individually or as whole. If we are all flowers within this garden and are coming into our summer solstice of florescence, we can choose to be a rose and bloom for as long as six months of the year, or we can be a lily which blooms for about two weeks.

As we enter into the summer solstice of this lifetime, as well as a period of enlightenment for the whole of humanity, we have the ability to realize our inner potential and actualize our dreams. As the summer solstice is Mother Nature's fifteen minutes of florescence, this period in our lives is our moment of glory, whether it lasts fifteen minutes or a thousand lifetimes. As Albert Einstein once said, "It's all relative."

⊕

Sirona Knight holds a master's degree in psychology from California State University (Phi Kappa Phi) and is a trained Third Degree Craftmaster in the Gwyddonic Druid tradition. She is the author of *Greenfire, Moonflower,* and *Starwind.* She is also the co-creator of *The Shapeshifter Tarot.* Currently, Knight is a contributing editor for *Magical Blend* magazine and a featured writer for *Napra ReVIEW, New Age Retailer,* and *Fate* magazine. She and her husband live in the Sierra foothills of California with their son, three dogs, and a family of cats.

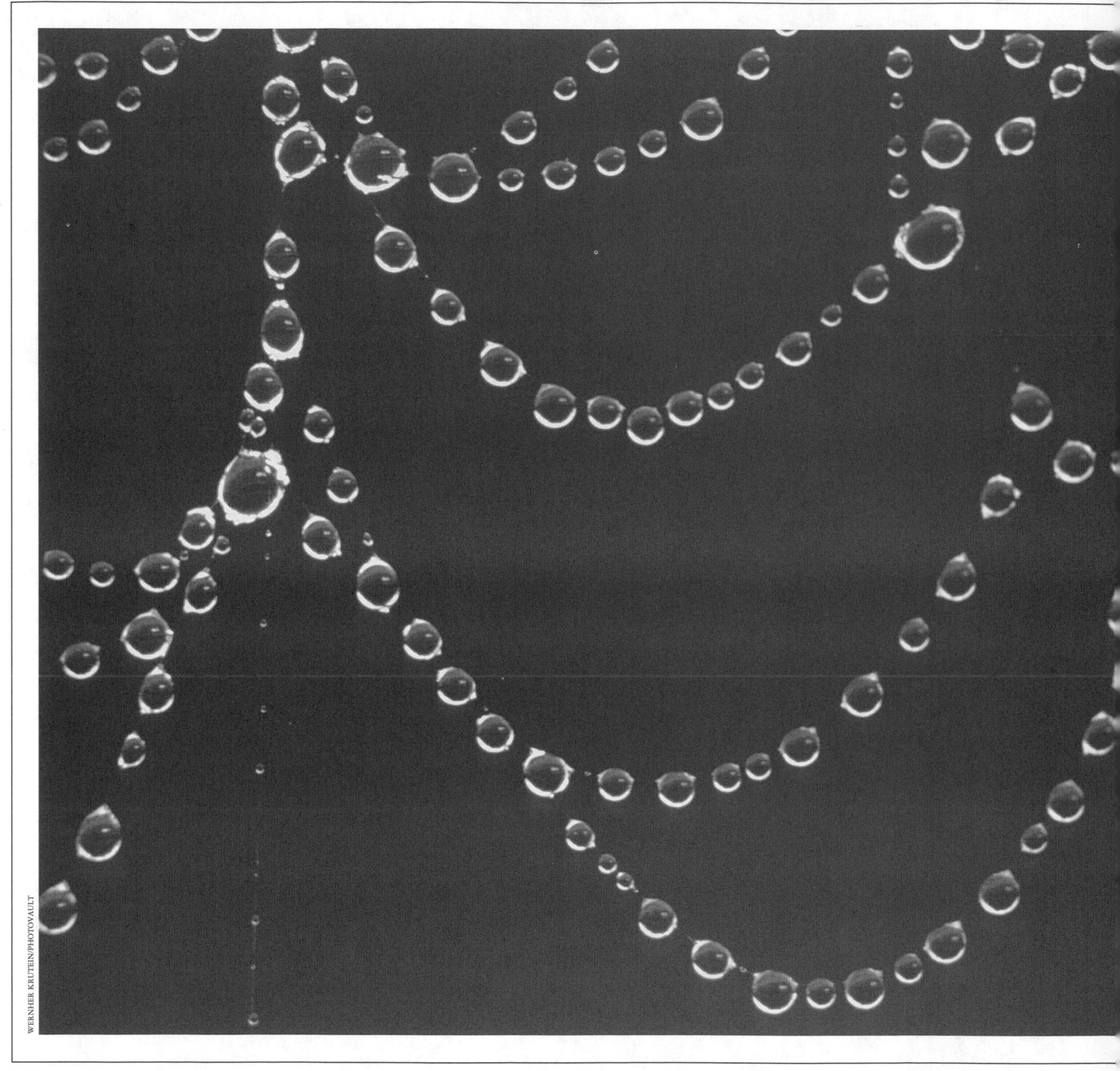

WERNHER KRUTEIN/PHOTOVAULT

Chapter Fourteen

WEAVING THE FUTURE WEB

by Laverne E. Denyer

It's interesting to note that with the revelations shared so far—as with our own thinking, feeling, and sensing—we have been creating a web of consciousness.

We all spin a web of awareness with our interactions, as the spider spins a web to gather the dew, to capture food, to create beauty—to interact with its outer environment. In the same way we spin a web of life: physical, mental, emotional, spiritual, and everything in between. We spin connectors between ourselves and others. All that you are and all that you do interacts with me. We are each connected to every other being on the planet, and through the dimensions to the "multiverse" and to the original source. This very intricate network of energies magically blends all of the energies together to create a powerful living circuit. When the circuits are secured and activated, our pattern flows in a productive and very rhythmic pattern. That's what we all seek; that's where we're trying to arrive. This goal hasn't been fully achieved yet, but we are making progress. At those moments when it does work, synchronicity lives. I am in sync with you, and you with my friend, and she with your plant, and all of us with her cat. When we are disconnected or are walled off, our web fluctuates, struggles, and some of the strands break. Are you a weaver or a drop-stitch? I often think of the chant that says, "We are the weavers, we are the web." We are both. We are part of what everybody else creates and the creators at the same moment. What are we weaving as we move into these changes? What will the web look like? How complex, how simple, how beautiful, how tangled will it be?

For a long time on this planet, the web that we have woven has carried a lot of pain,

"We all spin a web of awareness with our interactions, as the spider spins a web to gather the dew, to capture food, to create beauty—to interact with its outer environment. In the same way we spin a web of life: physical, mental, emotional, spiritual, and everything in between. We spin connectors between ourselves and others. All that you are and all that you do interacts with me."

separation, and fear. Many of the currently incarnated souls have woven individual cocoons around themselves. Like a chrysalis, they figure that, if they withdraw into a cocoon formed from these webs of energy, they'll be safe. They withdraw. Most are still at least partially accessible, but many have completely walled themselves off. They live a nightmare of fear and pain and separation. It is said that fear is love that forgot to grow up. When we cut our threads or wrap them too tightly around ourselves, we are walling ourselves off from the possibility of that love, keeping us in fear and hate. And, when we live that way, we create prejudice, violence, and anguish with our "less than" and "win/lose" mentality. I would like to think that we are ready to move out of these isolation cells, these cocoons, to where we can freely roam the web.

For those walled off, their interconnecting threads grow weak and tattered. The separateness of their thinking and feeling are tearing at that primal fabric of life. Remember, your feelings affect me, and my feelings and actions eventually affect you. Have you ever pulled just one little corner of a spider web and seen how the rest of it vibrates? Or seen a breeze blowing through the web, or a dewdrop dropping on it? Our every thought, feeling, and action has that kind of effect. Everybody has heard of the World Wide Web (an electronic network that mirrors the web of life). By linking computers, which are mostly related to our physical brains, we have figured out how to tap the rich resources of the entire world instantaneously. Through one terminal, an individual—one mind—can access data and solicit opinions from other minds anywhere in the world—except from those who continue to be walled off and isolated. The information can be downloaded, and then shared in person with groups, or inputted back onto the web, spreading that net of communication even further, so that it begins to look like a global brain.

In our own bodies, our neural net or brain—our own central processing unit—interfaces with the central nervous system, informing, distributing data, analyzing data. This neural net then communicates with the rest of the nervous system (including the autonomic nervous system) and our physical bodies in a web of constantly flowing information. Think of all the bits of information running across that neural net at any moment, and you can begin to get a picture of how the energy of life runs across the spiritual web at any moment. Experiencing the world as individuals, we interact with other beings through this complicated web of communication. Opening our awareness to this web on a physical level, through telephones, fax machines, through the Internet, our web of life expands through this direct mind-to-mind contact. And, through this process, groups of beings, cultures, and environments communicate with each other. The web grows tighter and broader every moment, linking us all together in this complex pattern. Tighter, in that we build more nets, more threads from place to place,

"For a long time on this planet, the web that we have woven has carried a lot of pain, separation, and fear. Many of the currently incarnated souls have woven individual cocoons around themselves. Like a chrysalis, they figure that, if they withdraw into a cocoon formed from these webs of energy, they'll be safe. They withdraw. Most are still at least partially accessible, but many have completely walled themselves off. They live a nightmare of fear and pain and separation."

WERNHER KRUTEIN/PHOTOVAULT

which in turn makes the web denser. Broader, because the web covers more distance, more things, more thoughts, more emotions, and more communications. Ours is a collective experience. What you experience eventually travels across the web and impacts my awareness. Your joy is my joy. Your pain lives somewhere inside of me. Also, your fear is as pervasive. Likewise, my reactions ripple across the collective web of consciousness and influence your life as well. Generally, the influences are subtle; occasionally they become very profound. The noticeable impact is broad. It may take us a while to become aware of it, but it's there.

Think of the "hundredth monkey" model, in which one monkey on a South Pacific island started washing its sweet potatoes because they tasted better. That one monkey taught a couple others, and they shared the information with just a few more. Then the information spread across their communication network, their web, and more and more monkeys began to come down to the water and wash their potatoes. The magic happened when this awareness reached critical mass with the hundredth monkey, and the behavior quickly spread to monkeys on other islands, who had no direct contact with the original band. It had reached the level of the species' collective consciousness. From this example, you see that we can make a difference by sharing our thoughts of peace, acceptance, growth, joy, and asking people to share them with others. And suddenly, when our thoughts reach critical mass, they will quickly spread beyond our personal contacts through the web to everybody. Joy, acceptance, and love can be spread this way, and so can fear. It is important to remember that your experience feeds collective awareness, collective memory, every instant of your life. Every instant makes a difference in this collective webbing. What do you want your pattern to look like?

We have connecting bands of energy that link us all emotionally, mentally, psychically, and even physically. Think of roads and telephone lines and communication forces like radio and television. We're connected. We live in bodies that have unique awareness. We all radiate patterns of vitality that connect us in this living web of experience. We assume responsibility when we start thinking of who we intend to be in the next moment, the next

WERNHER KRUTEIN/PHOTOVAULT

day, the coming millennium. There have been a lot of predictions, a lot of speculation on who we are becoming as a species. We take individual responsibility by spreading along that communication web what we wish to have returned to us. We are all the hundredth monkey. So send out only joy. We are moving through a process of evolution, and that evolution occurs as we shift from our place of planned ignorance—and it was very well planned—to a place of conscious awareness.

I ask who you intend to become next because we are being asked to prepare ourselves to move into our next learning opportunity as a species. The time of transformation is upon us; we're going through it right now. We will have lots of opportunities to let that take us, but change we must, change we are. The shift will be profound. It may be immediate or more gradual. We may not even notice the major change until it has happened. We may breathe one moment here and the next moment in another dimension. It all depends on the decisions we are making. Our collective consciousness, that web we are weaving, is taking on a unique pattern that has never been experienced here or on any other planet, in any dimension, in any way. We have the opportunity to create something new and magnificent, something totally unique. What do we want it to be?

"We have connecting bands of energy that link us all emotionally, mentally, psychically, and even physically. Think of roads and telephone lines and communication forces like radio and television. We're connected. We live in bodies that have unique awareness. We all radiate patterns of vitality that connect us in this living web of experience. We assume responsibility when we start thinking of who we intend to be in the next moment, the next day, the coming millennium."

We're being asked to integrate our light bodies, our high-soul selves, with our physical being. That means two things must happen. First, as we're already experiencing, our bodies must be prepared for the intense energy frequencies they will be required to accept. Second, our soul energies must find a way to manifest through physical form. Both changes require very intense recalibrations of energy. A lot of our brothers and sisters have found this task overwhelming, and have decided not to continue living through the changes. There has been a mass exodus of souls leaving their physical being in a variety of ways: through war, sickness, and violence. Some have just quit living. Some of those souls have moved to higher energy realms and dimensions to act as our guides and our helpers. Most have probably returned to other times or dimensions to complete their learning experiences. Within the last decade every soul has been given an opportunity for choice, whether to live or die. I would expect that every reader of this book has, at some point within the last decade, come close to leaving the planet at least once, and several of you, multiple times. Every soul incarnated on the planet today has chosen whether to stay or leave. However, that choice isn't cast in stone. Everyone can change their minds at any point. We can handle the shift in many ways, but the most important aspect has to do with an awareness of how our shifting thoughts affect that web of consciousness.

It is important to note that many of us are going through a lot of physical change. In past experiences on this planet and others, in this dimension and others, when this kind of evolution has occurred, the physical body was shifted significantly. We seem to be finding a way for these physical bodies to increase in frequency so that our high-soul selves can become more manifest. We're expecting a great deal from these physical bodies. We aren't specifically designing anything brand new for this integration; we are adapting what we already have and moving with it. Historically, there has never been an experience where the bodies of living entities were transformed to house full-wisdom energies or high-soul selves. It's remarkable, it's exciting; nobody knows what to expect. But we must not worry ourselves about what to expect, how to prepare, or how to react. Our high-soul self is already taking care of that. What's important is to be conscious, and that our intent be to gain the greatest wisdom we can and to become as connected as we can with all other beings. We must build that web. The angelic beings remind us that we are all wise beings and very brave. We've each chosen to be here. We've each selected a growth path with these very unique challenges. They commend and support us all. With their guidance we can get through it.

As we live through these changing times, move your fears—which manifest as prejudices—into a state of openness. You aren't expected to move into a state of love and rapture immediately. That's where we're headed. Your first challenge is to open every wound of fear, every wound that fear has turned into hate, every wound that hate has turned into violence, and cleanse it as you would cleanse a boil.

It's up to you to challenge your views, not for anybody else. When you live in the isolation of fear, you cannot communicate across the web and discover what others have to offer you. Poke at the old fears, find out where they came from, their place of origin in this life and in others. You don't always have to know the original cause, just the original feeling. And forgive yourself for feeling that way. For me, forgiving means "giving forward" to that universal source. Giving forward to God, to the Tao, to the one mind, to the center of the web—whatever you may call it. But give it forward because you don't have to deal with it anymore. When fear burdens you, forgive it, give it forward. Forgive yourself for feeling that way. At the time you first had those feelings, you probably had a reason. But you've matured now, and you no longer need to hold on to those limiting bindings of fear. Cut them. Thank them for having been there. Ask what you've learned from them. Ask what you want to learn next. And then release them. It is unnecessary to carry the burden any longer. As you release your fears, you open more threads to this great web of consciousness. You begin to remember more when you remove those blockages. Know that all energy is good and powerful. It is only destructive when it becomes stagnant as in fear, when it is held captive against the natural flow, when you hold it too firm, when you try to control it too much. That is when good and powerful energy turns stagnant and destructive and needs cleansing. Go in and slowly release the energy, forgiving yourself and those who created the situation. Every hole will fill with something. It's up to you to fill it with something good and positive. Some new fun experience instead.

This may sound very simplistic, but my inclination is to look at very practical, everyday ways to bring the higher-wisdom self into balance. One way is to look at fear as immature love that you can forgive by giving it forward to another source and opening yourself to peace. That creates a very practical space in your life for doing something productive. When energy is trapped in fear, and you are constantly battling to control it so it doesn't run your life, you're expending a lot of energy just holding it together. There isn't time for contemplating the meaning of life or who you wish to be, or who you may have been, or who you're becoming. There isn't time. There isn't energy. There isn't space to become who you choose to be. You're simply fighting battles, trying to maintain your situation. "Control over" is a losing situation. Nobody wins. When you release the fear, you create an opportunity for healthy energy to come back into your life, to flow across the web with freedom. You are empowered by all the other energy moving at the same pace, and are moving into new places because you are empowered. You can respond and play without having to control. "Power over" is control; empowerment is "living with." As you move into empowerment, you win, I win, everyone wins, and we build higher and greater levels of enjoyment and wisdom. You suddenly have all of that free space in your life to move into healthy, playful, joyful, loving places. That gives you space to have a healthy physical and mental body, a healthy spiritual body, and a healthy social body. That's practical. When you choose freedom, your communication ripples come across the web, empowering me, those that you care about, and even those you don't. They each become empowered on a more joyful level. Then suddenly your life and your environment are more comfortable, as is mine and everybody else's. We are now living in a synchronistic flow with the whole. Synchronicity lives as this web builds and flows.

As you begin to feel more comfortable living in this place of empowerment, the next task is to share it. You can share it with a smile or a kind deed. You can share it by teaching. You can share it by example. You can share it by playing. I would challenge you to share your new sense of self at least a couple of times a week, so that you purposefully do what the bumper sticker says: "Practice random acts of kindness." That kindness will flow across the web, through consciousness, and flow back to you stronger than when it was sent out. When it travels out on that web, others pick it up. Some hold it to themselves and say, "Ahhh, this is wonderful!" Some take it and say, "This can't be true" and reject it. Enough hearts and minds find it and say, "This is wonderful and I'll build my joy on it." It spreads, and by the time it comes back to you, it has been magnified and made stronger. So you have more joy coming back to you than you sent out with that original act of kindness. That's being cosmic on a very real day-to-day basis. The point is that it always comes back stronger than you send it. If you want love back, send it out. Create and recreate your own world by being kind. We're building to that critical mass where suddenly everybody begins to shift.

The third trick is to pay attention and to be conscious. Pay attention to what is flowing out of you, around you, and back to you. Tune into the web. What's traveling across it right now? When you are conscious, you can choose which bits of data, which bits of energy to collect, and which to either derail and send back to the God for recycling, and which to shift, or enhance.

With intent, you selectively choose that which you want to become. This is a threefold journey based on the fact that your bodies are changing, your consciousness is shifting, and you're becoming new—brand new energy beings. You simply cannot help it. You chose to come into this life at this time, on this planet, in whatever situation you find yourself. You did that for a reason. Figure out what that reason is and what you want to do about it, and how long you want to stay here. Then purposefully connect, using that intent. Tune yourself with whatever focus technique you use—be it prayer, meditation, deep contemplation, or listening to music—and purposefully practice those random acts of kindness. Purposely direct the energy, recreating the world as you want it to be, as your high-soul self inspires you to create it. The ego or personality, created by the bonding of spirit and body, can oftentimes interfere. That's one way fear is created. I am suggesting that you commune with your high-soul self regularly. That you bring that great wisdom into yourself and broadcast it on the net so that others may have the opportunity to pick it up and use it. Once you have gathered, listened, and shared, you can then move with purposeful intent out to the greater essence and the greater good. Then you will know why you are here, where you are headed, and what you want to do about it.

We'll experience all of these transitions together. This is your opportunity to nurture your connection with every other part of the divine power, the divine pattern. You can reach forward and grasp your power, discover what you're capable of doing. Manifest it through all the realities. It's all real. We say that this world is an illusion, yet as you experience it, it's all very real. Overcome your mortal prejudices and fears. You can do the things you imagine, you just need to want the power and accept it. Begin small and let your powers build. You're a creative God-force, walking in partnership with a physical being. Look at the magic you hold. It's now time to prepare for what lies ahead by using these simple tools—just a reminder of what you already know. You made the choice to come here. You made the choice to experience this realty. You even made the choice to pick up this book and read it. On some level you felt ready for new growth opportunities. They are upon you and they will continue to accelerate.

Connect with your purpose. Bring forth your high-wisdom self. Let it be manifest. Become an ascended master, if that's the term you use. Move into the white hole. We've fallen into the black hole of "taking away," so now move into a place where we release the void. Out of that void comes the spinning procreative process of the white hole where we create. Move into the white light of re-creation with grace, dignity, courage, and intent. We are all at last ready and willing. You are remembering. You are taking action. Be you in all of your glory. Let your soul's highest essence manifest through you, of you, and with you. Be yourself. Be. All that we can do is simply be. That's the plan. Blessed be!

⊕

Laverne E. Denyer is a high school teacher, counselor, lecturer, self-described computer junkie, and business woman with degrees in Psychology, Religious Studies, Philosophy, Education, and Drafting. Her writings range from technical manuals for public education, through metaphysical self-help, to poetry. In 1975 she began working with automatic writing, combining her interest in spirituality and writing. She lives in Yuba City, California, with her husband of 34 years and is the mother of "two terrific grown daughters."

WERNHER KRUTEIN/PHOTOVAULT

"I see sexuality as the final frontier of enlightenment. Sacred sexuality is a path of healing, of manifesting our higher purpose and connection with the one heart. The most joyous state of erotic innocence comes from acceptance of our bodies and our sexuality as natural and precious. We can experience pure delight in our bodies, savoring our sexuality in its wholesome sacredness. The time has come for the reenchantment of the body as the temple of our Essence Self."

Chapter Fifteen

Our Harmonic Resonance with Joy

by Marina Raye

In this time, unlike any other on Planet Gaia, we have front-row seats for the hottest event ever in this neighborhood of the galaxy: The Awakening of the Human, an awakening from the collective dream of unconsciousness. By accessing the harmonic resonance that we share with all life—the frequency of joy—this solstice shift is intensifying the process of remembering our true identity. As I meditated during the solstice shift, I felt Gaia herself asking me two questions. They are so simple that I could imagine Gaia smiling as she spoke, "What is standing in the way of your joy? Right now, in this moment, what is keeping you from being fully present?"

I had rather expected to receive profound new information in seeking Gaia's assistance. Like many in the consciousness movement, I have taken the job of personal and planetary evolution quite seriously. As an overachiever, I have often felt that I needed to read just one more book, attend one more workshop, or have at least one more healing session for all the cosmic tumblers to click into place. At this point, I could hear Mother Gaia reminding me, "These tumblers you've been waiting for are already in place. What is now clicking into place is your awareness—you are remembering more and more of yourself. And you often take this awakening process so seriously. Lighten up and access the frequency of joy!"

Since my seriousness was too intense for the moment, I performed my favorite lighten-up ceremony. I took my gallon jug of bubble solution and my double-bubble blower into my front yard and made big, sensuous, bubbles within bubbles, connected to other bubbles. Some reflected a rainbow world as they sailed over the treetops, while others consciously chose to pop over my head. All the while I asked myself, "What is standing in the way of my joy now?"

I did some serious work preparing for this writing assignment. I was born human into a dysfunctional family. Most of my fifty years have been spent trying to fill the holes in my psyche created by well-meaning, albeit unskilled parents. When we are not validated as children, we spend years trying to fill our emptiness with people, possessions, and a myriad of addictions. Yet the answer to this lifelong search is quite simple. When we surrender to the emptiness, we can access joy from within ourselves.

In the past I would have thought accessing joy involved affirming away my woundedness and pretending that none of it ever happened—putting a smile on my face, no matter how badly I hurt. The game of denial will only postpone the inevitable, profound, inner homework that must be done. What is keeping me from feeling joy now? When I am honest with myself, I have to admit that I am the only one standing in the way of my joy. My lack of compassion and forgiveness for myself keeps me from being gentle with my awakening process. This realization offers yet another gift of awareness: a reminder to surrender to my wholeness rather than beat myself up with my perceived inadequacies. To quote Nelson Mandela in his inaugural speech, "Our deepest fear is not that we are inadequate. Our deepest fear is that we are powerful beyond measure."

I would like to explore what we humans are experiencing in this initiation into wholeness, our harmonic resonance with joy. With the intention to embrace our wholeness, we set in motion events that cause us to feel as though a spinning confusion is whirling us out of our fixed certainties into the unknown. Every aspect of our lives—lifework, physical well-being, relationships, and especially our sexuality—must be evaluated for its harmonic resonance with the frequency of joy. Our deep shadow issues will no longer tolerate denial. We cannot intellectualize our way through the turbulence of the next few years. We must do the profound inner homework of healing our emotions for our personal evolution and for raising humanity's collective consciousness. Every issue that we process and heal on an individual level produces transformative change on a planetary level. We are individually and collectively undergoing a rite of passage from which we will emerge as more than third-dimensional human beings: a shift in reality so dramatic that only surrendering to our Essence Self will protect us from complete overload. This is the final stage of our initiation as cosmic citizens able to move consciously through time and space as multidimensional beings. We are embarking on the grandest adventure of all time. I recommend posting a sign on your refrigerator, "Welcome to the deep end!"

Are you excited to be a part of this awakening experience, or does it feel scary to be human? Does it feel as though the very fabric of your life is coming unraveled? Our personal crisis is a mirror of the planetary crisis, and both personal and planetary changes are intensifying. Time as we know it has speeded up and will continue to move more quickly until our notion of time collapses, as the past collides with the future. The by-product of this time shift is that life can feel intensely chaotic. And it will get more intense, more chaotic. We are being tested by the waves of change that grow more powerful and more ominous. Our personal and planetary crises are breaking down fear patterns that have kept us stuck in the old paradigm. This chaos is leading to a breakthrough to freedom, to joy, and to reunion with our wholeness.

There is a joyous urgency to complete our preparations for this journey of initiation. We need to travel lightly, releasing the emotional baggage that keeps us from accessing the frequency of joy. There are three areas that weigh down our collective shoulders. First, we carry a great deal of baggage around the issue of work. The Judeo-Christian programming that we must earn a living by the sweat of our brow has kept us working for a paycheck. We have been selling out our joy for this paycheck. Many of us have recently taken the leap by cutting the corporate umbilical cord. We are reinventing our lives to honor our bliss and to dance on the razor's edge, trusting that we'll be able to make ends meet. Does your present line of work bring you joy? Do you feel a harmonic resonance with your colleagues? If not, it is now vital to make the leap into living your bliss, and not five years from now when you can afford it. Just do it. The evolution of consciousness demands that we "give" a living in a harmonious way, one that allows others to give to us. It works.

A few years ago a participant in one of my workshops shared that he had spent time meditating on Mt. Shasta and that people began sending him money. He said it was that simple. My life partner Charlie and I almost scoffed at the idea. Yeah, sure, people would send money to the mountain. We were well-programmed to believe that we had to go out and make, really make things happen. Now, three years later, we are living on a mountain, and yes, people are sending money for Charlie's Native American flutes and my music albums. Charlie and I no longer focus on making a living. Instead we are giving a living. It takes courage to walk through our fears to a place of total surrender to a life of joy. We deserve to live our bliss. Nothing less will do. How joyful are you feeling right now? What is standing in the way of your giving a living by doing what brings you joy?

WERNHER KRUTEIN/PHOTOVAULT

"With the intention to embrace our wholeness, we set in motion events that cause us to feel as though a spinning confusion is whirling us out of our fixed certainties into the unknown. Every aspect of our lives—lifework, physical well-being, relationships, and especially our sexuality—must be evaluated for its harmonic resonance with the frequency of joy. ...We must do the profound inner homework of healing our emotions for our personal evolution and for raising humanity's collective consciousness."

WERNHER KRUTEIN/PHOTOVAULT

"Joy comes from living simply, from releasing expectations and trusting in the guidance we receive by surrendering to living our heart's purpose. We will pay the rent, feed the cat, and make all the payments. In the process, we are unraveling ourselves from the intricate web of conformity that kept us a slave to the system for so many years. This deep surrender to our bliss allows us to live in a state of joy. It is a process of undefining ourselves, becoming lighter, clearer, more in touch with our Essence Self."

A test of my belief in the goodness of the universe and my deserving of abundance has involved letting go of who I think I am and who others perceive me to be. I've played all the games about fulfilling expectations, living my life so that others, especially parents, will be proud of me. When I was touring the country giving workshops in a different city every week, my dad suggested that I should settle down and at least get a part-time job! I felt hurt because he didn't understand why I had left the corporate world. Yet no explanation is necessary. Joy is necessary.

Joy comes from living simply, from releasing expectations and trusting in the guidance we receive by surrendering to living our heart's purpose. We will pay the rent, feed the cat, and make all the payments. In the process, we are unraveling ourselves from the intricate web of conformity that kept us a slave to the system for so many years. This deep surrender to our bliss allows us to live in a state of joy. It is a process of undefining ourselves, becoming lighter, clearer, more in touch with our Essence Self. When we become so clear of emotional baggage that we are transparent, we will have made the leap into our wholeness. We will be living as the Ascended Self.

The second area where we carry a lot of unprocessed emotions is in the physical body. When it is out of balance, it can prevent us from accessing our joy. How does your body feel now? Does it fill you with joy to have the miracle of human form? Stress, physical pain, and disease are all signals from our body's inner wisdom. These signals remind us to pay attention, to become present in our lives. We are reminded to relax into our breath and let go into the moment. Physical pain always contains a gift of understanding and an opportunity to transmute the energy of pain into joy.

The quickening consciousness is revealing valuable information on high-level wellness and life extension. However, what follows is the quantum leap into life consciousness. I believe that we can free ourselves from the myth of having to die. The reality of death is a collective lie that we have been acting out for thousands of years. Our salvation as a species will come from bringing the light of consciousness into every cell in our body. The next few years will bring greater understanding of how to utilize the vibration of love and joy to maintain the light of pure awareness at a cellular level. Our bodies must adapt to the higher frequencies that are sweeping over us like a tidal wave. Like a snake shedding its skin, we are rebuilding our bodies to accommodate this quickening, crafting our light body for the journey home to our Ascended Self. This home is not some distant star system. Home is right here. The earth is our ascension ground.

The third area of emotional baggage is fraught with more hidden agendas, societal and religious abuse, and exploited by more beer commercials than any other issue we face. This is our sexuality. Does your experience of your sexuality feel like a sacred gift or an aching wound? Do you yearn for a richer, more meaningful level of intimacy? Do you long to explore new worlds by riding the wave of sexual bliss? On any given day, I can personally answer each of these questions affirmatively. But sometimes the weight of my sexual woundedness feels so overwhelming that I avoid the issue altogether. It is hard not to get stuck in this area of profound inner homework.

I see sexuality as the final frontier of enlightenment. Sacred sexuality is a path of healing, of manifesting our higher purpose and connection with the one heart. The most joyous state of erotic innocence comes from acceptance of our bodies and our sexuality as natural and precious. We can experience pure delight in our bodies, savoring our sexuality in its wholesome sacredness. The time has come for the reenchantment of the body as the temple of our Essence Self. As we release our addictive sex patterns and experience our bodies as sacred, we open ourselves to true ecstasy. What steals our joy is that sexuality also holds our greatest pain and denial. Consequently, healing our sexual woundedness frees an enormous amount of energy that opens us to our creative juices and to our joy. The shame, guilt, and fear uncovered in this healing work provide a rich compost for our personal evolution. We now have the opportunity to heal our sexual issues and return to an erotic innocence of joy and delight.

Forgiveness has been the most important aspect of my own healing from sexual woundedness and my return to innocence. Forgiveness does not condone the acts of our abusers. It is vital to release our karmic tie to these individuals, which opens us to profound healing. We have spent years building a type of psychological armoring, which closed us off from our feelings. We protected ourselves from pain because it was too intense to bear. Yet we also armored ourselves from our joy. When we can recognize our abusers and others who have wronged us as our sacred teachers of forgiveness, we will be able to live more fully alive and more fully in our bodies.

I have a simple process I like to call my "forgiveness ceremony." I begin by drumming, dancing, or chanting to get the energy moving. Then I sit quietly and focus on the energy that I feel in my body. I spend time breathing in the life force energy of the kundalini through the base chakra, up the spine in a circular movement, bringing it to the crown chakra and down the front of the body. There are many variations on this form of breathwork. The most important part is getting in touch with how our body is feeling by bringing the awareness of the breath to each chakra.

Then, placing my hand on my heart chakra, I focus on self-forgiveness. I release the grudges, the impatience, the judgments that I hold against myself. I ask myself aloud for forgiveness; I breathe in and grant that forgiveness to myself. There is immeasurable power in the vibration of the spoken word. Allow yourself to trust the process. It works.

Next, I focus on those I ask to forgive me. I speak each name aloud and ask them to forgive me. For example, I would say, "Donna, forgive me for trying to project my expectations onto you. I release you to be you." I repeat this refrain for each person. Sometimes I respond for them and reply, "I forgive you."

I next ask, "Whom am I willing to forgive now?" I wait until individuals and circumstances come to mind that I have held in nonforgiveness. Then I speak aloud, beginning with the person's name. For example, "Richard, I am willing to forgive you for abusing me." Breathe deeply and allow yourself to feel your body. Feel the emotions that come up and express them in whatever way is appropriate for you. I use drumming, dancing, deep breathing, or shouting and screaming to release the woundedness into the light of forgiveness.

This forgiveness ceremony can be done on a daily or weekly basis. It can be done quickly or at length. Practiced regularly, it helps to keep us clear. This process offers healing in all areas: our lifework, physical well-being, relationships, and sexuality. Once we work out the deep issues, we can more easily deal with the daily irritations and polarities.

The planetary shift demands that we release the woundedness of our past. It's time to perform this forgiveness ceremony with Mother Gaia, asking her forgiveness for the wrongs that we have done individually and as a species. The destruction caused by humans carries a legacy of fear and disaster, the loss of precious life forms. Find a place where you can lie on the earth, feel her heartbeat, and tell her you are sorry. Then breathe in her forgiveness, her love, and her healing energy. She invites us to taste her tears as they blend with our own. Open to the harmonic resonance of the one heart. Open to the frequency of joy.

Setting an intention to live in harmony and joy is a radical choice. Every shred of unfinished business, all of our emotional issues will keep reappearing like unclaimed baggage on an airport carousel. This truth has never been more apparent in my life than while writing this article. I spent the two days of solstice shift observance in a time of silence and fasting. In meditation and in ceremony, I held the energy of this shift along with the other authors of this book and many others around the world who drummed, prayed, and performed ceremony. At the end of the two days, I completed the rough draft of this chapter and was opened to a flood of emotions that turned my life upside down. Every aspect of myself not in harmony with joy came up to be processed. All of my fixed certainties came loose from their moorings as I felt myself shifting through time. It seemed that the trickster coyote was peering at me from every unhealed shadow issue. It felt as though I were being crushed in the collision of my past and my future. There were times the pain was so great that I felt I would die, or that the joy was so intense I felt certain I *had* died. This material was rewriting my life, helping me to midwife my awakened self at light speed. Resistance to the chaos that I felt brought excruciating pain. Surrender into emptiness allowed the old skin to shed and a more consciously conscious self to emerge. The chaos that I experienced has led to a breakdown of the old hardened beliefs and resistance. This solstice shift has caused a breakthrough to my harmonic resonance with the Oneness of all life. It is an experience of innocence and great compassion for me and for all my earth family. My message is simple: as we surrender more deeply into life, we no longer need to seek joy. Joy is our Essence Self.

We are being quickened during this transformative time, and our shift in consciousness affects the collective reality of all. We are the dreamer and the dream, the awakener and the awakening of consciousness. We represent the transformative power of lightning, burning away the old realities and rebirthing ourselves and all of humanity. It is we who are the miracle of the solstice shift. As we attune to the frequency of joy, we are midwifing the new human. Together we are ascending into the frequencies of the golden octave. Together we are vibrating in the harmonic resonance of joy.

⊕

Marina Raye is the author of several books, including *Brainware, Sexuality: The Sacred Journey,* and *Do You Have an Owner's Manual for Your Brain?* She is also a recording artist, who has been called the "Feminine Voice of the Native Flute." Her albums include *Gentle Medicine, Heart of the Mother, Earth Ascending,* and *Wolf Sister.* Her most recent album, *Star Visions,* is "the story of the prophecy of the ancient ones of the great shift in consciousness that we are living now." Marina Raye lives in the Colorado mountains with her life partner, Charlie Oakwind.

"I believe we discarded these male guardian roles at the end of the Paleolithic era about 12,000 years ago—in the Garden. About 6,000 years ago, all of us, men and women alike, were captivated by the negative male—creating our realities based on suppression of the female. *...It was in losing the positive male—warrior of the hearth—that we forgot how to care for Gaia and to forge an existence in harmony with her."*

Chapter Sixteen

THE AQUARIAN AGE ACTIVATION

by Barbara Hand Clow

By means of astrological analysis, I realized about twenty years ago that a new geometric field of light would begin forming in the spring of 1996, one that would help us integrate the energies of the coming Age of Aquarius—the next great age when we would shed our Piscean passivity and activate our true creative potential. As you will see in a moment, this activation phase occurred during the period between the spring equinox and the summer solstice of 1996—with the actual new field fully in place during the month of August 1996. So, when Michael Langevin asked me to contribute to this group sharing of solstice '96 experiences, I was excited that others were now sensing the momentous shift.

In the late 1970s, David Spangler, a most revered spiritual teacher, had also seen that great change would come in 1996. Because we both saw this potential twenty years ago, I took this future energy coalescence even more seriously. In the back of my mind, I made note about this powerful time and then went on happily observing the wave of cultural transformation that was occurring during the 1980s. The changes we were making during this period fueled my hope that humankind could finally move beyond a passive and limited sense of self. The Harmonic Convergence in August 1987 ushered in a wave of consciousness that potentiated a new morphogenetic field for the planet—earth's galactic synchronization—which expanded into a larger and larger field. Following that great event, new grids of light were manifesting and generating electromagnetic fields that could potentiate stellar knowledge in human awareness while we were still in physical bodies. The formation of these grids has given me a childlike hope for greater human freedom and ecstasy. As a result of this light activation, many brave individuals in the late 1980s and early 1990s were processing their emotional bodies and making firm commitments to integrate Spirit. Yet most did not realize why. This processing of dross—negative emotions—in our chakra system by emotional-body clearance is the time-honored method to enhance our electromagnetic fields.

During this period, the spontaneous clearing of emotional baggage by so many individuals activated the planetary potential for initiating a critical leap in human evolution.

For when we as individuals seized the moment, Gaia could align with us! This harmonic alignment in 1995 catalyzed the healing of our *mental bodies* at the global level, even though personal emotional processing will always be needed. This shift in our *mental* fields is what will teach us how to breathe with the etheric body of earth and pave the way for group activation of our Gaian minds. We are becoming conscious of the actual processes needed for catalyzing our species' next evolutionary state. This process was so intense during 1995 that many of us felt adrift, but by early 1996 the agenda shift became palpable. Waves of new biological creativity infused the grids, and even a comet heralded the arrival of a new phase of speciation. This was a *nexus point*—when extraordinary time lines converge and there is a shift in how we perceive everything. At first nothing seems to have changed, but it has. We are moving out of the Age of Pisces and into the Age of Aquarius, accessing the biological codes of *Earth's Original Time Line*—the "first time" of ancient Egypt/the primordial Garden of Eden. My goal here is to clarify this species-level integration of new human potential that suffused the planet between spring equinox and summer solstice of 1996 and into August.

As the time for the ceremonies came closer in early winter 1996, I knew that one whole phase of my life would end. I kept breathing deeply and asking Gaia to help me trust more than ever. The great force coming in was so intense that I sought out the small pleasures in my life, my family and friends, to ground me. As an astrologer, I knew that Pluto moving through fiery Sagittarius (1995 through 2008) and Uranus moving through airy Aquarius (1995 through 2004) would create radical levels of alchemical transmutation. After all, in 2012 A.D., we are coming to the end of a 26,000-year cycle based on the Mayan Calendar. The planetary transits of the spring equinox and summer solstice 1996 reveal that our male parts of consciousness—warriors for planetary harmony—would reassume their essential guiding roles. I believe we discarded these male guardian roles at the end of the Paleolithic era about 12,000 years ago—in the Garden. About 6,000 years ago, all of us, men and women alike, were captivated by the negative male—*creating our realities based on suppression of the female.* This regression locked us into an insidious passivity, and now Gaia, sensing that we are ready, groans for a new active direction for humanity. It was in losing the positive male—warrior of the hearth—that we forgot how to care for Gaia and to forge an existence in harmony with her.

We astrologers know that, as one astronomical age ends, a total loss of direction is always experienced by humankind. As we release our old beliefs so that the old order can die, we lose our vision of a future and chaos reigns. But, during these transitions, the space is also created for the activation of a new field. When the Age of Aries ended with the birth of Christ heralding the Age of Pisces, Rome lost its belief in its own warlike, controlling, global culture. And, as this new Piscean age was ushered in, a space opened for humankind to develop empathy—feeling in our emotional bodies. Now, as we prepare for the Aquarian infusion, a planetary heart opening is occurring as the Christ within activates our feeling bodies, resulting in a complete awakening of our biological ecstasy. Yet, this empowering spiritual nurturance—tectonic goddess/birthing powers—will implode our personal life-force energies unless the ecstatic birthing waves are contained and supported by the active male grounding faculty. As any seductive female can sense unexpressed love and pleasure in the male and then allure him into her arms, Gaia knows how to awaken the great male force—Pan, Min, Dionysus, Shiva. In 1996 she unleashed these gods of the earth at spring equinox, deepened them during summer solstice, and then encoded them into our planetary dreaming bodies during a truly rare Grand Square in the sky.

The Grand Square is the most potent activator of new forms in earth, and the one in August 1996 was composed of five planets and the lunar nodes. This great activating structure formed in the sky during an extremely long period of planetary tension. Normally such a pattern lasts only a few days, but in August 1996 both Mars and Venus were the fourth point in a T-square formed by Chiron on the lunar north node, opposed by Saturn on the lunar south node, and squared by Jupiter. First Jupiter was opposed by Mars and then by Venus. It was this astrological configuration—which I saw coming almost twenty years ago—that had the power to draw new and subtle Aquarian vibrations into clear and undeniable earth manifestation. Many people, sensing this vibrational shift, gathered together during the 1996 spring equinox and summer solstice. Unconsciously, they were preparing for the Aquarian light infusion during the coming Grand Square, when the qualities of the coming changes would be clearly evident. As a Mayan Elder, I was drawn to teach during the spring equinox in Crete and Egypt. However, it was when I was asked by The Findhorn Foundation to teach with David Spangler in Scotland for the summer solstice conference called "Imagining the New Millennium," that I knew the change was truly upon us. These kinds of synchronicities are guiding lights.

The Grand Square indicated that we would receive the powers of the equinox/solstice 1996 shift by having *our female sides demand the healing of our wounded inner males.* Equinox/solstice ceremonies were instinctively created to answer that demand; it was by reactivating our magical males that we would heal our wounded male sides. We would finally be able to recognize the violence, abuse, and control by the Global Elite—the negative-male, patriarchal system that creates control patterns

WERNHER KRUTEIN/PHOTOVAULT

"Equinox/solstice ceremonies were instinctively created to answer that demand; it was by reactivating our magical males that we would heal our wounded male sides. We would finally be able to recognize the violence, abuse, and control by the Global Elite—the negative-male, patriarchal system that creates control patterns based on survival and scarcity concerns. ...It is time to refuse to participate in survival/scarcity patterns and destroy the old order, so we can again create a world of unlimited potential."

based on survival and scarcity concerns. The female shadow side or negative female is fear-filled passivity that paralyzes us in the face of evil. We do not object without the support of the active male principle. To move beyond this stasis, our inner males must contemplate the limitations and violence in our belief systems. It is time to refuse to participate in survival/scarcity patterns and destroy the old order, so we can again create a world of unlimited potential. It is our male sides that must banish cynicism and weakness so new birth can come. As I began my ceremonial preparations, I was certain spring 1996 would be a time to remember.

First, the guidance said I must teach in full partnership with my mate of more than twenty years, Gerry Clow, for the first time. We are both Aquarians, not codependent, and so I wondered about this prospect. I followed guidance, as I always do. We agreed to teach together in Crete during the spring equinox for a conference called "The Opening of the Age of Aquarius," conducted by Power Places Tours. This would later culminate in working alone with our groups in ceremonies in the Great Pyramid. Without going into detail about the work in Crete/Egypt, it is interesting to note that according to magical traditions, monumental events on earth are heralded by comets, asteroids, meteors, and other portents in the sky. As we worked to coax the reluctant and deeply wounded male into warrior mode, Comet Hyakatuke hovered above the Giza plateau in alignment with Venus conjunct the Pleiades. According to my Mayan brother, Hunbatz Men, the energies received during the equinox are implanted at north latitudes during the subsequent solstice. The sudden appearance of the blue comet indicated that truly prodigious knowledge would infuse the northern latitudes during the 1996 solstice. While working in the Mediterranean zone at the spring equinox, my mind was constantly drawn to a sea vortex north of Scotland—the vortex that holds the primordial Atlantean mind—and I began to realize that this infusion would actually be the opening of the Original Time Line of earth.

I've been working on a book about a great cosmic catastrophe that occurred in 9500 B.C., which scientists in many fields have been reporting. This caused the widespread decimation of species and huge geological catastrophes between paleolithic and neolithic cultures—the prediluvial dichotomy. This new understanding is heavily based on the latest findings about earth history from asteroid research. As an explorer of human consciousness, I'm interested in how this event affected our minds. This was when we lost paradise—the Garden of Eden—in the Great Flood. In my opinion, our species suffered a great shock: we were dislodged from our etheric bodies—our connection to spirit while grounded in the earth plane. We are only now beginning to process deep inner fears created in the chaos of these dark days. This relatively recent shock is what

WERNHER KRUTEIN/PHOTOVAULT

". . . 'The surges of my awareness that will move through your feelings in the coming years will be of the same magnitude as the waves of physical forces that you've felt during my past great catastrophes. You must open yourselves and open unlimited space, and trust your partners and loved ones. Only with this unconditional opening can I ripple through you and awaken the New Age of Aquarius.'"

crippled the protective male.

When I've told groups the story of this catastrophe, I've watched people ripple through waves of unprocessed fear as this memory awakens. I believe the apocalyptical and millennial tendencies in fundamentalist movements (including the New Age) are actually a projection into the near future of that deeply repressed 9500 B.C. catastrophe. Of course, we could destroy our planet by means of out-of-control inner fear, since we do have the means to do it. *We can destroy our world with thought now that we have the Bomb!* Ironically, Gerry and I would next celebrate the summer solstice at Findhorn, where, in the words of the conference brochure, "we'd focus on finding ways to handle the rapid levels of change to avoid 'millennarian dis-ease'—a sense of personal anxiety and disempowerment in the face of apocalyptic scenarios, seemingly irresistible forces of global change, and a bewildering choice of visions for our next steps."

The Findhorn Community is a center for spiritual and holistic education based on nature's intelligence. It is also one of the world's most powerful sacred sites for remembering the powers of the positive male—trust, cocreation, and conscious crafting of new realities. What better place to complete this ceremonial cycle? When I got there, I discovered that this community had indeed managed to activate the positive male: Findhorn is based on very high spiritual ideals that are totally grounded in the everyday reality of growing and preparing food, processing sewage with anaerobic bacteria; that is inhabited by members who build their own buildings and run their own businesses. Centered deep within these mundane realities are sacred temples in the form of indoor and outdoor meditation spaces that sucked me right down into the bowels of earth. The keepers of these sites—animals, devas, plants, and insects—assist humans, and they readily came forth while we were meditating. They offered us memories about the "Dream of Earth." The glue that holds Findhorn together is a deep love of God and earth that is palpable and audible.

Gerry and I arrived with knowledge about the awakening male gathered at the spring equinox, knowledge that did not come without struggle. After the equinox in April and May, the tension coming from the newly activated (but not actuated) male felt to me like an incipient psychosis. The most difficult and delicate phase of a new energy awakening exists in the shift from an exciting idea into a real form. I must admit that my faith was greatly tested about the real potential of my deepest and most secret hopes. As we arrived in Scotland, all that I really knew was that Findhorn could teach us something about how to activate this great force of Pan and make it part of our world again. After all, Findhorn means "find the horned god" and is a center for global consciousness. If we could discover Pan there, we could find ways to support the remembering of this true maleness.

On the day of the solstice, I taught a "Pleiadian agenda activation," based on my latest book, *The Pleiadian Agenda: A New Cosmology for the Age of Light.* During these activations, students experience being in the earth field while also being in touch with the stellar realm—Goddess Alchemy. I connect earth and sky because this opens a pillar of light from the crystal in the center of the earth to the Galactic Center. The movement from one age to another is greatly facilitated by this kind of energy circulation, and there is considerable evidence that these kinds of ceremonies have been performed in the past to ease the tension during these shifts every 2,160 years, the average length of a great age. Personally, I perform this activation because it enables me to enter the crystal in the center of earth to learn about the special qualities of a particular age. I have done this during many transitions from one age to the next.

During summer solstice 1996, the earth crystal spoke to us:

> *"I am groaning and wrenching under your old yokes of limitation and lack of belief in my plenitude. I will move and stretch to release your control patterns on me. My way of moving your energy through you is e-motional. The surges of my awareness that will move through your feelings in the coming years will be of the same magnitude as the waves of physical forces that you've felt during my past great catastrophes. You must open yourselves and open unlimited space, and trust your partners and loved ones. Only with this unconditional opening can I ripple through you and awaken the New Age of Aquarius."*

As these visions moved through me, I saw a complex of great lines of light reaching through Findhorn from the center of earth and moving out to many distant locations on the planet. I next saw another comet coming, one that would brighten the skies of Findhorn, in spite of the enveloping winter darkness this close to the Arctic Circle. I felt and imprinted an amazing tectonic male vibration—a force equal to Gaia—as her voice thundered through me. The cells in my body imprinted these vibrations and held them until they could be released into each one of us during the August Grand Square. On the night of the summer solstice, the Findhorn Community built a great fire in Community Field, and we all danced around it in the eery, never-ending light of the Arctic night. The sun set at 11:00 p.m. and rose at 5:00 a.m., but the light was never totally eclipsed because the sun was always close under the horizon. This constant light oscillated my cells, helping me to absorb this new awareness. As I watched the people dancing around the fire wearing old Celtic clothing, a storyteller told about the coming of the White Buffalo while flames consumed the great Druidic bonfire. Wine brought from Glastonbury by Serena Roney-Dougal and bread made by The Findhorn Community were shared.

As people danced with eyes glowing in the hot fire, we sipped single-malt Scotch, and I thought about my Scottish clan codes. My Irish magical teachings, Scottish totem blood, and Cherokee initiations are my blood and spiritual heritage. I thought of this book and of the other writers who were tuning into Gaia. During the solstice itself, the new forms coming to the planet were so powerful that I couldn't yet imagine expressing them in written form. However, during the Grand Square of August 6 through 20, the enormity of what had transpired during summer solstice 1996 finally became palpable. I can tell you this: the namby-pamby control and manipulation of our planetary powers is passing, and the male that respects, honors, and guards the female is coming back again. And the unconditional love and joy of the feminine for the exquisite male phallic power is rising again. The time has come for the opening of the mystery play of the earth god and the goddess of the stars.

⊕

Barbara Hand Clow is an internationally noted astrologer, shamanic teacher, editor, and author of *The Mind Chronicles Trilogy* consisting of *Eye of the Centaur: A Visionary Guide into Past Lives; Heart of the Christos: Starseeding from the Pleiades;* and *Signet of Atlantis: War in Heaven Bypass.* Her other published works include *Chiron: Rainbow Bridge Between the Inner and Outer Planets; Liquid Light of Sex: Kundalini Rising at Midlife Crisis;* and *The Pleiadian Agenda: A New Cosmology for the Age of Light.* Barbara Hand Clow conducts workshops worldwide, teaching advanced multidimensional perceptual skills and techniques for integrating higher states of human potential. She and her husband, Gerry Clow, maintain homes in Connecticut and New Mexico.

WERNHER KRUTEIN/PHOTOVAULT

Chapter Seventeen

THE STORM BEFORE THE CALM

by Neale Donald Walsch

Interesting energy, I thought. Very open, very expansive energy. Hmmmm. I wonder what will come of this. . . .

Walking with my wife Nancy in the moonlight along the beach on Jekyll Island, Georgia, I watched the Atlantic Ocean majestically rise and abruptly crash upon the shore, my ears welcoming the familiar thunder of a billion particles of water pounding a billion particles of sand. That sound cannot be heard too often. It's one of the magical sounds of the earth. It's one of the declarations of her glory.

Suddenly, finding myself caught up in the wonder of the moment, in nature's gregarious display—and over-

"Walking with my wife Nancy in the moonlight along the beach on Jekyll Island, Georgia, I watched the Atlantic Ocean majestically rise and abruptly crash upon the shore, my ears welcoming the familiar thunder of a billion particles of water pounding a billion particles of sand. That sound cannot be heard too often. It's one of the magical sounds of the earth. It's one of the declarations of her glory."

whelmed with love for my wife as the night breeze toyed with her hair and sent its fragrance to me on invisible wings—I tore off my shirt, climbed out of my pants, ran with the joy of a six-year-old, and jumped into the waves. Nancy was at once shocked, amused, and just slightly scandalized by her crazy husband's actions.

I wanted to be One with it, that was all. One with the ocean, with the beach, with the smell and the sounds. I wanted to be One with the totality of it.

You see, I was at the beach on assignment. I'd been asked to take a moment on the summer solstice in June 1996 to "get in touch with" that "totality," to let it speak to me about the movement of the human race into the new millennium. That weekend Nancy and I were attending a United Church of Religious Science conference, where I'd been invited to be the keynote speaker. Earlier in the evening, Nancy had grabbed my arm and whispered, "C'mon, let's walk the beach." She had sensed that the time was at hand.

So there I was, in that wonderful moment, in an incredible setting with an incredible person, feeling the power of this solstice shift and the energy of that moment completely—so completely that I felt compelled to unite with it. Which was exactly what my editor had asked of me: to join with other writers and teachers in a grand experiment of unified consciousness.

Now, as I write this chapter many weeks later, I recall that the overwhelming impression I got in the ocean that June night was an extraordinary sense of unity. That was the single most pervasive feeling. Unity. The Oneness with which I sought to merge was everywhere and in everything. And I walked away from that experience with the unshakable belief that our future will be more "One" than it has ever been. More whole. More unified. More "together." Our days of separation are coming to an end.

Still, I know as I ponder these reflections, that the years just ahead of us will be, in a very real sense, the best of times and the worst of times. To many it will indeed seem as if we are living a "tale of two planets." I feel that, on the one hand, the next 25 years will see a widening gulf between some groups of people, while there will be a new unity between others—perhaps a greater unity of purpose and unity in action than we have ever witnessed.

As I gaze into the future, I see us living, as the lyrics of the old song go, "in two different worlds." There will be the planet of the "haves" and the planet of the "have nots," the home of the hopeful and the home of the hopeless, the world of believers and the world of nonbelievers. There will be those who have a grander vision of the future and those who are blind to anything but the past. And I see the energies of love and the energies of fear, perhaps more clearly defined than ever, driving the activities of men, women, and children everywhere.

It feels as if we are giving birth. All of us. We have made love with life—real, passionate love: the kind of love which hurts and which leaves it mark, the kind of love which is at once a joy and a struggle, a crucible and a celebration.

Having made love with life, we will soon give birth to a new century. We are in labor now. Nearly everyone has felt it. The new millennium is kicking and growing inside of us, and it is ready to be delivered. The birthing will go flawlessly but not painlessly. As with all births, we will forget the pain soon after delivery,

"As I gaze into the future, I see us living, as the lyrics of the old song go, 'in two different worlds.' There will be the planet of the 'haves' and the planet of the 'have nots,' the home of the hopeful and the home of the hopeless, the world of believers and the world of nonbelievers. There will be those who have a grander vision of the future and those who are blind to anything but the past."

WERNHER KRUTEIN/PHOTOVAULT

"The human race is about to . . .insist upon—not long for, not hope for, not pray for, but insist upon—a way for all of its members to live in peace, in harmony, in dignity, and in oneness. It is about to demand that we acknowledge the obvious truth: that the only real love is love which is unconditional; that the only real acceptance is acceptance which includes the deepest compassion and the highest understanding, and which embraces our differences with tolerance as it embraces our commonalities with joy."

WERNHER KRUTEIN/PHOTOVAULT

when our discomfort turns to joy at the miracle of what we have created. Having created new life (and a new way of life for most people on this planet), we will have an opportunity to nurture it and to watch it grow. In this, too, there will be some growing pains, which is an essential part of the cycles of life, part of its celebration.

Our movement into the twenty-first century will be a time of reappraisal and redefinition, of restructuring and realignment, of renewal and, ultimately, of reunification. We will be reunified with ourselves and with our highest hopes; with each other and our highest collective ideals; with God and with our highest truths. Yet, before this reunification is complete, there will come, there must come, a disassembly. This is what my moment on the beach told me. And, as the waves came crashing down on my naked body, I knew instinctively that there is always the greatest chaos before the greatest calm. Chaos is, in fact, the harbinger of calm.

And so, I know now that I must prepare for the chaos.

I know, too, that I am free to make those preparations without fear, knowing that chaos is natural, a natural turn of events. A necessary ingredient. A harbinger, yes. It is a sign, to be sure, but a good sign. A healthy sign. A welcome sign.

Seeing it approach is a clear indication that we are moving in the right direction. That is why, even in the face of the weary and seemingly unending pronouncements of so many doomsday predictors, I hold great hope for our future.

I am enormously optimistic because everywhere I look society is disassembling itself. I see governments reinventing themselves. I see political, economic, and religious constructions—which have held up for centuries—now falling apart. I see old scientific assumptions being set aside, long-standing philosophical arguments losing favor, and ancient spiritual paradigms shifting.

All of this dismantling reduces itself to one word: change. And yet change has been a basic component of the human experience from the beginning. Why is it so different now? The difference is that we are seeing, and are going to see, change on a grander scale than ever.

The human race is about to grant itself its greatest wish. It is about to insist upon—not long for, not hope for, not pray for, but insist upon—a way for all of its members to live in peace, in harmony, in dignity, and in oneness. It is about to demand that we acknowledge the obvious truth: that the only real love is love which is unconditional; that the only real acceptance is acceptance which includes the deepest compassion and the highest understanding, and which embraces our differences with tolerance as it embraces our commonalities with joy. I sense that it is about to require that we live up to our potential and become, in our actions as well as our self-congratulatory descriptions, an enlightened species.

I knew on that beach in Georgia that this insistence, this demand, this requirement will not be an overt action of particular people, but a covert result of the combined actions of all of us.

We are all losing patience with ourselves and beginning to act on it. That this is happening collectively, perhaps for the first time in 2,000 years, is what packs the experience with such power, endows the moment with such opportunity, and ensures the outcome with such certainty. For when the human race collectively comes to conclusions and moves to action, the result is inevitably titanic.

So get ready. We're about to rock the boat.

The largest area in which we are about to produce great and lasting change—indeed, enormous upheaval—is in our way of being with each other. We are about to eliminate the contradictions and the hypocrisies, the half-truths, and the secrets from our daily lives, and from our political, economic, religious, and social systems as well.

We are about to insist upon a new watchword in the conduct of human affairs: transparency. That's what I "got" on that moonlit night on Jekyll Island. It is about being naked, about being seen: no more cover-ups, no more hiding out, no more masks and shields and cloaks and daggers. That is what I felt, what I saw and understood, standing knee-deep in the ocean; its very essence washed me clean of every old thought that would have ruled that moment in former days.

For me it was a baptism. A baptism by my mother and life-giver, earth. And now I could be born again, born into the new world of the new millennium, where there will be no hidden agendas, no under-the-table dealings, and no duplicity; no more "what they don't know won't hurt 'em" and "let sleeping dogs lie"; no more "company secrets," national security "deletions," medical profession or blue-uniform "codes of silence," and individual word-of-honor "confidentialities." Far from being honorable, such behaviors will be seen as just the opposite.

In this new millennium, we will also create a new paradigm around the matter of personal choice. We will evolve into a society of limited laws and unlimited personal freedom. There will be only three guidelines, or "rules" by which we will be asked to live: awareness, honesty, and responsibility. We will be challenged to move to a new level of awareness—deep awareness—of the impact and the effect of our thoughts, words, and actions upon one another. We will be asked to be totally honest with ourselves and others as to those thoughts, words, and actions. And we will be invited to accept full responsibility for all outcomes fairly attributed to them.

There will be no other laws or legislation, although there will be "systems" put in place (such as a system of traffic lights in most areas), which will allow us to better facilitate our own movement to awareness, honesty, and responsibility. Under such a system, for instance, one would never be stopped and given a ticket for absentmindedly running a stop sign. If no one was hurt, there would be no "offense."

If, on the other hand, there was an accident resulting in injury to another's person or property, all parties would be given an opportunity to resolve the situation within the framework of the three guidelines: 1) Were you aware of the stop sign your community has placed at that corner to give traffic a better opportunity to regulate itself? 2) When you honestly assess what happened and how it happened, what, if anything, do you believe your actions caused? 3)Are you willing now to take responsibility for those outcomes, and what does responsibility now call upon you to do?

Will it be possible for people to live this way? Can human beings (much less corporations and governments) operate within such a paradigm? On the beach that night, I knew that the answer was yes. Not only can the human race do it; it now understands that this is the only way it can evolve any further. We know we have come just about as far as we can with our present system of withholds and deceits, judgments and condemnations.

The division, which I see coming before the unity, will be between those who cling desperately to the old ways and those who point urgently to the new. Many of those who "have" will not want to share with those who "have not." They will not see us all as One, but rather, will continue in the old paradigm of "every man for himself." As with so many individuals, neither will many nations see themselves as One, but rather they will continue in the old paradigm of "might is right" and "to the victor go the spoils."

Yet the new millennium and its energies will not be denied; even now there are those who agitate for a grander view, a larger vision. More and more of us are pressing for that vision, and it is this growing divergence between the two camps that will produce the storm before the calm.

And so for a while the waters will be choppy. Yet that is not what drags us down. This is what I learned on that delicious night in June of 1996. We have been swimming in the waters of life with all our "stuff" on, and have been drowning. It is time to throw off everything, accept what is true about us, and swim free at last.

⊕

ROGER HOLDEN

Neale Donald Walsch's long and varied career in the communications field has included stints as a newspaper reporter and managing editor and as host of a nationally syndicated radio talk show. In the pursuit of his vision of a world in which people no longer live in fear of God and each other, he has written two books: *Conversations with God, Book 1,* and *Conversations with God, Book 2,* which have appeared on the *New York Times* Bestsellers list, and he has two new releases in the fall of 1997: *Conversations with God, Book 1 Guidebook* and *Meditations from Conversations with God, Book 2*. He lives with his wife Nancy in southern Oregon.

STACEY BAIRD/PHOTOVAULT

Chapter Eighteen

THE NEW MYTHS FOR OUR TIME

by Jean Houston

All over the world myth is bursting through its chthonic barriers. Many of us were raised in the time of the dying of the myth, while others were raised in the time of non-mythic science or print culture, wherein principles of continuity, uniformity, and repeatability were elevated over the more mythic and organic principles of discontinuity, simultaneity, and multiple associations. Now, in science, the mythic flavor of the more ancient, organic perspective is returning; chaos theory is being lauded as the way things work.

We now look for flow patterns rather than for linear cause/effect explanations. Quantum views of the universe tell us that we are absolutely ubiquitous through time and space. Every bonded electron has knowledge of every other bonded electron; everything is dynamically interwoven with everything else. Resonance has become far more important than relevance, and nothing is truly hidden anymore. Reality has become mythic.

I remember working with my friend Ed Mitchell, the sixth man on the moon; my husband and I were trying to help him remember some of the peripheral things he saw on the moon. After trying a variety of techniques, he finally said to me, "You know, Jean, it's not what we saw on the moon that's important; it's what we saw coming back to earth. Coming back to earth, there she was, that beautiful blue and silver planet floating in that womb of ocean, the oceanic womb of the cosmos." And then he said, "I felt such nostalgia for what the world could be. My hand hit the stereo button, and the music of "Camelot" came on. There she was, Camelot, the

"there is the unique fact that women are rising to full partnership with men in the whole domain of human affairs. This is changing everything! Everything! It is the single most important event of the last 5,000 years. Because when women, with their rich mind-style—which has been gestating in the womb of preparatory time these many millennia—begin to emerge, what happens to education? To governments? To economics? When the emphasis is on process rather that on product: on making things cohere, grow, and develop, what happens to everything? It's a seismic shakeup."

once and future earth. I went up an astronaut and came back a 'psychenaut,' devoted to inner space. And you know, of course, lunacy was in no way a metaphor. Many of the astronauts went quite crazy. Because, finally, we had come back to a concrete, mythic reality. And suddenly we were catapulted into the next myth."

I really think there's something monumental about the year 1969. When the astronauts, representing our species, left for the moon, we were born out of that womb of our mother as her fetus, and when we came back as her partner, everything accelerated. Look what has happened since 1969. Planetization. There has been this extraordinary exchange of cultures; we have leaky margins with everybody. And, of course, with this cross-fertilization comes the acceleration of all of the old myths—almost as a catharsis to get to that next stage—where we suddenly have a multicultural reality. Haven't we seen the myths of the two brothers rising up as a catharsis? Bosnia and Serbia. North and South Ireland. And the list goes on and on. Just look at how we dress. My shoes are from Italy. My watch is from Australia, and my undergarments are from Taiwan. And just imagine what's happening to our minds? It's almost as if our minds have leaky margins to other mythic realms as never before in history. Many people, whether they like it or not, have become fascinated by myth in the last ten years. For many the old stories have been rising up to be regrown. Something profound is happening in the cosmos of the psyche.

Then, of course, there is the unique fact that women are rising to full partnership with men in the whole domain of human affairs. This is changing everything! Everything! It is the single most important event of the last 5,000 years. Because when women, with their rich mind-style—which has been gestating in the womb of preparatory time these many millennia—begin to emerge, what happens to education? To governments? To economics? When the emphasis is on process rather that on product: on making things cohere, grow, and develop, what happens to everything? It's a seismic shakeup.

And just look at the leaky margins in the media. With the daily revolutions in technology, the media is becoming the matrix of culture. How many of us are going to be on the Internet? I, for example, have been enjoying it immensely. I'm a computer nerd myself. I am so fascinated by computers, and I've even taken my mythical interests onto the Internet. One of my identities is a fifteen-year-old boy, playing "Dungeons and Dragons" with other fifteen-year-olds, who think I'm their age but with a weird vocabulary. Another me is known as the "Queen of Comedy" because I inherited my father's joke file. I have friends who go out on the Internet, and they take on shamanic power. They call themselves "Flaming Mensch" or whatever. They really take on these archetypal identities with remarkable powers. And there is a little girl of fourteen who took on an oceanic name. Through the Internet, she gathered together hundreds and hundreds of people to help save the oceans. They all thought she was thirty-five. What is happening in this extended media role is that we are not only extending our nervous system electronically, we are extending parts of our souls. We are discovering new identities.

How are people experiencing the nature of this new reality? The rising of the depth-currents of all times, all cultures, all experiences, and all potentials? Its effects are being felt worldwide. I have one small claim to fame. I'm one of the best-traveled human beings who's ever lived, which isn't hard at the end of the twentieth century. Sometimes I travel 250,000 miles a year. I have been working with international development agencies all over the world, like The Institute of Cultural Affairs, and with UNICEF in Bangladesh and Burma. I work with cultures, especially indigenous cultures, trying to help them preserve themselves while they move into the next century. Some of the things I'm finding are a fascination with myth the world over; the seeking of spiritual experience; the revival of the knowings of indigenous people; the beginnings of a world music which incorporates and sustains the knowings of many regions; styles of clothing that mix and match continents on a single body. I even find the shadow side rising—the last stand. The old tribal gods in their varying fundamentalist postures rising before they are swept—not away, nothing is ever swept away—into a new amalgam in which they become part of a larger story. Today, and for all of us, all parts of the planet are catching all parts of the planet. To prepare for these world changes, the human psyche, I believe, is manifesting many different singularities of itself as it helps the planetary movement towards convergence and transition. Psyche may look very different 100 years from now. In fact, I think if schizophrenia is the disease of the human condition, then polyphrenia, the orchestration of our many selves, may be our expanded health. That's why it is critical that we begin to mythologize rather that pathologize.

Ego, as we understand it, will become but one image of the multiple images of the psyche. We are so polyphrenic that if there is a weakness in one part of the psyche, other parts of the psyche simply do not have that weakness. Furthermore, the psyche has the capacity for autonomous creative structures. Take a man like Mozart, who was very silly in many ways but was of course a highly skilled musician. They said to him, "Sir. How does it happen that such a silly little man like you can compose such extraordinary music?" He said, "Ha, ha! It's because when I sit down to play, I enter into the realm of music, and I play what I hear. And it comes there all at once...zusammen." All of us have, at certain depth levels of the psyche, these autonomous, creative structures that seem to rise and demand their creative time, their creative impetus, from the mythic structures that are the substrata of the human psyche.

Psyche, right now, is moving at remarkable speeds past the limits that most of us have lived with for thousands of years to perhaps an utterly different state of being. A dream-like reality in which it is difficult to tell what is news and what is drama, what is matter and what is myth. We live in self-created chaos to hasten our own meeting with ourselves.

All over the world, in virtually every culture I've visited, I find that images that were once relegated to the unconscious are becoming conscious. Happenings that belong to extraordinary experiences of reality are becoming more common. Many of the maps of the psyche and its unfolding are undergoing awesome change. Buddhist cybernauts share realities with secretaries who hold black belts in Kung Fu. Female Episcopalian priests draw ancient mazes on the floors of their cathedrals and lead their parishioners to the sacred geometry of the dromenon. United Nations economic advisers practice deep meditation and find the solutions to the tribulations of countries in inner space.

And then there are the children. Among the children the myths are rising. I once made a study of very young children who had not been exposed to television or radio. I wanted to see what kind of stories they would tell. I found one little boy who was quite vocal, who was just under three. I said to him, "Jimmy, tell me a story."

"I don't know any stories."

"Yes, you do. Tell me a story," I insisted. "Tell me a new story."

"Okay. Once upon a time there was a little boy, and he had a mommy. He loved his mommy. So he married his mommy. And they had many babies."

"Oh God! And what happened next?" I asked.

"I don't remember."

"Yes you do. I know you do."

"People got mad at him," he said.

"Come back here...What happened to him?"

"He went away with his sister."

"And then what happened?"

"He talked to everybody, and they liked him again...I'm gonna go play with the doggy now...."

And he ran off. Then I thought of that famous Jewish joke: "Oedipus shmoedipus, as long as he loves his mother." He was telling us the full story; he didn't stop where Freud stopped. He went on to the story that Oedipus, led by his sister/daughter, Antigone, goes around the world. People are shocked, but they think, *Oh! He has gone as far as you can go. Him we can tell everything! He is more wounded than anyone. Oedipus! Wait for me! Have I got a story for you. You've got to help me.*

Until, finally, rich from having shared his woundings and listening to the woundings of others, he finally ends up at the grove of colonists. There the great priest/king Theseus says, "Welcome, great man, you who have suffered so much: you who have learned so much. Be for us the wise man of Athens. Be our counsel."

And Oedipus says, "Thank you. I will."

And then the gods say, "Ooh! These people are getting frightfully sophisticated. Do they actually have more experiences than we

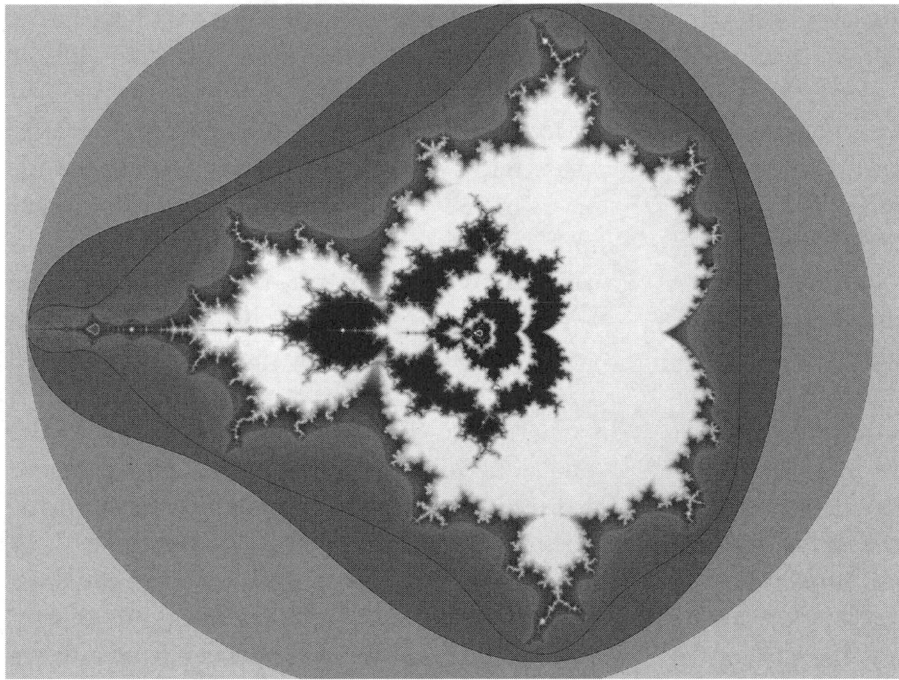

WERNHER KRUTEIN/PHOTOVAULT

"Many of us were raised in the time of the dying of the myth, while others were raised in the time of nonmythic science or print culture, wherein principles of continuity, uniformity, and repeatability were elevated over the more mythic and organic principles of discontinuity, simultaneity, and multiple associations. Now, in science, the mythic flavor of the more ancient, organic perspective is returning; chaos theory is being lauded as the way things work."

do? We need a shrink. We need Oedipus." And, of course, there's this tremendous earthquake, and Oedipus is taken up and becomes a god.

That's a true story. There was something in that child's mind that remembered. Now, if this had just happened once, I would say, "Ah, this was some kind of fluke." But it happens over and over again. And whether it is that children seem to know the ancient stories as part of a kind of diaphony to the collective unconscious, or whether it is something that is accelerating in the psyche of our time that gives children this remarkable knowing, I don't know.

I believe that it is our privilege and our particular challenge to witness and assist a new story coming into being.

As actors in this new story, we are seeing the rise of new archetypes, or perhaps the evolution of old ones. I've seen very similar things happen among the aboriginal people with whom I've had the great pleasure of living in Australia, as well as the Maoris in New Zealand. One thing that happens with the changing of the story, be it our own or the culture's, is that wounding happens. Whenever you leave an outmoded condition, wounding is central to the story. The wounding pathos of our own local story contains the seeds of healing and even of transformation. This is an often-told truth and is woven into all the classic tales of the human condition. Witness Greek tragedies in which the gods force themselves symptomatically into consciousness at the time of wounding. All myth has wounding at its core. Artemis must kill Action when he comes too close. Job must have his boils. Dionysus must be childish and attract Titanic enemies who rip him apart. An abundance of sacred wounding marks the core of all great Western myths and their attending gods and humans. Adam's rib. Achilles' heel. Odin's eye. Orpheus' decapitation. Innana's descent and torture. Prometheus' liver. Zeus' split head. Pentheus' dismemberment. Jacob's broken hip. Isaiah's seared lips. Persephone's rape. Oedipus' blinding. The killing of Osiris and the extraordinary grief of Isis.

We are drawn to these stories over and over. We do not flinch before their terrors because they mirror our own. Also, they carry us into the mystery, the marvel, the uncanny, the announcement that, with wounding, the sacred enters into time. Each of these stories prefigures a journey: a renaissance. Each of the woundings is a turning point in the lives of gods and mortals. From the point of the wounding, the journey of gods and humans proceeds towards new birth. And with it unfolds a sensuous acuity to the needs of others that was, until then, impossible. Being more vulnerable, we reach out. We extend our hands and our hearts to others who are wounded.

It is only at such a pass that we grow into a larger understanding of what life is about and act therefore out of a deeper and nobler nature. It is difficult, challenging, and yet extremely necessary at the time of wounding to "revision" our situation so that its larger story is revealed, and we don't just fall into paranoia, or cynicism, or a block against all and everything. This means that we must stop repeating to ourselves the datum of local events or personalities that have caused us pain. This is not to deny the fact but to move out of the easy seductions of tunnel vision and into the broader landscape that reveals potent opportunities for growth.

We then ask ourselves, "Are we in a cauldron of pain or a chalice of opportunity?" Shall we fret and whine and kvetch, or can we see our suffering as the hand coming from the gods to pull us into a new story? By viewing our humiliations, illnesses, accidents, and acts of violation in this way, we take our story from the local, "here's me, this is me" level, to the archetypal and mythic level.

I always ask my students to ask themselves the great and terrible question, "Where and by whom were you wounded? What or who is trying to be born in you from that wound?" I ask them to tell the story again, not as a repetition of historical detail but as myth, in which the wounding is only the middle of the story, and the ending of which is the birth of a new grace.

I say to myself repeatedly, "If I had not been wounded on any number of occasions, I would not be able to do the work I do. If I had not been wounded, I would not have the hypersensitivity to the human condition and to cultures and ideas that I had. If I had not been wounded, I would not take the risks and challenges that I do." And everybody can say very much the same thing. If you had not been wounded, you would not have tapped the depth of life force that is trying to emerge in our time. You would not have the interest; you would not have the compassion. There's no question that wounding opens the doors of our sensibility to a larger reality that is blocked to our habituated and conditioned point of view. Pathos gives us eyes and ears to see and hear and feel what normal eyes and ears and feelings cannot. Moreover, wounding is the traditional training ground for the healer and the teacher. The shaman healer is often wounded and marked as part of his or her preparation. Those who have, through accident or illness, vividly confronted the reality of their own death, often return with a renewed sense of wonder and strength.

By allowing my wounds to remain open, I can be more helpful to others who are seeking to revision their sufferings in a more profound and useful way. My own experiences of wounding—physical, psychological, emotional; loss of status, prospects, friends, and what had been my place in the world—have led me to understand that, in times of suffering when I feel abandoned, perhaps even annihilated, there is occurring at levels deeper than my pain the entry into a reality at once more subtle and more evolved. Thus I offer the conundrum that, as baby-making occurs through the wounding of the ovum by the sperm and the sperm's explosion and dying into the ovum, so cell-making occurs through the wounding of the psyche—quite possibly by the gods. And by gods I mean, not old atavisms, but those psycho-spiritual potencies yearning at the threshold of existence to enter into our lives to redeem the higher dream that is trying to emerge into time. Maybe the gods also suffer and even die as we do: die out of their old archaic selves to be rebirthed as emergent culture, art, story, and spirit. It was Kazantzakis who said, "We must become the saviors of the gods."

A new story is emerging in our time. A new story is coming out of the woundings of culture, of crisis, of consciousness. It is a new story. It may be a new mythology. It's not yet in shape. You might say, "Can we ever really invent, or reinvent a myth? Can we actually bring it in to time?" Go beneath the surface crust of consciousness anywhere, of anybody in the world, and you find repositories of the imaginal world: the mundus archetypes that the Sufis refer to as the "El Lam el Mithal." It's a whole energetic system with its patterns of creation yearning at the threshold to enter into time. You find within everyone a teaming terrain of myth and archetype: holy men, wise women, flying horses, talking frogs, sacred spaces, rainbow serpents, and death and resurrection. The journeys of the heroes and heroines are a thousand, yea, a million faces.

Having taken depth probings of the psyche of many people the world over, I know this to be true. I know, for example, that in the West we have moved from the Promethean myth, a great wounding myth of snatching fire from heaven—and our materialistic accomplishments and our high tech civilization—to the myth of Proteus, the shape shifter. The sea god Proteus was capable of taking on all manner of shapes, forms, and purposes at will. This is us today, suddenly like Proteus, having to take on other cultures, other ways of being, ways of knowing. We have to become Protean, highly resilient and creative, able to adapt to the ever-changing story, especially in the light of constant challenge and ever-present peril.

As Robert J. Lipton, who has written wonderfully of the relevance of the Proteus archetype for our time, has said, "Without quite realizing it, we have been evolving a sense of self appropriate to the restlessness and flux of our time." That's why I really believe we are evolving a new psyche. And this is also why myth is changing. Mythic structures not only support the work and help of any culture, but allow the psyche its own healthy development.

In the past, personal identity and cultural identity tended to be consonant with each other. Now the psyche is adrift because the old stable stories are not as operative as in earlier times. Myths, after all, contain the greater story that never was but is always happening. Myth serves as a manner of explanation, but it is also a mode of discovery. For myth, I believe, is the coded DNA of the human psyche. I think it is a structural form that is both in the psyche and perhaps in the body, as Joe Campbell believed. It is the stuff of the evolving self that awakens consciousness and culture according to the needs of time and place. It is the promise of our becoming.

When we undertake consciously to work with great old myths, a rich and buried world of experience opens to us. We can travel with Odysseus and make a tragic mistake just like him. Instead of going home to his wife after conquering Troy, a decent two-week trip, he says no, "Let's go north and sack the Sacconians." Wrong! Ten years' travel.

How many of us have done that? How many of us have made the real mistake? Why did you marry that woman or that man? Have those children? Go to that school and not another? Why? So we could enter the great journey and be worthy of Penelope when we finally arrived home. We can experience the passion play of Isis and Osiris, rendezvous with Percival in search of the Grail. Make the great mistake: take our Ph.D. in Knightcraft, and we have the big opportunity to assay, "Who serves the Grail?" Or, "Who does the Grail serve?" We say, "Mmmm, I'm a good knight. A good and perfect knight doesn't ask questions." Wrong! Seven years travel and with no passion, too. Ever do that? Miss your big kairos and spend seven years doing your job with no passion?

Within the ritual spoken or ritually enacted myth, we can allow our lives to be writ larger. The personal particulars of our local existence find their amplification and elucidation in the personal universals of the greater story. Most of us who work with myths find that our students and our clients, having entered the realm of the ancient stories and their persona, seem to inherit a cache of experience that illumines and fortifies their own. They are no longer an encapsulated bag of skin dragging around a dreary little ego. They are organic environments, symbiotic, not just with myths, but with the realm of knowledge as such. Myth seems to be the key to the larger mind of being. It seems to be the entry point. They discover that they, too, then, are valuable characters in the drama of the world and in the drama of the world's soul. Pushing the boundary of their own local story, they gain the courage to be and do so much more.

This is part of my work; I use myth as a journey upon which to then weave the exercises/processes of our own becoming. You can teach people thousands of processes to wake up human potential, but they won't keep them if they're not embedded in great story. You need the story to sustain the muchness of the learning of human becoming.

How, then, can we change patterns so deeply woven into the structure of the psyche? Until recently I doubted that anyone could do more than alter certain details. Now, however, in a time of whole system transition, when everything is deconstructing and reconstructing, where everything and everyone is wounded, myth also requires its redemptions. Most of us live anywhere between five to a hundred times the amount of sheer experience of our ancestors of a hundred years ago—for which we have not been prepared. We've been prepared to be white males living in the year 1926. And the only people who are good at that right now are Asians, and they're getting very nervous about it, too.

So I'm saying the reweaving of the myth also requires its redemption. This may be as critical a task as one could attempt at the cusp of the millennium. The task is how to enhance the dominant myths by guiding people into the realms of the psyche, where they have the power to change their own essential story.

I work with a premise that all of the world's psyche is now emerging larger than ever. We're experiencing the harvest of all the world's cultures: belief systems, ways of knowing, seeing, doing, being; what had been contained in the so-called unconscious over hundreds of years is now up and about and preparing to go to work. What had been part of the collective as the shared myth or archetype is now finding new rivers of unique stories flowing out of the passion play of individual lives, not just lives caught up in a collective. This does not mean the dismissal of traditional myths, but rather that now, as the myths of the ancient traditions no longer fit exactly the personal territory to the degree that they once did—owing to the radical change of our time—we must live our lives with the mythic

WERNHER KRUTEIN/PHOTOVAULT

vibrancy of those who inhabited the ancient stories. We have become mythic ourselves. We are mentored and informed by the ancient myths, but we are also in an open moment—a jump time—when myth is recreating itself from the stuff of personal experience. For the development of the psyche, this is as monumental as when people stopped depending on the meanderings of the hunt and settled down to agriculture and civilization. And as we are now capable of discovering our own personal mythologies, we are becoming required to discover them. In so doing, we can add our own deepening story to the emerging new story and with it the new planetary civilization.

We are in jump time. A few hundred months from now we're going to be out there as stewards of the solar system, terraforming Mars and creating biospheres around the solar system. What are we doing in nanotechnology? Little vacuum cleaners are going down our bloodstream. How many of us may live to be well over a hundred? Our children? Our children's children? Perhaps they will live even much longer than that. This is a reinvention of society. This is a reinvention of everything. How do we become stewards of the process? We need a story that is feisty, greening, rich enough to sustain us. And a few thousand months from now we may be joining a galactic milieu, for all we know. I sometimes think that this planet, located in an outer arm of the galaxy, is the experiment school, that this is Godschool. This isn't the center where everything happens. This is where the experiments are made.

"I work with a premise that all of the world's psyche is now emerging larger than ever. We're experiencing the harvest of all the world's cultures: belief systems, ways of knowing, seeing, doing, being; what had been contained in the so-called unconscious over hundreds of years is now up and about and preparing to go to work. What had been part of the collective as the shared myth or archetype is now finding new rivers of unique stories flowing out of the passion play of individual lives, not just lives caught up in a collective."

We are being prepared to go out and create stuff. We are becoming cocreators in our time. And also, with so much personal history behind us, with so much more experience behind us and within us, so much more wounding, we have achieved what is surely an extraordinary evolutionary achievement: the ability to continuously receive, recreate, and extend our experience. This new Protean capacity of the self is virtually a new structure in mind, brain, and psyche. It grants the capacity to view ideas and systems, whether social, intellectual, political, philosophical, or spiritual, with a freedom that was not ours in the past. Now we can view them, as Lipton suggests, with a new ease that stands in sharp contrast to the inner struggle people in the past endured with such shifts. Our creative capacity has thus technically grown exponentially, as has our capacity to deal with complexity that would have driven our forebears quite mad. Whether we use it or not is something else. What is emerging the world over, owing in part to the rise of myth again, is the technology of the sacred, a high art form as well as the once and future science. It is everywhere. Look at the bookshelves. Look at the seminar announcements. It finds its theory in practice and in the teachings of the mystery schools of old: the shamanic trainings and initiations, the rise of the deep knowledge of indigenous peoples, as well as in the modern laboratories of consciousness research on the cutting edge of psychotherapy. While fiber optics, interactive television, global computer networks, and other information superhighways give us access to the world's mind, groups of artists and scientists are arising who are providing us with the highways to the world's soul.

New powers open as we learn to reframe our story, see our story in mythic light, and take on the larger life of myth and of the unfolding of the loaded, coded dream: finding within our own bodies the metaphors for both conflict and conciliation; discovering power objects, personal shields, inner allies; and reconnecting to the myths of generations past. We are luminously led to become a pioneer in the undiscovered country of the myths of times to come. Since culture is everywhere being newly reimagined, nothing is more necessary than a rebirth of the self. These are the times that are meant to breach our souls, unlock the treasures of our minds, and through the divine act of demythologizing, release the purpose, the plan, and the possibilities of our lives. It is so great that it is only a myth that can give us the pattern, the blueprint, the guide. We are regrown to greatness then and take our place with Percival, Penelope, White Buffalo Woman, the Lady of the Lake, Quetzalcoatl, Bridget, and Mr. Spock. And the name of this new character out of the myth is "you." The name of the myth is "your story," reframed in the light of the understanding that has come from this process and reconceived for the renewal of self and history. "Thank God our time is now," poet Christopher Fry says, "when wrong comes up to face us everywhere, never to leave us till we take the longest stride of soul men ever took. Affairs are now soul size. The enterprise is exploration into God. Where are we making for? It takes so many thousand years to wake, but will you wake for pity's sake?"

And I believe that the strides our souls are taking must carry us through every shadow towards an open possibility, in a time when everything quite literally is up for grabs. We can do no less. The psyche requires its greatness as do our times. This adventure is mythic, both ancient and personal, very original, and an exciting way to greatness. Or should I say "responsible living of the life we are given"?

⊕

MARTHA SWOPE

Jean Houston is an internationally known philosopher, author, cultural historian, and teacher, who, after many years of work as a behavioral scientist, has developed and continues to develop revolutionary new ways of unlocking the latent human capacities existent in every human being. With the late mythologist Joseph Campbell, Dr. Houston frequently co-led seminars and workshops aimed at understanding interrelationships between ancient myths and modern societies. She is the author of 15 books, including *A Mythic Life; The Passion of Isis and Osiris; Life Force; The Possible Human; Godseed; The Search for the Beloved;* and *The Hero and the Goddess.* For the past 30 years, she has co-directed with her husband, Dr. Robert Masters, the Foundation for Mind Research.

WERNHER KRUTEIN/PHOTOVAULT

"In the inner worlds, energies and qualities do not just move through empty space, like radio waves or radiation traveling through the stars. They are embodied. The transfer is from one being to another, from one life to another. In talking about new energies coming to the earth, it's not as if some ray is being beamed to us from some far distant star system. A much more accurate metaphor would be to say that a living essence is being shared and transferred to us through a process akin to touch."

Chapter Nineteen

EARTH SHIFTS

by David Spangler

Some years ago an acquaintance of mine underwent extensive plastic surgery to give himself a new face. This is not an especially unusual procedure, except that he did it entirely without anesthetic. "I didn't want to just wake up to a new and unfamiliar face," he told me later. "I was birthing a new identity for myself, and I wanted to be conscious throughout the process. I wanted to experience the transition from the old me to the new me so there would be continuity."

I had to admire his courage and resolve. The idea of letting someone carve up and rearrange my face while feeling every moment of it is not my idea of a good time. On the other hand, my friend in his wisdom knew the importance of conscious participation in a transformational process. He knew that, for himself at least, unless he could participate in the transformation, he would be unable to inhabit fully the new identity he was creating.

Early in my career as a teacher and lecturer, I also learned the importance of staying conscious, present, responsible, and participatory. Much of my training came from nonphysical, spiritual beings who acted as mentors and colleagues for me. Our mode of communication was always a conscious one; I have never entered any kind of trance state. Both they and I preferred it that way. During one period, though, when I was working as an intuitive counselor, I felt very strongly the responsibility of dealing with the problems and issues that people brought to me. The work of being a mediator between their needs, my own wisdom, and sources of spiritual help within the inner realms required a lot of effort, attention, and precision on my part to ensure accuracy. I began to envy friends of mine who were traditional trance mediums. They simply went to sleep, allowed some other entity to speak through them and answer their clients' questions and problems, and then they woke up, not having to worry about what had happened in between. I, on the other hand, had to measure each word, each thought, to ensure that I was perceiving and communicating accurately what I was seeing on the inner. It was hard work!

So, one day, I asked my inner colleagues if they couldn't arrange it so I simply went into a trance state and woke up after the session was over. That way, I reasoned, my own thoughts and feelings wouldn't get in the way and perhaps create errors in the information. Their reply was very clear: "We would rather have errors than unconsciousness." They then went on to say, "The object of our working together is to put you in touch with your own wisdom and inner perceptions; if you can learn to trust yourself, you will not need us. But that trust will not come to you in an unconscious state. You must earn it by participating in the process."

I think about my friend's new face and my own inner training when I think about the New Age. I have found a tendency in New Age thinking to imagine that some great shift or transformation is going to happen, and that because of it, we will all wake up one morning to discover that we have a new consciousness and are living in a new world.

This is a tempting image. It is like getting something for nothing—like winning the lottery, for example—and we all can appreciate the attractiveness of such an occurrence. Yet, in this process, something is lost. There are connections that are not made. As my nonphysical friends implied, consciousness is impoverished through lack of participation. If humanity is entering a new world and a new consciousness, if a transformative shift is truly going on, then, like my friend, we must be awake to it and be part of it; we cannot just wake up one morning with a new face and a new identity. We would not know how we got there, and it would be just a surface event; an outer change but not necessarily an inner one. We might be in a new world but we wouldn't know how to inhabit it.

My own inner contacts have stressed over the years that humanity is going through a time of transition, but that the nature of this transition is different from others which it has experienced in the past. One of the differences is the degree to which the details, the process, and the outcome of this transition are an outgrowth of our consciousness, reflecting our own choices and actions. Put simply, the fundamental nature of the transition is not the emergence of a new world but the emergence of a new spiritual and incarnational maturity. It is the emergence, not of new powers of awareness necessarily, but of new depths of responsibility, integrity, accountability, and connectedness.

For this reason, the new world is not something that can just happen for (or to) us. We cannot be magically transported from where we are to a better place. We must forge the path ourselves, for in knowing how we arrived in that better place and what we had to go through to get there, we will have developed the knowledge, the wisdom, and the maturity to know how to sustain it.

It is not uncommon for individuals to have experiences of sudden, spontaneous enlightenment; it is much more rare, however, for that experience to last. Nearly everyone I have talked to who has had an experience of suddenly entering a higher consciousness has told me how it faded after a few days, leaving them with a feeling of emptiness and longing. This is because something in that person's life was attuned enough or strong enough to empower a breakthrough but not integrated, attuned, or strong enough to sustain the new level of complexity and energy once it had been touched. To make such a new level permanent, one needs to live out its elements in everyday life, to anchor its qualities within oneself through choices, actions, and attentiveness. This can take time and work.

Within this context, I believe we need to be careful when we talk about "shifts" in the earth's vibrations or new "energies" coming into the world. It is very easy for this kind of language to become quite abstract and meaningless while still engendering a feeling that something is going to happen that will bring the New Age about without our needing to do anything. I have had people in New Age gatherings come up to me and say with much excitement, "A shift in the planet's energies is going to happen this coming solstice!" or some equivalent statement with the same happy anticipation as if they had said, "Christ is appearing next month and all the world will be transformed."

The problem with such an attitude is twofold: it can be disempowering because it leads us to look outside ourselves for something or someone else to do our work for us, and it is not a precise enough statement to mean anything. After all, what does a "shift" mean? What is shifting? How is it shifting? How will that affect us? What are the new "energies" that a "shift" might bring? How are they propagated throughout the world? How do they work? What impact will they have? These are all important questions to at least consider if we are to use such language with precision and with the hope that it actually will have concrete meaning that will be useful to us in making choices and taking actions.

The fact that something is shifting in the world around us does not mean that suddenly everything will be taken care of for us, and we will happily be in a new world. We still have our work of awareness and participation; we still have our tasks of dealing with the world. What the idea of inner shifts can mean is that the work we need to do will become easier or that we will have more resources to draw upon.

For example, when AIDS first became recognized, little attention was paid to it. It seemed confined to a minority population (one that was not in great favor with the general public anyway), and it was not seen as a general public health problem. For this reason, very few resources were made available to deal with this disease. However, over time, with much more evidence and public education and awareness, this perception changed. There was a shift in consciousness, and as a result, a great many more scientific, medical, and financial resources became available. The actual work of research, experimentation, and treatment still needs to be done. The shift in public awareness has not changed that at all.

When I look at the world inwardly, I see it as being made up of a complex mixture of qualities and forces at work. Like most other people engaged with metaphysical ideas, I often simply call these qualities and forces "energies." But what exactly does this mean? In physical

WERNHER KRUTEIN/PHOTOVAULT

"What the idea of inner shifts can mean is that the work we need to do will become easier or that we will have more resources to draw upon. For example, when AIDS first became recognized, little attention was paid to it. . . . However, over time, with much more evidence and public education and awareness, this perception changed. There was a shift in consciousness, and as a result, a great many more scientific, medical, and financial resources became available."

science, the term energy has a very specific meaning: it is a measure of the capacity to do work. This might also be described as the capacity to make something happen or to allow it to happen. It is a measure of the capacity for activity. Thus, biological energy allows work to be done or things to happen or activities to occur within biological systems. Nuclear energy allows activity within the structure and relationships of atoms and their components. Chemical energy allows molecular and atomic interactions to occur, and so forth.

Spiritual energy, to my mind, is no different. It also allows work to be done, such as creating, sustaining, connecting, empowering, and so forth: work that sustains, vitalizes, and extends the very beingness and structure of creation. Perhaps when we talk about a shift in the earth's energies, we are really talking about a shift in the ease with which we can do such spiritual work. Such a shift might enable us to be more creative, more loving, more connected, more empowering, for example. But it doesn't guarantee that this will happen. It simply increases the possibility or the potential that this will be so. The fulfillment of the shift occurs only when we take action, both inwardly in terms of how we monitor and shape our consciousness and outwardly in terms of how we act in the world.

When we talk about these inner shifts, there is a tendency to see them as special events; this is particularly true when they are tied to specific dates, such as the summer solstice of 1996. We might think of them, for example, as equivalent to an earthquake where the ground suddenly jerks and slides and assumes a new contour. But for the most part, the influx of new or different spiritual energies into the world takes place gradually over time. For example, most of the "shifts" that sensitives and intuitives discern occurring in our time are part of a larger current of "energy" that began to manifest itself within the earth approximately 500 years ago and which will continue for at least another 500 years. Of course, on the time scale of the earth, this is a mere instant, but on a human time scale, it is a long time.

Within this larger current, there are times, such as the present, when the energy surges and is more intense and its effects are more noticeable, and times when it is less intense. So, to our human discernment, a particular spiritual quality may seem to impact us suddenly or over a very short period of time, when in fact, it has been impacting us for a much longer time but we simply have been unaware of it.

One metaphor for such a shift might be a hurricane. It begins as a slight stirring of a breeze, then builds in intensity until its full force bears down upon us; then it begins to lessen and the winds slow down as it passes on. It is important, for reasons I will expand upon in a moment, that we think of such inner shifts not as sudden events but as processes that have a period of buildup before and a period of integration after.

There is an implication when talking about these spiritual or vibrational shifts that in some manner they will exert a force that will sweep human consciousness along in a particular direction, like foam carried on the current of a river. In some ways, we each do register, to some degree, changes in the earth's vibrational field because it is in the nature of a holistic system that all of its parts will experience whatever affects the whole. It is also possible for a particular quality or energy to be "targeted," so to speak, towards a particular element within the earth, such as humanity. However, the actual integration of new energies into our planetary auric field and substance is more like water soaking into a landscape, with each part of that landscape absorbing what it can, than like a river rushing along its surface.

In effect, this means that where humanity is concerned, not everyone will register the full quality of the new energy at the same time. Collectively and individually, we respond to it and absorb it in various ways. Think of the new energy as being metaphorically a white light. Then, each of us individually and all the various collective groupings of humanity absorb different frequencies of this light. Some may absorb the blue bits, some the red bits, and some the yellow. Some may absorb combinations of colors, drawing in green or orange qualities, while some may in fact absorb the whole thing and experience it as white. However, humanity as a whole, and through us, the world as a whole, will experience the whiteness of the energy, for as each of its parts absorb this bit or that bit of color, collectively the colors are blended back into the white.

The changes that come in the world are not usually caused directly by the initial encounter with some new energy but by its absorption, integration, and expression within the body of the world. For a true shift to take place, everything in the world must participate in some degree in embodying and expressing the essential qualities which that shift brings into focus.

In other words, the idea of an "earth shift" or a shift in "the planet's energies" can be misleading if we continue to think of the planet as an environment within which we live and act rather than as a being whose life we share. It is not that the earth is shifting in some inner way and we must respond to it. We are part of the world, interwoven into its consciousness and being. Holistically speaking, it is we who are shifting as well. But this cannot just be an abstract idea. If a shift is to take place, we must experience and embody it.

This idea may be more clear if I put it this way. In the inner worlds, energies and qualities do not just move through empty space, like radio waves or radiation traveling through the stars. They are embodied. The transfer is from one being to another, from one life to another. In talking about new energies coming to the earth, it's not as if some ray is being beamed to us from some far distant star system. A much more accurate metaphor would be to say that a living essence is being shared and transferred to us through a process akin to touch. Just as I may, through my presence, share love or friendship or peace or some other quality with you through a process of induction and resonance, so the earth, both as a living being in its own right and as a cocreative community of living beings, shares and receives qualities from other lives who share its cosmic environment. I don't "beam" peace to you, for example; I am peaceful, and you pick up on and share that quality with me by discovering the peacefulness within yourself. There is a shift in your feeling and thinking, but not because I have "sent" you something. It happens because

"In physical science, the term energy has a very specific meaning: it is a measure of the capacity to do work. . . . Spiritual energy, to my mind, is no different. It also allows work to be done, such as creating, sustaining, connecting, empowering, and so forth: work that sustains, vitalizes, and extends the very beingness and structure of creation."

WERNHER KRUTEIN/PHOTOVAULT

my example or presence enables you to find the same quality of peace within yourself. You choose to participate in a state of peacefulness.

So inner shifts occur within consciousness and within beings, not within environments. For energy upon the inner realms is always an expression of life, not simply of some blind force.

Taking on new energies and undergoing shifts of consciousness are not things that can happen in spite of us or without our participation in some way. We cannot be spectators to the process. Instead of saying, "There will be a shift of the earth's energies in June of this year," to be more accurate, we should say, "I am going to shift my energies in June of this year." Instead of saying there will be new energies coming into the earth in the year 2012, for example, I should say, "I will express new energies in the year 2012." But when I put it like that, the question arises, "Why can't I express new energies now?" And the fact is, we can.

Of course, there are issues of timing. There may be qualities I cannot immediately bring into play because I don't know enough about them yet or do not have access to them, just as medical researchers into AIDS did not have access to large amounts of funding until public attitudes changed and the money was made available.

On the other hand, nothing stops me from doing more with what I have or with seeking out new perspectives and new behaviors that are available to me. I can right now become more loving, more empowering, more attentive, more accountable, and so on. I do not have to wait for an earth shift of some kind in order to do these things. I can act in new ways right now. And taking small steps of change may be what is necessary before I can truly resonate with, or be aware of, larger potentials of change in me or in my larger world. Simply waiting for some earth shift to happen or for some new energies to come makes no sense at all, and in fact, can cut me off from that larger unfoldment in the life of the world.

Which brings us back to the ideas of participation and consciousness with which I started this chapter. These are important qualities. Without them, our capacity to change and the world's capacity to change are both limited.

There is another reason why this is true. We often see the New Age within an evolutionary context, or we talk as if humanity were evolving into a new state of being, a new consciousness. But what is this new state, this new consciousness?

My understanding of the new energy we are beginning to express is that it is a blend of love and will manifesting as a quality of synergetic or holistic freedom. By this I mean a greater state of individual freedom of soul and consciousness to embody and express more fully the unique configuration of sacredness that each of us represents, but at the same time, including a greater awareness of our participation in larger wholes, from our families on up to all of humanity and beyond, to the community of planetary and cosmic life itself. This awareness leads us to express our freedom in ways that willingly and consciously create connections and interdependencies and community.

The thrust of the "new" energies active within the earth at the present time is towards enhancing the experience of personal freedom on the one hand and the experience of being part of a larger wholeness and having a responsibility to that larger wholeness on the other. There is a tension between these two states, and the new order of being arises from the loving and willing acceptance and resolution of this tension.

Indeed, many of the challenges we face in the world today arise from humanity (and individuals) responding to this energy of synergetic freedom in extreme ways, either through a heightening of selfishness or a heightening of a desire to give oneself over to a tribe or group: rampant individuality and rampant nationalism, and the tension between the two. Yet in between these extremes lies an ability to appreciate and love both the self and the whole and to understand the nature of the cocreative relationship between the two.

It is the energy of this cocreative consciousness that I believe is the energy of the new world, the New Age. And by its very nature, we cannot embody or understand it except by consciously working through the tension between the self and the other and learning to participate in cocreative relationships. In particular, this means we need to cocreate the very New Age that we desire. It cannot be handed to us, for the very quality that makes the New Age new is a quality that arises only through participation and consciousness. We are like my friend: to become a new identity, we must go through the process of earning that new identity. No earth shift, no new energy is simply going to hand it to us. This might have been possible in past periods of human evolution, but it is not possible now given the very nature of what seeks emergence within us.

The qualities of loving and mindful participation, a consciousness that seeks an inner and outer attunement, and wisdom that allows for successful cocreation are available to us now. Our process is not that different from the kind of spiritual and practical awareness that all the great religious faiths have sought to inculcate in us in their best and highest efforts. We do not need an earth shift to embody that awareness; that is a choice we can make now. It just demands a willingness to follow through. But as we do embody it, then we become the earth shift, not just for a solstice or an equinox, not just for some special year or other, but for all our days and all our years. And that is what will give us a true New Age.

⊕

David Spangler is a philosopher, writer, and educator whose work deals with the blending of spirituality and spiritual development, leadership and personal empowerment, the "new sciences" of holism and complexity, and personal and cultural transformation. His books include *Revelation: The Birth of a New Age; Emergence: The Rebirth of the Sacred;* and *Reimagination of the World,* co-authored with cultural historian William Irwin Thompson. His most recent books are *Everyday Miracles,* published by Bantam; *A Pilgrim in Aquarius,* from Findhorn Press; and *The Call,* from Riverhead Books.

WERNHER KRUTEIN/PHOTOVAULT

"The greatest, most practical expression of that {samadhi} experience is seen in those moments we are truly compassionate with ourselves and others. We listen to and acknowledge human work. We participate in society. We see the light of love in all beings and respond in ways that support well-being and peace. We nurture ourselves with actions that support who we know ourselves to truly be."

Chapter Twenty

Finding Your Bliss

by David Merritt

We humans are innate observers, explorers, and innovators. We watch the seasons change, the plants bloom and fade, and the animals forage. We watch each other and ourselves as we interact with the environment to get our needs met: hunger, partnership, self-fulfillment. As a species we have created a society so technically advanced that any part of our planet can communicate instantaneously with any other part—a phenomenon undreamed of just decades ago. We have the ability to feed ourselves with little fear of the famines and pestilences that were commonplace just a century ago. And when civil war and drought recently caused widespread starvation in rural Ethiopia, the nations of the world joined together to combat the problem. We are now in the process of honoring the connection between all humans, with the possibility that everyone's survival and social needs can be met.

It should be no wonder, then, that so many people are eager to move on to the next level of human evolution. People who are hungry or sick have a very hard time contemplating higher orders of communication, and spiritual discipline remains out of the question for them. But today we see that people around the world are studying mystic and occult practices, psychic control, holistic healing, cooperative communication, environmentalism, etc. There is a great hunger for the kind of knowledge that arises from the depths of people seeking to understand themselves and each other, and that comes only when they have seen the futility of striving for ever-increasing material and emotional control over their environment. Having acquired sufficient means of support, people are now venturing into the unknown potential of transformations in consciousness.

I asked a swami at the Vedanta Society what he thought about the progress we are all making toward a more spiritually evolved society. He was not nearly so hopeful as I had expected. "Our technological advances," he said, "cause us to attach ourselves to another layer of the external instead of the internal." While technology provides opportunity for communication, research, and cooperation, it also generates a whole new level of material and psychological attachments. Furthermore, people become dependent upon the hardware itself for solutions to life's dilemmas rather than looking within themselves.

WERNHER KRUTEIN/PHOTOVAULT

"I asked a swami at the Vedanta Society what he thought about the progress we are all making toward a more spiritually evolved society. He was not nearly so hopeful as I had expected. 'Our technological advances,' he said, 'cause us to attach ourselves to another layer of the external instead of the internal.' While technology provides opportunity for communication, research, and cooperation, it also generates a whole new level of material and psychological attachments."

Society may indeed advance while its members continue to identify themselves with their possessions, skills, and desires.

However, the major risk we run is that, while exploring new levels of consciousness, we may merely reinvent our egoism and desire for pleasure and domination in different packaging. Religious traditions have always been criticized for perpetuating this pattern. Insights lead to practices, which lead to ritual, which lead to traditions, which become the very objects of attachment and desire the original insight sought to obliterate. "The more things change, the more they stay the same" is a concept which has not been deleted from our repertoire of unconscious behavior. When the Buddha says, "We are our thoughts," he does not mean just our conscious ones.

Pursuing the spiritual requires letting go of the human compulsion to want and to have, or we will continue to be like children riding through the store in a grocery cart saying, "Gimme! Gimme!" Paradoxically, you must also observe your deepest desires and allow them to reveal their essential value. You can't tell a young mother she's wasting her time raising children, that she should be giving her full attention to meditation, charity, or philosophy. Imagine the response to such a suggestion! Acknowledge the devotion present in the relationship between mother and child. That is real worship.

Sri Ramakrishna asked his visitors, "Do you believe in God?" If they said yes, he'd ask, "Do you believe in God with form or without form?" Sri Ramakrishna never judged them for their responses. Instead, he used this information to move his guests toward a realization of their own source of devotion and peace. For a mother, God may equal her child. For a professor, God may equal his or her studies. God may be thought of with qualities like goodness and strength or without any qualities: beyond any human definition. The task of spiritual discipline is to unfold that image of bliss and pursue it to its natural conclusion. The highly revered Srimat Swami Shraddhanandaji Maharaj of the Ramakrishna Order once surprised a group of us devotees while we were enjoying bowls of ice cream after working in the monastery gardens. He raised his bowl with both hands and gazed upward while chanting enthusiastically, "Oh! Beautiful ice cream! You are the source of all my joy! How I love you! Your sweetness and purity are infinite and blissful! Let me enjoy your presence forever!" Everyone laughed uproariously while inwardly imbibing his potent message: all paths lead to the same goal. Know what path you have chosen and follow it.

It is important to distinguish this instruction, "Find your bliss," from the mere hedonistic indulgence of sensual desire. Many Christian denominations, for example, teach that physical nature is profane, vulgar, and sinful, and that the only hope for salvation is to forego pleasure on earth to enjoy it in heaven after death. By contrast, Vedanta, like modern physics, teaches that there are many dimensions to reality. Each dimension is imbued with divinity. The closer we examine our own experience, the more clearly we can appreciate divinity in all its forms, and the freer we are to choose those activities which best serve us.

John Calvin, a seventeenth century Protestant theologian, added to the Christian problem of attaining salvation by declaring that God favors those he loves with material wealth, and that those who live in poverty or pain are merely manifesting their condemnation by God. Thus, those Protestant denominations who base their teachings on Calvin's *Institutes* place their members in the untenable position of desperately desiring wealth, which proves they are among God's chosen people, while simultaneously suppressing any visible hint of pleasure—which may result in their eternal damnation in a lake of fire. From this teaching, we can see their justification for the extermination of Native Americans and the enslavement of Africans: their plight was merely the result of God's condemnation. Heathen savages! The same argument supports the massive devastation of wildlife and ecologies by industrialists eager to earn their salvation by accumulating wealth and power.

Of course Calvin is not the sole creator of shame. Every culture has its taboos and overzealous constraints on self-expression. And every industrialized society crosses the boundaries of ecological balance and healthfulness. The surprise for us children from Christian homes is that this shame has been institutionalized in our families' language, customs, and beliefs, insidiously sabotaging our tendencies to explore and understand ourselves. And these cultural traits, which have caused so much hatred and bigotry over the centuries, are still a subtle part of the way we think and process information. The struggle is to remember that it's permissible to be tired, sad, curious, angry, afraid, happy, ecstatic, or blissful. When we suppress these feelings, we also destroy any chance of learning by experiencing the consequences of those feelings. It may help to realize that these thoughts are not the invention of the soul, but that they have been passed down though generations of guilt-ridden, fear-driven people trying to prove themselves worthy of God's love by stifling their native curiosity and conforming to cultural patterns which result in the domination and destruction of their neighbors and their environments.

For Christian-born spiritual seekers, the Protestant ethic shows up in our endless striving. Not allowing ourselves to feel the peace derived from spiritual discipline, we work at it until we get it right. When we start from an unconscious core belief that we are undeserving of God's grace, it's no wonder that we import this thought into centering practice, worship, and contemplation. We seek divine bliss to the point of exhaustion because we unconsciously believe we will never seek it adequately. Depression results, often masked by grandiosity and arrogance. Christian-born devotees find themselves in the difficult position of inwardly celebrating an experience of their inherent divinity while outwardly tiptoeing around their fear and resentment that other people might judge them to be among the condemned. Their real task is not to gain external approval, although it may sometimes seem that way, but to conquer internal fear and resentment.

But today people from diverse cultures are communicating with each other, telling us that we can no longer tolerate abuse and destruction on the planet. We are all connected beings: physically, mentally, spiritually. Hurting any one of us hurts all of us. Conversely, our cooperation in generating global healings can result in the attainment of higher levels of consciousness. This requires that each person find the work that best suits his or her nature and that best serves the needs of the planet. It means communicating clearly and completely with people: with our immediate families as well as strangers. It means finding the highest source of joy and examining it, living inside it, allowing it to be born in the heart.

There is no escape from this planet until our work is done. People who have had near-death and out-of-body experiences tell us that we all have work to do here. That's the point of the cliche, "I saw my life flash before my eyes." The emphasis of the Bhagavad Gita is not on attainment of monastic values: it is on getting on the court, into the fracas of daily life, and overcoming the demons of fear, grief, and regret that hold us back from full participation. In that dialogue between Lord Krishna and the warrior Arjuna, Krishna berates Arjuna for his cowardice when Arjuna says he'd rather become a monk than go into battle. The highest form of spiritual discipline, according to the *Gita,* is to do one's work with a spirit of detachment. The Buddhists have a saying, "Before enlightenment I chopped wood and carried water. After enlightenment I chopped wood and carried water." There are no higher goals on this planet than peacefully coexisting with other humans, finding the right work, and finding your own bliss.

The chorus of Beethoven's Ninth Symphony continues to elicit strong emotions. It was played in Berlin the night the Iron

WERNHER KRUTEIN/PHOTOVAULT

"There is no escape from this planet until our work is done. People who have had near-death and out-of-body experiences tell us that we all have work to do here. That's the point of the cliche, 'I saw my life flash before my eyes.' The emphasis of the Bhagavad Gita is not on attainment of monastic values: it is on getting on the court, into the fracas of daily life, and overcoming the demons of fear, grief, and regret that hold us back from full participation."

Curtain crumbled. Beethoven wrote it after a series of political revolutions spread across Europe, replacing monarchies with republics. The lyrics he used, Schiller's "Ode to Joy," evoke peace with the image of the brotherhood of humanity nurtured beneath the gently fluttering wings of the goddess. In every age and society, whatever crisis and calamity befalls us, we each experience in our heart the truth our nature-oriented ancestors knew: we are the reflection of love and capable of bringing love into every situation.

The most challenging instruction in the wisdom literature was stated by Jesus, "You have heard it said, 'Love your neighbor and hate your enemy.' I say to you, love your enemy as well." Think of how often we say to each other, "I love you for being so helpful, kind, beautiful, etc." We are capable of much more. We can add, "I love all parts of you, who you are, and what you bring to our relationship." Even the things that cause us discomfort allow us to better understand our thoughts and reactions and to appreciate other people's enjoyable traits all the more. What makes this instruction so challenging is that it requires that we fully accept all aspects of ourselves: our bodies, thoughts, behaviors, and potential. It requires that we know the divinity within us.

The masters of every religion declare that God can be seen and known. Jesus said, "Seek and you will find. Knock and the door will be opened." Sri Ramakrishna demonstrated, by following the spiritual instruction of several traditions (Christianity, Islam, Tantra, Advaita, and other Hindu systems) that God can be known both with and without form, and that this knowledge can be acquired. Even those traditions which do not address a god with form nonetheless provide techniques and philosophies for realization of "truth," "self," and "emptiness," concepts which are similar to Jesus' "Lord," Ramakrishna's "Brahman," and the Native Americans' "Great Spirit."

The Upanishads describe the glories of the infinite imbued in every level of consciousness. By meditating on the five coverings of the Self, we can find methods of approaching our Self-discovery. First, we realize that matter is the stuff that makes up everything. Look at yourself. Your body is made up of skin, flesh, organs, bone, and fluids; this is quite different from plants and animals. At a deeper level, however, we discover that all matter has many things in common. It is comprised of molecules, atoms, and smaller objects called quarks. There is but one matter, and it is permeated by the Self.

Swami Shraddhanandaji told us devotees to gaze at our face in the mirror each day, and to think of our face as the face of all humanity. He said to look at the image in the mirror and substitute it for another image, so that we actually see a face other than our own. This was long before Michael Jackson's hit music video, *Black and White,* created the same effect using computer graphics morphing to make people and animals of all colors change shape into each other. We are all one. Our egos alone make us seem separate from each other.

Desiring a deeper level of knowledge, we realize that the universe is perceived as one vast pool of energy. All matter is set in motion by that energy. We experience energy in the beating of our heart and the rise and fall of our lungs. At a subtler level, we see it in the wind, in blossoming and fading plants, and in our feelings when around or away from other people. Energy is permeated by the divine. James Redfield's *The Celestine Prophecy* gives many examples of how to experience energy. In the martial art Aikido, energy is given and received in the form of grasping a wrist or shoulder and being thrown or getting out of the way. Attacks can be met head on if you're faster than the attacker, or can be led away by turning in the same direction of the attack and pushing as the attacker passes by. It is the same energy that moves all matter.

Next we discover the level of universal mind conceiving all action. Mind has its own vibration. When we consider the nature of our thoughts and their similarity to other people's thoughts, we perceive the thought inherent in energy and matter. Those in tune with nature have long known that plants and animals seem to think. Attuning the mind is a goal basic to all spiritual practices.

At the level of intelligence, the creative consciousness is celebrated and observed to be present throughout the universe: generating choice, invention, and strategy in human behavior, as well as in the inherent order of the cosmos.

At the level of bliss, our experience of pleasure, happiness, joy, and ecstasy is perceived as the same experience by all beings. Contemplating the levels of bliss and extending our thought to include all beings leads us to a personal experience of the divine.

At the center of these five coverings is the ineffable Self, "higher than the highest, deeper than the deepest depths. Thou art the light of love, the fount of truth, the home of bliss." There are no words to describe this level of consciousness, but people from many cultures have reported experiencing it. It is without thought, breath, vision, or sensation of any kind. Though permeating all creation, the Self is not changed by it.

The greatest, most practical expression of that experience is seen in those moments we are truly compassionate with ourselves and others. We listen to and acknowledge human work. We participate in society. We see the light of love in all beings and respond in ways that support well-being and peace. We nurture ourselves with actions that support who we know ourselves to truly be.

Having witnessed the ineffable, the ego's competitive and selfish characteristics fall away. Everything and everyone are perceived as part of the same unity. There is nothing to fear, nothing to resist, because the individual and the whole become one.

That is how we will move into the next century because that is who we really are. Wars, pestilence, crime, pollution, and cosmic disasters will call forth appropriate and responsible action. Peace, prosperity, justice, purity, and cosmic harmony will call forth appropriate and responsible action. No response is perfect, justified, or necessary. It just is. We just are.

⊕

David Merritt is an editorial associate of *Magical Blend* magazine and a long-time student of the East-West dialogue. His inquiry has led him from graduate studies in western psychology and theology to various martial arts,

and finally to the teachings of Sri Ramakrishna (1836-1886) as presented by the Vedanta Society, where he has been a devotee for the past twelve years. Those interested in more information on Swami Shraddhananda (1907-1996) can read his posthumously published work, *Seeing God Everywhere: A Practical Guide to Spiritual Living* (Vedanta Press, Los Angeles).

"Growing up in the modern world, most of us have experienced a profound disconnection from our spiritual selves and from the universal source, leaving us empty and insecure. . . . Spiritual healing occurs as we begin consciously to reconnect with our essential being—the wise, loving, powerful, and creative entity that we are at our core. Through this connection, we begin to reexperience our oneness with nature and with all other beings. The more we experience this essential oneness, the more we feel a sense of safety, trust, and fulfillment, of belonging in the universe."

WERNHER KRUTEIN/PHOTOVAULT

Chapter Twenty-one

HEALING OURSELVES, WE HEAL THE PLANET

by Shakti Gawain

As we rapidly approach the new millennium, life on our planet seems to be intensifying. Most of us are faced with challenging personal problems in our jobs, our relationships and families, our finances, and our health. We're unsure of how to best meet these challenges. Traditional ways of living, working, and relating to each other and to our environment no longer serve us very well, yet we have few role models for effective new modes of being.

Even more overwhelming are the problems confronting humanity as a whole. On a planetary level, everything appears to be getting worse and worse. We wonder why there is so much pain, suffering, and struggle. Most of us have no idea of how we can help, so we do little or nothing.

Changing our lives and changing the world cannot be accomplished either by focusing exclusively on external solutions or by following a transcendent, spiritual path that denies the reality and importance of the physical world. Rather, we need to choose an alternative which I call *The Path of Transformation,* in which we integrate our spiritual and human aspects and live as whole beings in balance and fulfillment on the earth.

Today's challenges can be effectively met only through a shift in consciousness, which is already happening worldwide. We need to recognize, to the depths of our souls, that we are all part of one whole and that what we do individually has a powerful impact on everyone. Our global crises mirror our individual processes. Only through healing ourselves on all levels—physical, emotional, mental, and spiritual—can we heal the planet.

The Four Levels of Existence

Human life consists of four levels which I define as spiritual, mental, emotional, and physical. *The Path of Transformation* involves clearing, healing, developing, and integrating all four of these levels within our lives. All are equally important. We can't skip or neglect one if we want to experience wholeness. As we heal and develop each one, all four levels naturally begin to balance and become more fully integrated with one another.

We may begin our consciousness journey at any of these levels. It's different for each person. For example, many people become involved in a consciousness process because they have a physical crisis: a disease, an accident, a weight issue, or an addiction problem. Or they develop a sharp interest in living a healthier life-style; they start learning more about nutrition and exercise. One thing leads to another, and eventually they discover new ideas and ways of living that leads them to explore the other levels.

For other people it may be an emotional crisis or need that brings them into the healing process. Perhaps someone seeks counseling over the loss of a loved one, and they begin to discover so much more about themselves that they want to explore even further. Or, because of an addiction problem, they join a twelve-step program (Alcoholics Anonymous, Narcotics Anonymous, etc.) which brings them into the consciousness journey.

Still others may enter the process on the mental level. Motivated initially by intellectual curiosity, they begin reading philosophy, psychology, or consciousness books. I have heard many stories about people who picked up a particular book by chance, and their life was never quite the same again.

The process may start in many different ways. Once we have begun, we may move from one level to another at different times, or we may work on two, three, or all four levels simultaneously. Each person's path is unique. Generally, however, no matter where we start our consciousness journey, or how we proceed with it, there's a certain underlying evolutionary process that unfolds from the spiritual to the physical.

At some point, we have a profound spiritual experience. Such an event may appear to happen by chance, even before we have chosen a consciousness path. In fact, that event may precipitate a crisis which, in turn, leads us to begin our journey. Or it may happen later, after we are already consciousness seekers. Whenever it happens, it changes our life forever. It gives us a glimpse of a higher perspective on life—the heights of love, power, and bliss that are possible to experience.

Having had these experiences, we are no longer content with a limited way of living; we are compelled to seek greater awareness. We try to understand what we've experienced so that we can repeat or expand it. This leads to experimentation with spiritual practices and to exploration on the mental level, as we release old ideas and open up to new ones. Eventually, after working on the spiritual and mental levels for a few years, we increasingly find ourselves bumping into the emotional level of our being. For many of us, the emotional level can feel like a wall that prevents us from fully living our spiritual beliefs in our daily lives.

Our emotional patterns seem to be keeping us from living these new philosophies. For example, we may have had moments of spiritual clarity or breakthrough in which we really felt that a higher power is caring for us. We may understand that idea intellectually and be committed to living our lives accordingly, trusting our inner guidance to show us what is needed. Yet we may repeatedly find ourselves wrestling with feelings of fear and terror, unable to release our old controlling patterns.

This is a perfectly natural part of the process. Experiencing something at the spiritual level and understanding it mentally doesn't necessarily mean we've integrated it at the emotional level. To heal and transform ourselves at the emotional level of our being demands an entirely different focus, requiring patience and compassion for ourselves. And, it usually requires help from other people as well.

Once we have done a substantial amount of work on the spiritual, mental, and emotional levels, we have the great challenge of integrating it on the physical level. Bringing everything we have been learning and discovering into our daily lives, we begin to live fully and freely, moment by moment. This often requires some healing of the body itself.

All four levels of being are closely related and affect one another. As we heal one level, we support the healing process of all the other levels as well. For example, fortifying our spiritual connection gives us the strength to face deep emotional healing. Doing emotional healing work also releases blocked energies on the mental and physical levels. And the more we clear our physical bodies, the more energy we feel on every level. We may begin the process on any level, exploring the others at different times in our lives. The ultimate goal is integrating all of them.

Healing the Spiritual Level

Spiritual healing occurs as we begin to consciously reconnect with our essential being—the wise, loving, powerful, creative entity at our core. Through this connection with our spiritual essence, we experience a sense of safety, trust, and fulfillment, a feeling of belonging in the universe.

Growing up in the modern world, most of us have experienced a profound disconnection from our spiritual selves and from the universal source, leaving us empty and insecure. Unconsciously we seek to fill this inner void in many fruitless ways. We may strive for money, power, and success as a way to feel secure, or we may devote ourselves to our families or careers to find meaning and purpose. Or, we may succumb to various addictive behaviors, using food, drugs, work, or sex to fill the feeling of emptiness. Unfortunately, none of them heal the underlying problem.

The lack of spiritual connection in our culture is at the root of many of our social as well as personal ills. Spiritual healing occurs as we begin consciously to reconnect with our essential being—the wise, loving, powerful, and creative entity that we are at our core. Through this connection, we begin to reexperience our oneness with nature and with all other beings. The more we experience this essential oneness, the more we feel a sense of safety, trust, and fulfillment, of belonging in the universe. We experience our inner emptiness being filled by the spirit within.

BILL GOIDELL/PHOTOVAULT

"Today's challenges can be effectively met only through a shift in consciousness, which is already happening worldwide. We need to recognize, to the depths of our souls, that we are all part of one whole and that what we do individually has a powerful impact on everyone. Our global crises mirror our individual processes. Only through healing ourselves on all levels—physical, emotional, mental, and spiritual—can we heal the planet."

This contact with our spiritual self gives us an expanded perspective on our lives, both as individuals and as part of humanity. Rising above the daily frustrations and struggles of our personality selves, we are able to see life from the soul's perspective. It makes our daily problems seem more manageable and our lives feel more meaningful.

Spiritual healing gives us a foundation from which we can more easily work on other levels. Without at least some spiritual healing, it may be very difficult, if not impossible, to find the hope, understanding, and strength to confront the difficulties and challenges of healing the other levels. Our inner guidance comes from the spiritual center within us. As we learn to trust and follow our intuition, we are building a strong relationship with our spiritual being.

Healing the Mental Level

The mental level of our being is the rational mind. To clear and heal the mental level, we must become conscious of our thoughts and underlying belief systems. We also need to educate ourselves about other ideas and beliefs, and eventually be able to consciously choose the ideas and beliefs that make our lives work the best.

To experience balance, integration, and well-being, our belief systems and thought processes (mental level) must be in harmony with the other three levels of our existence (physical, emotional, and spiritual). We need to have a spiritual understanding or life philosophy that gives meaning to our lives; we need to have an understanding and acceptance of our own emotions; and we need to know how to care for our physical bodies in a healthy way.

If you believe that your physical body is inferior to your spiritual self, for example, and that it is unworthy of your care or attention, you have a mental attitude that will eventually create a lack of well-being in your system. But, if you were to reeducate yourself on the importance and worth of your physical body and learn to take good care of it, you would find more balance and harmony in your entire system.

In the process of becoming more conscious, we are constantly learning new ideas, viewpoints, and philosophies, comparing them to those we already hold. Gradually, we begin to let go of the old ideas that limit us, retaining those that still serve us, while incorporating more expansive, deepening, and empowering ones.

Many people are confused about the process of healing the mental level. They think they must always practice "positive thinking," using that technique to block out their negative thoughts. They're afraid their negative thoughts will hurt them. At one time in their lives, they may have been stuck in negative thoughts and feelings. Now that they are feeling more positive, they don't want to acknowledge any negatives for fear of slipping back into depression or despair. So they deny or repress all their negative thoughts and concentrate only on the positive ones. For some people this will work fairly well for a while, but eventually all those denied or repressed thoughts and feelings come to the surface, one way or another. Many people who start to practice positive thinking are quite surprised to discover that their efforts have actually made matters worse. Rather than diminishing their negative thoughts and feelings, they find themselves caught up with them even more.

The first step in any healing process is always acknowledging and accepting your present state. We don't heal anything by trying to block it out or pretending it doesn't exist. We heal it by accepting what's there, and then becoming aware that there are other possible choices. So we need to acknowledge and accept our "negative" thoughts as part of who we are, and at the same time recognize and develop other, more expansive perspectives.

Some people have been wounded on the mental level by being told they were stupid as children, or by having their abilities compared unfavorably with a sibling or classmate. Many girls were given the message, directly or indirectly, that females are less intelligent, or that they are less important than males. And many people with more intuitive, holistic, right-brain learning styles were never supported by our left-brain, logically oriented society and school system; as a result, they may have drawn the mistaken conclusion that they are less intelligent than others.

People who have suffered such traumas in early life may have learned to doubt, discount, or deny their own intellect. In this case, the mental healing process must involve reclaiming one's own natural intelligence and learning to trust it. Remember that there are many different kinds of intelligence. Our culture tends to validate only certain types of abilities. An acquaintance of mine is not very educated or articulate, but he is brilliant at fixing mechanical things and finds great joy in his work.

Our society tends to reward only one kind of intelligence: book learning. But there are actually many different kinds of intelligence. In his book, *Raising a Magical Child,* Joseph Chilton Pierce talks about the seven intelligences. In each there is a clue to the gift we have come here to give. Every one of us has our own gift, from the agile rock climber to the "fix-it genius," to the single mother who raises three healthy kids and maintains a full-time job. Ironically, we are often the last ones in the world to see and acknowledge our own gifts or areas of intelligence. Most of us are pretty blind to what we do best; we live with our genius every day, and it just seems "normal" to us.

If you had an early negative experience of being discouraged or belittled, start reaffirming your abilities by recognizing that your special gifts and unique intelligence are often found in those interests toward which you naturally gravitated in your early life. The inner compass that pointed in that particular direction is rarely, if ever, wrong. If you need to do some healing in this area, look for ways to develop those early interests. Pursue skills and knowledge that interests you through taking classes and trying new things.

Healing The Emotional Level

Our feelings are an important part of the life force that constantly moves through us. If we don't allow ourselves to fully experience our emotions, we stop the natural flow of that life force. Energy becomes blocked in our physical bodies and may remain there for years, or even for a lifetime.

For most of us, exploring the spiritual realm is primarily a pleasant, expansive experience. And, because we are such a mental culture, we are fairly comfortable with the mental aspect of our journey. However, a great many people are stuck at the emotional level. Most people are frightened by the prospect of doing deep emotional healing work.

We live in a society that's generally terrified of emotions. Our patriarchal mentality is highly suspicious of the feminine aspect of our being—the feeling, intuitive part of us.

Our rational side is trying to ensure our safety in the physical world, and it fears the loss of control that deep emotions bring. Since our culture admires the male approach to life and has little respect for the feminine, feeling side, we have all learned, to one degree or another, to hide and deny our feelings—even from ourselves. We've learned to bury most of our feelings deep inside and show the world only what seems safe.

Most of us are particularly uncomfortable with what are commonly considered "negative" feelings, such as fear, hurt, sadness, grief, and anger. In reality, there is no such thing as a negative feeling. We call things negative when we don't understand them and therefore fear them. These feelings are natural and important to us. They each serve a meaningful function in the human experience. Rather than rejecting and avoiding them, we need to explore and discover the gift each offers us. To fully feel anything, we have to feel the fullness of its opposite. For example, to feel real joy, we must be able to embrace our sadness. To open to love, we need to accept our fear. Interestingly enough, we are often as afraid of too much "positive" feeling as we are of the so-called "negative" ones. We don't want to feel too much love, joy, or passion. We prefer the cool middle ground where we feel in control.

While most of us have learned to repress our feelings, some people have the opposite problems; they are too easily overwhelmed by their emotions and have difficulty maintaining any emotional equilibrium. They are often carrying the repressed emotions of the people around them, feeling everyone else's as well as their own. Other people are stuck in one particular emotion and are constantly reacting from that place: anger, perhaps, or fear. These are all symptoms of an emotional imbalance that needs healing.

Due in part to our fear of feelings, there is a great deal of ignorance and misinformation about healing the emotional level. Many people don't even acknowledge that emotions exist! How many times have you heard reference to the "three" levels of existence: body, mind, and spirit? The emotional level is not even acknowledged but is simply lumped together with the mind category. This derives from the traditional transcendent spiritual approach, where the importance of the human experience is minimized, and emotions are dismissed as fabrications of the mind.

Many teachers and healers confuse the mental and emotional levels, or treat them as one. For example, you may have heard a discussion of how our thoughts affect our physical health, with no reference whatsoever on how our feelings affect it. Yet, in my experience, blocked emotions are one of the main causes of physical ailments.

Of course, our mental and emotional energies are quite intertwined, as are all levels of our being. But thoughts and feelings, while certainly connected and strongly influencing each other, are very different. Healing the emotional level requires learning to distinguish between thinking and feeling.

When we were infants and children, we had many strong feelings. What we needed was to have people acknowledge and respond to these feelings in appropriate ways. For example, we needed to hear things like, "I know you're angry that you can't play with your friend. I can't let you do that right now, and I know you're feeling frustrated about that!" Or, "I can see that you're feeling really sad about not getting to visit Grandpa." In essence, as children we needed validation of our feelings from our parents, families, teachers, and the surrounding world. We needed to be assured that we had a right to our feelings, that our feelings weren't wrong or bad. We needed to feel that others could understand and empathize with us when we were experiencing strong feelings. In short, we needed to be allowed to have our own feeling experience.

Even as parents, we may find ourselves treating our own children in the same way. We tend to pass on the same attitudes and patterns acquired from our parents. If we never healed the belief that anger or fear was an "unacceptable" feeling, we will tend to pass that lesson on to our own children. And they, in turn, will have the same confusion about their feelings.

No matter how hard parents try, children inevitably experience some degree of emotional hurt, neglect, and abandonment. Because we are so vulnerable as children, we are deeply wounded by these experiences and carry our wounds inside us for the rest of our lives—or until we do our conscious emotional healing work.

In emotional healing work, we learn to give ourselves, and allow ourselves to receive from others, whatever we didn't receive as young children. We learn to accept and experience our feelings and, when appropriate, to communicate these feelings in a way that allows others to understand us. We open the way to our emotional healing by having at least one other person hear, understand, and empathize with what we are feeling.

If we have denied or stuffed our feelings, we need a safe place and an experienced guide to help us get in touch with, experience, and release them. Then we need to develop tools for staying present with our feelings, acknowledging and experiencing them as they arise. It is important to recognize the needs expressed by our feelings and to learn how to communicate them effectively. Those basic needs are for love, acceptance, security, and self-esteem. We need

WERNHER KRUTEIN/PHOTOVAULT

"My message for the coming of the new millennium is simple. Each one of us makes a real and substantial difference on this planet. By making a commitment to your own consciousness journey, you are indeed playing a significant role in the transformation of the world."

to acknowledge the vulnerable child who still lives deep inside each of us and learn to become its loving parent.

To experience the full range of our being, we need to heal the emotional wounds from our childhood and early life. This deep level of emotional healing takes time and cannot be rushed or forced. Sometimes it takes years to move through the deeper levels. Fortunately, as each layer is healed, life becomes more and more fulfilling and rewarding.

Our feelings are an important part of the life force that is constantly moving through us. If we don't allow ourselves to fully experience our emotions, we stop the natural flow of that life force. Energy becomes blocked in our physical bodies and may remain there for years or even a lifetime, unless it is released. This leads to emotional and physical pain and disease. Repressed feelings = blocked energy = emotional and physical ailments.

Accepting our emotions, allowing ourselves to feel them, and learning to communicate them constructively and appropriately allow them to move through us easily and naturally. This enables the full, free flow of the life force through our physical bodies, which brings emotional and physical healing. Experiencing feelings = free flowing energy = emotional and physical health and well-being.

I use the analogy that our emotions are like the weather, constantly changing—sometimes dark, sometimes light, at times wild and intense, at other times calm and quiet. Trying to resist or control your feelings is like trying to control the weather— an exercise in futility and frustration! Besides, if all we ever experienced were sunny days of exactly seventy-five-degree temperature, life would be quite boring. When we can appreciate the beauty of the rain, the wind, and the snow, as well as the sun, we are free to enjoy the fullness of life.

Healing the Physical Level

The overall process of physical healing takes place as we learn to feel, trust, and listen to our bodies again. They communicate clearly and specifically to us, if we are willing to listen. We must cultivate the art of interpreting their signals accurately.

Since the spiritual, mental, and emotional aspects of our being are housed in our physical body, healing work on the other three levels is reflected in our physical health and well-being. Our body is where we integrate and express all four levels of our existence. Consciousness acquired on the other levels is reflected in how alive we feel and how we actually experience living. As the other levels are healed, our consciousness is freed to be more present in the moment. We naturally feel more in touch with our body and are able to live in it more fully.

Of course, the physical body has its own specific healing process as well. As with the other levels, there are certain basic principles, common to everyone, yet each person's needs are also unique.

Today we are not generally encouraged to respect or be sensitive to our physical bodies. In fact, many of us are quite disconnected from our true physical needs. As our bodies are physical manifestations and vehicles for our individual consciousness, so the earth is the physical manifestation and home for our collective consciousness. Thus, our relationship to the physical plane is reflected in both how we treat our bodies and how we treat our earth body.

One reason why we are disconnected from our physical being is modern civilization's increasing emphasis on the intellect. In the twentieth century, the development of the technological age has tended to cut us off from awareness of our natural, physical selves.

Another contributing factor has been the attitude toward the body fostered by the traditional, transcendent spiritual approach embraced by most world religions. The body is seen as the enemy of spirit, the seat of human needs, emotions, attachments, and passions. And it is the goal of these religions to subdue and rise above these human needs. Therefore, the body is seen as lowly—inferior to mind and spirit, or even downright evil. Thus, our bodies are ignored or denigrated.

We are all born with a natural awareness of our bodies' needs and feelings, but we have learned to literally tune out the body, to ignore it completely except when it's in extreme distress. So the body quickly learns to get sick or have an accident in order to get attention. And even then, we try to mask or get rid of the symptoms as quickly as possible to resume our unconscious life patterns. We avoid looking deeper to the root of the problem: what the body is really trying to communicate to us.

Many of us think we're paying positive attention to our physical health because we are interested in nutrition, exercise, and perhaps stress reduction. All too often, however, we are following a mental agenda, eating a rigid diet or performing a strenuous exercise program, rather than listening to our bodies' real messages. Even conscious relaxation programs, designed to reduce stress in our lives, can be used to block out the body's messages rather than making us more conscious of them.

The overall process of physical healing takes place as we learn to feel, trust, and listen to our bodies again. Our bodies often know what they need. They communicate to us clearly and specifically, if we are willing to listen. We must cultivate the art of understanding and interpreting their signals accurately.

How do we heal the physical level of our being? The first step, especially if we have an acute or serious ailment, is to obtain the most immediate and effective treatment. The second step is to learn how to maintain and strengthen our physical health. This might include treatment and support from the appropriate medical and/or alternative practitioners. The third step, which can be done simultaneously with the first two, is to examine the contributing emotional, mental, and spiritual factors, and then seek help to heal those areas.

Remember that our physical bodies are wonderful communicators. They let us know what they need. Cultivate the art and practice of feeling, sensing, and listening to what your body is saying. As we respond to our bodies' needs, we gradually become attuned to our own natural rhythms and those of the earth.

I am convinced that life in a physical body is meant to be an ecstatic experience. Through commitment to our healing and transformational process, we can open to more and more of life's many gifts.

Integrating the Four Levels

A key word on *The Path of Transformation* is "integration." Simply stated, this means "joining together into one functional whole." Within our present context, it means becoming more fully realized beings, developing, expressing, and embodying all aspects of God/universe/life as fully as possible in our daily lives. Living on earth successfully means embracing and integrating our animal (physical), human (emotional and mental), and divine (spiritual) selves.

Life is trying to teach us how to open the door and look at those parts of ourselves that frightened us, that we've hated, that we think are bad, ugly, awful, and scary. Life is helping us discover the hidden aspects of ourselves that we need and want, and that we can't really live without.

There is a simple universal principle that few of us really understand: everything in the universe wants to be accepted. All aspects of creation want to be loved, appreciated, and included. So, any quality or energy you refuse to experience or express will keep coming up inside or around you until you recognize it as a part of you and integrate it into your personality and your life.

My message for the coming of the new millennium is simple. Each one of us makes a real and substantial difference on this planet. By making a commitment to your own consciousness journey, you are indeed playing a significant role in the transformation of the world. These thoughts are further developed in my books, *The Path of Transformation* and *The Four Levels of Healing,* from Nataraj Publishing.

⊕

WERNHER KRUTEIN/PHOTOVAULT

Shakti Gawain is the best-selling author of *Creative Visualization, Living in the Light, Return to the Garden, Awakening,* and *The Path of Transformation.* Gawain gives lectures and leads workshops, seminars, and retreats internationally. For nearly twenty years, she has guided thousands of people in learning to trust and act on their own inner truth, thus releasing and developing in every area of their lives. She and her husband, Jim Burns, are co-founders of Nataraj Publishing. They live in Mill Valley, California, and on the island of Kauai.

STEVEN FLESCH/PHOTOVAULT

Chapter Twenty-two

The Consciousness Shift

by Robert B. Stone

The shift in planetary consciousness should be painless.

Contrary to the predictions of many psychics and futurists, this shift will not be necessarily announced or even accompanied by earthquakes, floods, or cosmic collisions.

Since it is a shift in consciousness, it will be nonphysical. Even those classical scientists whose intransigence has acted as ballast to the status quo will hardly know that a shift is taking place.

One definition of classical science is "thus far, and no further." To this extent, we need to defend classical scientists in their apparent near-sightedness. Why should they be concerned with the existence of a higher intelligence when their business is the physical realm?

What the rest of us are preparing for is none of their business.

Our consciousness tends to foresee a sort of comeuppance for those who have ravaged the earth and closed their minds to a

"Is the Higher Intelligence that fills the universe filling our planet in higher concentration? Or is our increasing oneness with the Higher Intelligence through conscious awareness and meditative attunement activating it?

"Is it from the outer in? Or from the inner out? . . .

"Higher Intelligence may be moving toward planet earth and humanity, while planetary and human intelligence moves toward Higher Intelligence. The joint movement may be one movement."

Gaia consciousness. But this author gets the "message" that they will merely wither on the vine of humanity after the shift takes place and no longer be either a plus or minus factor.

But until then, the rest of us need to keep meditating, attuning, loving, communicating, searching, intuiting, creating, praying, and doing what we are moved to do to pave the way for this shift.

Early Symptoms of the Forthcoming Consciousness Shift

Some years ago a sensitive, with talents for time regression, claimed that the earth was originally populated by life forms from Venus who decided to play a game called Limited Love, Limited Money.

We earth-bound humans have been living our lives with limited love, limited money, limited energy, and many other limits. Let's not forfeit the credit. It is all ours.

We are especially skilled at demonstrating lives of limited opportunity, lives of limited skills and abilities, lives of violence, lives of immorality, lives without scruples, and lives of total independence from God.

The following conversation between a minister and his son shows a likely source for most of the troubles on earth today. Watching his father write a sermon, the son asks, "How do you know what to say, Dad?"

The minister replies, "God tells me."

"Then how come you are scratching out so much?"

We are all scratching out too much. Higher Intelligence is sending us solutions, guidance, energy, and everything else we need, but either it does not get through to our conscious mind or if it does, we, in effect, redline it.

Our right-brain hemisphere is our connection to the creative realm. Unfortunately, for most of us, it has become the equivalent of a vestigial organ. Our mental functioning has been endowed with two emergency means of access for Higher Intelligence: our right brain is stimulated about one second every minute while we are awake and about fifteen minutes every hour-and-a-half while asleep.

One of the first symptoms of the consciousness shift will likely be an increase in right-brain participation. But there will either be some physiological changes such as more right-brain attunement during both wakefulness and sleep, or else the current availability intervals will be subject to more intense usage.

More and more people will get flashes of insight. More and more people will get meaningful dreams.

At a recent conference on alternative forms of healing, the summation included this important finding: slowing the brain waves has some important therapeutic results.

Then the report added, "But we don't know how to do that yet."

Where have these particular observers been? We have been slowing brain waves with the passive meditation techniques of Transcendental Meditation, the dynamic meditation techniques of the Silva Method, and a number of variations and adaptations for years.

Next: a quantum leap in right-brain usage in normal thinking, resulting from an increased focus by Higher Intelligence on life here on planet earth.

Separateness Blurs, Togetherness Blends

It is difficult to tap into new concepts without their vocabulary becoming one-and-the-same as used for old concepts.

By turning off the material world and using right-brain relaxed visualization, a whole new picture emerges, usually without a vocabulary. Feelings that accompany the mental pictures must then be drawn upon to yield words.

I have received warm feelings. These feelings indicate that feelings of separateness between neighbors will blur. People will forget minor differences. Countries will forget minor disagreements. A feeling of oneness will sneak into billions of rifts, creating a togetherness that might be considered obscene today. Working together will take a quantum leap forward. Competition will not exactly become obsolete, but cooperation will become more prominent. The power of synergy will be more understood. Working together toward a common goal will accelerate global progress.

With apologies for using the word "spiritual"—as true spirituality is still several shifts in planetary consciousness away—materiality will take a step backward and spirituality a step forward. Just the way water takes the path of least resistance, flowing into previously carved channels, so will it be with Higher Intelligence.

It is enveloping us now, but tapping it is a skill known to few of us. Tomorrow it will be almost as easy to tap as breathing—for almost everybody.

Wave Good-bye to Vested Interests

About a half-century ago, I lived on Long Island and decided to help organize a symphony orchestra, more for compassion for music lovers who had to travel to Manhattan to enjoy a concert than for any personal interest.

There was a great deal of local support, but I was amazed by the opposition which came from existing New York musical groups. Question: who could possibly be against a symphony orchestra? Answer: vested interests.

When writing the book *Jose Silva—The Man Who Tapped the Secrets of the Human Mind*,[1] the author realized how this inspired founder of the Silva Mind Training had fought vested interests every step of the way.

Scientists invited him to present his approach and then gave him the silent treatment. Physicians in his audiences challenged him. In one instance, when questioned about his method of pain control, even the sticking of a pin into a subject without a flinch to demonstrate its effectiveness evoked only the sarcastic question,

[1] H.J. Kramer, Inc., Tiburon, California, 1990.

WERNHER KRUTEIN/PHOTOVAULT

"What do we do now? Go back to medical school and start over?"

The church itself must have felt threatened, too. Word of Silva's healings and parapsychological training sessions caused him to be brought before the Catholic monsignors and threatened with excommunication. But it was his very connectedness to Higher Intelligence that allowed him to congenially ask them key probing questions. This resulted in the monsignors eventually agreeing, "If this is what God wants, nobody is going to be able to stop you." Had Jose's approach been more adversarial, the outcome would have been quite different. As

"A shift in consciousness will forestall the ravaging of the planet in the interests of human comfort and pleasure. It will be in the direction of the American Indians' love of the earth as a living aspect of the Great Spirit. As a result, the current denuding of land, which has come close to dealing a death blow to the forests, will cease and a reversal will be fostered."

it was, many members of the ministry eventually took the Silva training free of charge.

The vested interests were not threatened.

The Force Behind the Shift in Planetary Consciousness

A few decades ago the growth of consciousness was termed *The Greening of America* in a book by that title, when actually green was the fastest disappearing color. To refer to the growth of planetary consciousness as "the greening of planet earth" is more in line with the facts.

A shift in consciousness will forestall the ravaging of the planet in the interests of human comfort and pleasure. It will be in the direction of the American Indians' love of the earth as a living aspect of the Great Spirit. As a result, the current denuding of land, which has come close to dealing a death blow to the forests, will cease and a reversal will be fostered.

If the shift in consciousness is pro-life when plant life is concerned, certainly it will be pro-life where humans are concerned. "Make love, not war" may be "the greening of humanity."

Anything that is pro-life—plant or animal—must be life-giving. The force behind the shift in planetary consciousness must therefore be the source of life. We have no other word for the source of life. We must use the word "God."

Infinite Intelligence is our measurement of God's "smarts." It is so far beyond our own wisdom that it is not measurable by us. In fact, we cannot even categorize it. God may even decide against humanity and in favor of ants, or even microbes. And, although absurd to human intelligence, it may be appropriate to Infinite Intelligence.

Disease-causing microscopic organisms are becoming immune to our so-called miracle drugs. New diseases are appearing. Diseases formerly thought to be wiped out are reappearing.

United States and Canadian health officials are currently mystified by an outbreak of infection caused by what they must call an "exotic" microbe. It attacks the intestines causing abdominal cramps, nausea, severe diarrhea, extreme fatigue, and a fever of up to 102 degrees Fahrenheit. As yet, there is no cure.

This microbe has been given the name "cyclosporat." Giving disease-causing agents a name is a necessary first step to controlling them—but not a guarantee. All it takes is a decision by Higher Intelligence, and teacher will have erased the blackboard.

The Best Way Available to Humanity

There are many who agree that a major shift in planetary consciousness is not only on the way, but is already taking place.

The religious say that the Second Coming of Christ has already taken place—in the consciousness of thousands of enlightened people.

Those with awareness are noticing an increase in coincidences and synchronicities in everyday life. This was confirmed in a recent survey of people in an around-the-world trip taken by my wife and me. Just about everybody we queried agreed that these coincidences and synchronicities were becoming more numerous. However, their explanations were different. Some felt it was God getting closer, others that our consciousness was already expanding and making us all more aware.

Is the Higher Intelligence that fills the universe filling our planet in higher concentration? Or is our increasing oneness with the Higher Intelligence through conscious awareness and meditative attunement activating it?

Is it from the outer in? Or from the inner out?

Such a question may very likely be baseless and the result of our anachronistic concept of separation.

Higher Intelligence may be moving toward planet earth and humanity, while planetary and human intelligence moves toward Higher Intelligence. The joint movement may be one movement.

Inner and outer join, and we are faced with the need to open our minds to it.

How? The answer appears to be trite to those of us already aware of the path toward a higher consciousness, because the best way available to humanity is the way upon which many of us have embarked.

Steps to Keep in Step

I recently attended a church-sponsored planning meeting to organize help for homeless people. The temporary chairman announced the procedure: the group would brainstorm ideas to raise money and attract support. We would then form separate groups for each idea to develop it further.

I raised my hand and when recognized said, "I have a great respect for brainstorming. We used it quite successfully when I attended MIT. But this is a church. Shouldn't we use a spiritual right brain approach instead?"

"You're right," replied the chairman. "Go ahead, Bob, lead it."

Not expecting that reaction, I nevertheless began, "Sit in a comfortable position. Close your eyes gently. Take a nice deep breath and, as you exhale, feel yourself letting go." Following several more relaxation steps I said, "You are now in the kingdom of heaven within. Mentally ask what this group can do to accomplish its goal." In about two minutes, the session was ended with the usual prayer of thanks, and all eyes were again open.

The chairman had a huge sheet of butcher paper ready to write down any useful ideas. He went around the circle, and so many rich ideas came forth that he had to use sheet after sheet.

Many of the ideas have since been implemented, and the organization has helped scores of homeless to put a roof over their heads.

Steps to keep in step are familiar to those interested enough to listen, but now all the more urgent.

We need to work together, harnessing the power of synergy for application toward a common goal. Those who say, "easier said than done" must nevertheless dive in and find out for themselves that it is the "done" that is really the easier part.

We need to daydream more—imagining solutions to problems. When we relax and use our visualizing factor, we are transcending physical limitations and functioning more in the creative, spiritual realm.

We need to solve problems—and not how we're going to move from third place to first place in bowling league, but problems having to do with making this a better world. This does not necessarily mean sharing the wealth, but surely it means sharing the knowledge and beating the drums for the phenomenal realm.

We need to help others to heal both emotional ills and physical ailments. If they do not know the general precepts of good nutrition and a healthy life-style, then relax and in the imagination, fix them up and "see" them well.

We need to think of Higher Intelligence more and more, feeling ourselves God-like, rising above petty limitations, and finding that the doors of our self-made prison were never locked.

As we move toward Higher Intelligence, Higher Intelligence moves toward us.

What Happens Next Is Incomprehensible Now

It appears inevitable that this shift in planetary consciousness will decrease the gap between heaven and earth, between the unmanifest and the manifest.

Does that mean Higher Intelligence will speak to us? We think so. William knows so.

William's business was failing. He made a rare visit to church.

"Dear God," he prayed, "let me win a sweepstake. It is the only thing that can save my business." Nothing happened. He went again and prayed, "Dear God, only a sweepstake win can keep my business from going bankrupt." Again, no help came. The third time he prayed he reminded God of his previous prayers, adding, "Now my wife is leaving me. Only winning a sweepstake can save me." As he finished the sky darkened, and a voice boomed, "William, please, buy a ticket."

It is impossible for us to comprehend an existence that involves increased communication between the manifest and the unmanifest. What form will it take? Will all the jokes being told about the voice of God become more truth than humor?

Already science is studying ways to improve communication between the living and the spirits of the so-called dead. Because tapes and television are involved, it is called "instrumental transcommunication."

Will we all be seers, psychics, and visionaries? Or is God adding more strings to make us more responsive puppets?

The antenna of our consciousness can tune into probability, insight, and trends. But it cannot give us the incomprehensible in any acceptable form.

And there is likely much in store, incomprehensible now, and that will be difficult

WERNHER KRUTEIN/PHOTOVAULT

"a small sign said to have hung in the office of the late magnate Howard Hughes. It said, in effect, 'The bumblebee weighs X number of grams. Its wings have an area of Y square centimeters. The dihedral angle of its wings is Z number of degrees. According to all the laws of aerodynamics, the bumblebee cannot fly. But the bumblebee does not know this.'"

to digest even then. When the planetary shift arrives it won't be all sweetness and light.

The Daily Word is an inspiring handbook published by Unity.[2] The reading for Monday, June 24, 1996, calls on more and more people to join in their vigil of prayer, so that the glow of faith and wisdom will burn ever brighter. It ends with, "Soon every person in every nation of the

[2]*The Daily Word,* 1901 NW Blue Parkway, Unity Village, Missouri 64065-0001.

world will be aware of the all-encompassing light of God."

Disagreement: the word "soon." Despite the soonness of the shift in planetary consciousness, this awareness will hardly be instant.

A key to this might be best expressed in a small sign said to have hung in the office of the late magnate Howard Hughes. It said, in effect, "The bumblebee weighs X number of grams. Its wings have an area of Y square centimeters. The dihedral angle of its wings is Z number of degrees. According to all the laws of aerodynamics, the bumblebee cannot fly. But the bumblebee does not know this."

Translating this into postconsciousness shift terms, albeit implying the converse of the Hughes idea:

"The inhabitants of planet earth now have an expanded consciousness. Their formerly accepted limits no longer exist. Energy is freely available. They are one with God. But the inhabitants do not know this."

⊕

Robert Stone is the author and co-author of 85 self-help books with millions of copies in print in 15 languages. His titles include *You the Healer* with Jose Silva, *The Secret Life of Your Cells, The Silva Mind Control Method for Business Managers* with Jose Silva, *The Power of Miracle Metaphysics,* and *Celestial 911*. Stone's books have evolved from body to mind to spirit and beyond. He says of his upcoming release, *How to Benefit from the Coming Alien Arrivals,* "There may be something beyond spiritual; it's on a galactic level." Stone has lived with his wife Lola in Hawaii for 25 years.

WERNHER KRUTEIN/PHOTOVAULT

"What exactly does feminization of a culture imply? For twenty years leading thinkers on the subject have seen it as collaborative leadership, empowered work relations, equity and balance in family demands, reawakened imagery of the sacred feminine in religion, honoring the interconnectedness of all species, and finally, a reverence for all stages of life including death and the regenerative potential."

Chapter Twenty-three

WOMEN AND THE FEMININE SPIRIT: SHAPING THE NEXT MILLENNIUM

by Peg Jordan

You are here in the West, Ma Kali.
I know . . . the ground is burning beneath my feet.

I ask the Fates, those three wise women, the weavers of destiny, "What is going to happen during this solstice shift? What can we expect in the new millennium?"

Anticipating my questions (they always do when an abundance of 9's line up on the universe's odometer), the Fates show me what will transpire: they have a grand cosmic lens in their clutches. Holding it up to Mother Earth, they are focusing the rays of a billion suns, scorching us with an intensity that exposes our divisional polarities.

This solstice shift into the next millennium is about an unrelenting, conscious light that insists we transform or die. For the Fates are ultimately dispassionate. They are neither the all-abiding Mother Goddess nor the wrathful Father God. Those deities are from the old millennium. The Fates of this next age know it's time to stop the cycle of domination. If we cling to our ridiculous dramas, then, like ants caught under the lens of the sun's magnified light, we will catch fire. A cosmic joke by destiny's forces? Too harsh an ending for the faithful? Not when you consider the consequence of refusing to transform.

As a journalist, I write in the father tongue, a language of immediacy, power, and status. I play the game of objective reporting, declaring what's so in a linear argument of full-fledged undeniableness. I report on the scourge of ecological disasters, the corruption of political actions, unchecked violence, domestic abuse, and the death of outworn institutions. I stack up my facts, yielding the sword of my father, a genuine Athenian, in his most ferocious coolly logical self. Educated with the discerning eye of dualism, I'm a rational, laser-directed, heat-seeking missile, judging right from wrong and insisting on order and boundaries: death sentences for heinous acts against the whole. I am the best of patriarchal protection, carving out the individuated state, glorifying the hero's journey. My head is above the clouds, my sight on the futuristic visions, the lofty goals of a next age. It is the view from up here.

As a woman, I communicate in the mother tongue, a soulful expression of what should be. I am maid, mother, and crone in a continuum of never-ending cosmic music, a voice for life-affirming acts of regeneration. Within me resides Hecate, goddess of the crossroads, who stands vigilantly committed to reconciling the polarities of life. Here is where my feet are firmly planted in the organic stuff of life. There is no avoiding it as a woman, just dealing with my blood cycle every month keeps me grounded. I comfort my sisters as they patch together their battered histories and dream of a time in this culture when the body will be as sacred as the spirit. I plant some tomatoes, pay a few bills, write another paragraph, and wipe the baby's butt. I feel the loss of relationships gone sour, the absurd promise of trying to be all things to all people: lovers, children, employers. This is the view from down below.

As a future resident of the next millennium, I seek to harmonize these two worlds. The masculine world I've learned to live outwardly, the feminine world of my retreat. And, in this time of tremendously accelerated change—social, political, economic, and spiritual reinvention—there is a desire to bring both worlds, both selves, into harmony and wholeness. According to the wise women, this solstice shift into the next millennium is actually a massive shift in how we consciously view the polarities of lightdark, goodevil, spiritmatter, sunmoon, masculinefeminine—a departure from how the human race has perceived them over the past 2,000 years.

This chapter focuses on the shifting polarities recognized by several women leaders, seers, healers, and priestesses, (as well as sensitive men in touch with their deep feminine) as we head toward the Aquarian Age. We see seven different signs appearing that promise a complete revamping of how we relate to each other and to the planet. It is possible to see glimmers of the emerging paradigm now as it comes into the light and settles into position over the next twenty years or so—for we can only estimate the exact passage from the Age of Pisces into the Age of Aquarius.

All seven signs have the distinctive mark of a feminine spirit shaping and molding their impact, and they affect all the significant questions in life, such as:

1) How We Know What We Know

We are shifting our epistemological groundedness from the head to the heart. Despite a wellspring of esoteric texts advising this for eons, we are finally convinced, based on new scientific findings, to allow the heart and positive emotions to serve as the central processor for intelligence.

A group of researchers, psychologists and physicists at the Institute of HeartMath in Boulder Creek, California, have been studying the electromagnetic fields surrounding the heart during states of positive emotions. This field is about five times greater than that generated by the brain alone and connects us to a celestial grid of cosmic intelligence. The researchers admit that they are somewhat reluctant to share the extent of the extraordinary findings with their scientific colleagues. Tapping into realms of immune system enhancement, disease reversal, future "filmstrip" envisioning, their research findings are an awesome validation of sacred scriptures such as "the heart is the kingdom," common insights, and even the wisdom by Saint-Exupery's *Little Prince:* "Only the heart can see clearly. What is essential is invisible to the eye."

We are leaving an age in which epistemology—how we know what we know—has been ruled exclusively by scientific method: the gathering, testing, and duplicating of observable data. Now, we are bombarded with an explosion of information, and we must intuitively map our way through the Information Age and move into the Consciousness Age, allowing our sixth sense to inform and guide us. What was once considered a quirky female characteristic is now taught in business seminars and employed in creative brainstorming sessions.

2) How We Tell Our Myth

We are shifting from the Conquering Hero to the Regeneration myth as the guiding mythos for this upcoming age. It is time to remythologize ourselves! Time to release the first myth of patriarchy: the Sumerian tale of Gilgamesh, slaying the feminine dragon, betraying Astarte, Queen of Heaven, and crowning himself the conquering hero. Conquest and rule, rule and conquest.

3) What We Honor

We are shifting from the heavens to the earth as the sacred eminent being. We resacralize matter, the body, and nature and recognize that we're already in the Garden. Unless we truly honor the body (and implied within that, woman, nature, organic life, death, and the earth), we will continue to live on this planet in self-destructive ways. The immanent—the deep honoring of the here and now—is being restored to its rightful place with the transcendent, and this is happening with and through the work of the divine feminine.

The transcendent nature of spirituality is not dismissed, but it is balanced with the wisdom of the immanent spirituality of the feminine. This not only develops in the world of organized religions but in the upcoming environmental resolutions. Ecofeminists such as Charlene Spretnak (Green Politics) have taken the lead in this pursuit, and they are now joined by ecopsychologists Theodore Roszak and environmental monk Thomas Berry *(Voice of the Earth).*

4) How We Stay Well

We are shifting from the allopathic to the integrative as a means for healing, from a reliance on technology alone to a holistic approach. It is significant that the four leaders in the new health age—the field of energy medicine—are women: Rosalyn Bruyere, Barbara Brennan, Donna Eden, and Carolyn Myss. Each has followed a system of scientific inquiry, intuitive processing, and personal transformative work in their investigations into subtle fields of energy. Biophysicist Beverly Rubik, Ph.D., Director of the Institute for Frontier Science and an editor and researcher with the Office of Alternative Medicine at the National Institutes of Health, believes we are learning to recognize imbalance and incongruence, and this will revolutionize the way medicine will be practiced in the West: "There is a new reverence for the subtle fields of energy, the invisible realities."

5) How We See Each Other

We are shifting from the concretionary, heterosexist poles of male and female to a fluid continuum for gender relations. We are learning from the native cultures such as the Zuni who recognize four genders (man, woman, man with a woman's soul, and woman with a man's soul). We celebrate the differences of biology: research into the intricacies of our hard wiring (for example, women having more fibers across the corpus callosum connecting the two hemispheres of the brain) that shows women more relational and more independently minded. We understand how education and upbringing can soften the differences, lending more unity and peace to our paths. Counselor and psychic healer Cheryl Self argues that marriage itself will change dramatically in the upcoming era. "We are moving into a time of accelerated change, it's rather outdated and impossible to think that one person can possibly remain with you during all the permutations you will undergo in your spirit and psyche."

6) How We Govern Ourselves

We are shifting from the polarized state of individuals versus fascist collectives—to a new collective state of individuals, with new global laws, a new system of justice, and personal law.

7) How We Recognize Truth

We are shifting from an era of post-modern deconstructionism and "constructed realities" to an era of more certainty about consensual truths.

In looking at these sweeping changes, it should be noted that we see the feminine spirit manifesting in every area of life: politics, the workplace, family balance issues, leadership roles, and even religious liturgical dictates. When forecasting researchers Patricia Aburdene and John Naisbitt followed up *Megatrends* with *Megatrends for Women* in 1992, they concluded that the trends were not apart from women, but rather were due to women and the feminization of the social, political, and economic life.

What exactly does feminization of a culture imply? For twenty years leading thinkers on the subject have seen it as collaborative leadership, empowered work relations, equity and balance in family demands, reawakened imagery of the sacred feminine in religion, honoring the interconnectedness of all species, and finally, a reverence for all stages of life including death and the regenerative potential.

Imagination and visualization are the tools of mastery for the next age. "It's that simple," explains Reverend Pamela Eakins, Ph.D. *(Tarot of the Spirit).* "We will not be establishing the new order by the rules of the old; we have to venture out, take risks, work outside the system, and use our imaginative abilities and deep intuition." Intuitive knowing allows us to know more than we understand or can prove by scientific method. Deep ecology, which is an intuitive connection with the planet and her natural systems, is the work of global environmentalists, teachers, and ecofeminists Joanna Macy and Margaret Pavel, who work with a small but growing Japanese force to halt nuclear plant escalation in Japan, a country with more than 300 reactors in an area not much larger than New Jersey. "You know in your bones that something is amiss—aside from the reams of facts and findings," says Pavel. For these women activists, creating sustainable systems is a passion that allows them to enter with full awareness into the despair and insanity of a disconnected mind-set that poisons the land, water, and air. "You have to go through the despair to come out the other side," Macy teaches. Connecting through the heart and positive emotions are the gateway for making a difference in the world, Macy and Pavel explain. Without these we become burnt-out embers of ourselves, and our best-laid plans for political action fall short.

Emotions, intuition, and intimate respectful connection are not necessarily feminine traits; but the corporate, legal, and political influences have shoved them aside—to the marginated feminine realms. The cost to men as well as women has been extraordinary. Men die earlier of heart disease for more than physiological reasons. "It just makes sense—what you've put down for millennia is bound to rise up again; it's the natural order of cycles, an irrepressible part of nature," explains cultural historian Elinor Gadon, Ph.D., author of *The Once and Future Goddess* and founder of the first women's spirituality graduate program at California Institute of Integral Studies (CISS).

But it's not just women who have been subjugated by the patriarchal system, explains scholar Mara Keller, Ph.D., researcher in ancient women's mysteries, and on the faculty at CISS in San Francisco. "There is no doubt that men have suffered greatly as well—after all, they've had to abandon the emotional connections in order to proceed with the initiatives of patriarchy."

In their gatherings with men over the past few years, Robert Bly and Michael Meade warned about the destructive nature of societies in which the three sectors of public authority—elite clergy, government leaders, and heads

WERNHER KRUTEIN/PHOTOVAULT

"{In the patriarchal system,} there is no room for the 'wild man' or the 'green man,' nor is the best of paternal nurturance honored and cultivated. The signs of this decay in compassion are evident today: the way we discard our infirm, incompetent, and aged. The roles of compassionate caretaker and dedicated teacher are among the lowest paid in status and salary."

of households—are males only. There is no room for the "wild man" or the "green man," nor is the best of paternal nurturance honored and cultivated. The signs of this decay in compassion are evident today: the way we discard our infirm, incompetent, and aged. The roles of compassionate caretaker and dedicated teacher are among the lowest paid in status and salary.

You cannot discount the contributions of the present paradigm: the birth of science, the flourishing of individuation, the achievements of linear-directed progress. But it is time to question the way we live (personal), the way we govern ourselves (culture), and the images and symbols we live with (mythological spiritual) that have been male-dominant.

In the macro-time line of human history, the era of the great goddess cultures, chronicled by archaeologists such as Marija Gimbutas and James Maellert, existed from the dawn of humanity to about 2,500 to 5,000 years ago. With the overthrow, reversal, and in some cases, integration of matrilineal cultures by patriarchal societies, the dynamic forces that attempt to control human interaction on the planet became male-dominant. "With the reemergence of the Goddess," explains Zsuzsanna Budapest, a founding mother in the contemporary women's spirituality movement and four-time best-selling author, "the time of the lunar-conscious male and the self-directed female is here. And together, this new masculine and feminine are weaving a new pattern, a new worldview. Consciousness is evolving."

What kind of leaders will be required as we redesign a gender-balanced worldview? Multiple ways of knowing will be honored on the planet, and they will be forged by leaders, women and men both, who know how to "tend the inner fires; heal spirit, body, and relationship; and bring a collaborative power into the larger community," according to Mara Keller, Ph.D., Associate Professor of Women's Spirituality at CISS. Keller's holistic vision is similar to that of her colleague Riane Eisler (author of *The Chalice and the Blade,* and more recently, *Sacred Pleasure)* and was one of the chief editors of Eisler's new book. Their vision pulls together the spiritual with the economic, political, and the interpersonal/relational dimensions of life in a very accessible way and speaks to this larger vision of cultural transformation.

"I believe that cultural transformation can happen very rapidly. And what we need to do is mainstream the alternative values and make them central—the values of partnership and the equality of men and women, and a new cooperative stance among economic relationships. That we mainstream peace, social justice, and ecological restoration. These are what we require to live as human beings in the 21st century, not some idealistic utopian fantasy. These are crucial for survival," Keller explains.

According to feminists like Keller, women's leadership in the next millennium is crucial because "we need to know how to feed the hungry, how to clean up the environment, how to care for the sick, how to do good mothering for the children and good care for the elders. It's women's job to be loving, part of the job description of being a spouse or mother. It's still our expectation, and we are socialized to live relationally." I asked Keller if this nurturance role isn't part of a compassion trap in which women have traditionally found themselves. She agreed that "there is a way that women can give themselves away and be a doormat by serving everyone's needs and neglecting ourselves. It's certainly worth the effort to learn something else. A big part of feminism is learning to take care of and heal yourself and find empowerment for what you need. And that is the best example we set for children and those who emulate us as role models and of course, for the men to see. We must be committed to our own well-being as well as others."

Remythologizing the New Millennium

It is actually an exhilarating time for the feminine spirit because the voice-on-the-margin has a certain freedom to be outrageous and act as an utter nonconformist—exactly what is needed when reenvisioning the world.

Take Jean Houston, for instance, a psychologist and philosopher, and author of fifteen books. Her latest, *A Mythic Life,* talks about "the lure of becoming." Houston believes that, "With the new millennium fast approaching, we are being called to re-invent the world while we re-invent ourselves. Thus we can become designers and weavers of a new pattern to re-envision and re-enchant the world."

A scholar of international renown, Houston is Codirector of the Foundation for Mind Research in Pomona, New York, and founder of the Mystery School—an institution that attracts students from around the globe to study history, philosophy, new physics, psychology, anthropology, and the human potential. Her transformational seminars are sought by the chiefs of state, UNICEF, and other international agencies.

For the past twelve years, more than 3,000 people have participated in communities of attunement with Jean Houston, acquiring the skills for implementing a new vision of a moral and ethical society. She inspires medical professionals to resource the healing process. She invites religious clergy to widen their spiritual orientation to multiple dimensions and artists to use shamanic states of consciousness to enliven their creativity. She inspires everyone with whom she comes in contact to engage in their own personal mythic dimensions.

Her call to create our own mythic life represents not only a strong vote in favor of deep intuitive knowing, but also a disappearance of the priesthood and a move toward recognizing truth on one's own, rather than accepting the canon from above. Houston takes off where Jung and her colleague Joseph Campbell left off. They may have awakened us to the mythic dimensions alive and well in the collective field, but it is Jean Houston's work as a personal, hands-on guide that helps us wrap our individual lives around the great myths, enter our own chrysalis, and emerge into a new world. An inspirational healer of renown, Houston encourages us to "give vent to the unbound labyrinth of the unconscious...," to journey to the "multidimensional nested ecology of allies," and "dissolve all barriers....There is a spiritual eros happening in the world....We are being partnered consciously. The emotional eros from our limbic emotional system of the brain activates a cadence of spiritual longing, and you find yourself well met—whether it's by Kuan Yin, Tara, Krishna, Jesus, or Mother Meera! This rising spiritual eros allows you to sense a high connection with an archetype partner, a unique individuation of the God-Self within." How do we accomplish this spiritual passion in our lives? By making contact. By spending time talking with and cherishing our chosen archetype. "We are acts of imagination before we are anything else," she quotes one of her favorite teachers. Houston teaches us how to be our own decipherer of the mystery, how to interpret our own oracle, and thereby bypass the intermediary priesthood of this passing age.

From Conquest to Regeneration

Women and men are weary of the story of the "lone conquering hero"—a tale that has been played out ad nauseam in these final gasps of a dominator age, including the blockbuster hits about tough guys kicking alien butt. "It's an old, outworn story," explains Vicki Noble, who has been researching and performing healing circles in sacred public rituals.

"I'm working very hard to help us imagine a new myth—one of Regeneration." Part of her workshop, "Sybils, Seers, Healers, and Banshee" is the telling of an Icelandic myth. "I introduce a modern version of the ancient mystery religion, combining healing, dance, and shamanism for transformational purposes. It tells about a war between the old and new gods, which represents the old feminine gods and the newer masculine gods, then goes into the hubris, the corruption and arrogance of patriarchal gods and then the world basically breaks loose." Noble describes battles, underworld diversions, and terrifying earthquakes and volcanoes—not unlike our present time.

"I've been plotting the number of earthquakes and volcanoes around the world, and they are on the rise dramatically," asserts Noble. "The awakening of this age is both personal and planetary." What is different about this myth? Noble says, "It's not apocalyptic. It's a regenerative myth. It teaches how the earth herself will regenerate, and in it will be a restoration of the old, correct ways. Ways of being in harmony with nature, not trying to live above nature."

The women I talked with who worked toward personal and planetary healing were not unaffected by the disruption and unsettling mood of the times. In fact, they often found it frightening to live with the "corporatization" of the world and the endless consumption. Noble asserts, "I listen to people with euphoric fantasies about computers and visions to download consciousness into computers—and it's hilarious, considering once the power goes out with a piddling little storm, then what? We live in a physical world, and as much as we try to deny it, the physical will take it back, and I love when it teaches us that. . . . If you can have a global view of what's happening, it's very hopeful. Then you can see how natural law supersedes multinational corporation law and governments." We grew to distrust natural law during the dawn of the age of reason, the splitting of the body and soul, and the world has since undergone the legacy of an unholy deal made between Descartes and the reigning pope. Some have been trying to close the dichotomous split ever since.

Governing Ourselves

During the Senate hearings of Clarence Thomas and throughout the Simpson trial, many women longed for a court of wise elders to inject common sense—a radical departure from the legal maneuverings and power-play gestures of a system that sometimes seems to lose sight of justice and truth. "Above all," Zsuzsanna Budapest explains, "the Fates want you to use your common sense in life's predicaments. If you don't, the three sisters will continue to serve up similar challenges until your soul manifests what it is fully capable of." Budapest's predictions are derived from legends of Old Europe and astrological shifts. In fact, several astrologers are predicting that we will undergo a tremendous revision over the next 100 years in how we elect to govern ourselves. Global agreements for handling trade and terrorism will emerge. Fair-minded laws to protect all human rights will be enacted on a worldwide scale; their conscious enforcement will be another story, but at least the laws governing human rights, which are even recognized in some parts of the world, will be a matter of record internationally.

"There is a pool of unseen energy into which we can tap during this transitional time. It has been fed by all the simple yet profound 'Rosa Parks moments.' Whenever a woman stands up for her own self-worth and halts the devaluation of her gender, we all take a step forward. Whenever a brother does not believe the lying story and puts down the gun, we take another step. We are reaching a point of critical mass in which this pool of energy has been permeated by enough feminine spirit to transform consciousness in a massive way."

While regions of distinct cultural flavors and customs will flourish, there will be a homogenized, democratized sense of what is fair and just. In other words, the Serbs and Croats will not really blend into one culture, but they will be able to respect the cultural boundary due to a new system of international law. Through advancements in telecommunications, the world will know when rights are violated, and swift consequences will be delivered. We are already seeing instances of this techno-watchdog in China, South America, and the Middle East. It is this application of technology by a guiding hand of consensual truth that makes this next age very exciting.

Recognizing Truth

Tony Rich, a founder of the futurist and holistic think tank, IdeasOne, says, "This new millennium will be a time of massive consciousness-raising for all societies. And, as the human species realizes more fully, with each passing day, that the salvation it created in its written word and esoteric texts shall come not from outside (as in waiting for the Messiah) but from within, it is then that we will once again embrace the wisdom of our ancestors."

This new vision we're crafting on how to live on the planet comes from the practical, roll-up-your-shirtsleeves, get-real, and go-to-work orientation that women have had to carry

WERNHER KRUTEIN/PHOTOVAULT

for the past several thousand years. The baby's butt has to be wiped (read healthy propagation, conscious childbearing), the kids have to get along (read global harmony), and the garbage has to be cleaned up (read ecological balance). And we might as well make it all sacred work. This resacralizing of the organic stuff of life is the unique contribution of women and the feminine spirit.

Pamela Eakins looks to the ancient kabbalah to recognize universal truths for the future: freedom, compassion, wisdom, and possibility. "When we realize we are free to change our lives, that wisdom begins to radiate outward, and gives others the impetus to also become free. New possibilities are created, and we can act with more compassion." Perhaps the great avatar for this transitional era is not one more guru promising enlightenment through asceticism, or one more New Age circuit speaker who promises no-limits living through his thirty-day program; but Rosa Parks, the diminutive black woman who refused to give up her seat on a city bus in Alabama, and thus became an empowering symbol for the civil rights movement. She took a stand for her own self-worth and touched the world's heart. The energy generated in that moment—something I call a "Rosa Parks moment"—radiated to the world, but Rosa did not steal our stage. She receded into the background and tended to her own garden, leaving each individual with the task of striving for his or her own freedom.

There is a pool of unseen energy into which we can tap during this transitional time. It has been fed by all the simple yet profound "Rosa Parks moments." Whenever a woman stands up for her own self-worth and halts the devaluation of her gender, we all take a step forward. Whenever a brother does not believe the lying story and puts down the gun, we take another step. We are reaching a point of critical mass in which this pool of energy has been permeated by enough feminine spirit to transform consciousness in a massive way. That's it: the Fates have spoken; the poles are shifting. We have but to imagine it.

Peg Jordan is one of America's most recognized health authors, journalists, and broadcasters. Her groundbreaking reports in the fields of health, fitness, self-improvement, gender issues, spirituality, and psychology have appeared in major newspapers and magazines. She is a former health reporter for Fox-KTVU in San Francisco and a frequent guest commentator for NBC *Today* and on CNN. Jordan is the editor and founder of *American Fitness* magazine and the editor of *Fitness: Theory & Practice,* a leading text for fitness professionals. She is the author of *Aerobics Today, Plyo Play for Kids, How the New Food Label Can Save Your Life,* and *Aerobic Injuries.* She was the 1991 winner of the coveted Health American Fitness Leader Award, and she is now serving on the first Governor's Council on Physical Fitness and Sports in California. Living and working in both Los Angeles and San Francisco, Peg Jordan is the mother of two teenagers.

About the Photo Illustrator

Wernher Krutein has had, since childhood, a reverence for a world he describes as "simply beautiful, enormously complex, and lovingly profound." Early on, he began to use the visual arts to express and share this feeling of reverence. His dream is both to capture archetypal images and to communicate his awe at the sheer majesty of being alive.

The producer and director of the award-winning short video *It's In Every One Of Us,* Krutein has also filmed countless hours of beautiful footage from around the world. He is the creator of a trademark formulae called *Painting with Time*™ for shooting exquisite time-lapse cinematography. In the late 1970s, he invented a visual cataloging system titled FLUID LOGIC™. This cataloging system is perhaps the most comprehensive yet simplistic slide filing system ever devised. His research into the "ultimate" photo search and retrieval system led to the creation of a visual resource library called PHOTOVAULT.

PHOTOVAULT, an exploration into the wonder and essence of the "Great Mystery," became Krutein's escape into spiritual realism. It is a warmly human and artistically inspired voyage into the wonder of life, containing a diverse variety of images from Aerospace and Astrology to Zimbabwe and Zoology.

With the goal to "visually document the Universe," he has made well over three million images. Krutein acknowledges, however, that the credit for his accomplishment is not his alone; since the late seventies, he has gathered a diverse and spectacularly talented group of photographers who have made invaluable contributions to the archive.

Based in San Francisco and rooted deeply in cyberspace, the archive is currently being digitized and can be accessed on the internet at www.photovault.com.

PHOTOVAULT's staff who have contributed to researching and preparing the photos in this book:

Bill Goidell .... Project Manager
Diane DePineres .... Research
Robin Thielen .... Administration
Khalila Wolfe .... Archiving
MeYou Krutein (Cat) .... Spiritual Advisor
Vern Krutein .... President

PHOTOVAULT

(415) 552-9682 ⊕ e-mail: tetra@photovault.com ⊕ URL: www.photovault.com.

Hampton Roads Publishing Company
publishes and distributes books on a variety of subjects,
including metaphysics, health, integrative medicine,
visionary fiction, and other related topics.

To order or receive a copy of our latest catalog, call toll-free,
(800) 766-8009, or send your name and address to:

Hampton Roads Publishing Company, Inc.
134 Burgess Lane
Charlottesville, VA 22902